Shakespeare's Reparative Comedies

Shakespeare's Reparative Comedies

A Psychoanalytic View of the Middle Plays

Joseph Westlund

The University of Chicago Press
Chicago and London

Joseph Westlund is associate professor of English at
Northeastern University, Boston.

The University of Chicago Press, Chicago 60637
The University of Chicago Press, Ltd., London

© 1984 by The University of Chicago
All rights reserved. Published 1984
Printed in the United States of America
91 90 89 88 87 86 85 84   5 4 3 2 1

Library of Congress Cataloging in Publication Data
Westlund, Joseph.
    Shakespeare's reparative comedies.

    Includes index.
    1. Shakespeare, William, 1564-1616—Comedies.
2. Psychoanalysis and literature.   I. Title.
PR2981.W47   1984   822.3'3   83-9305
ISBN 0-226-89413-4

Contents

Preface

This book is written for the general reader, as well as for those familiar with psychoanalytic criticism. Shakespeare's comedies are so well known, and so excellent, that special terms and theories seem intrusive. I proceed in the traditional mode of Shakespeare criticism, and exile most of the psychoanalytic underpinning to the footnotes. Rather than discuss psychoanalytic issues all at once, I introduce them one at a time and at the point where they help to clarify the work at hand. The effect, then, is cumulative—and the drawback is that readers who dive into a discussion of their favorite play may find it somewhat unclear.

Specialists in psychoanalytic criticism may want a general account of my theoretical approach, and I offer it here. Psychoanalysis dwells upon guilt and conflict, and with good reason. Still, we need a clearer sense of how it is that people transcend this painful state. This need becomes especially pertinent in a study of comedy's effect upon an audience. The theorists I rely upon focus their attention on early, preoedipal states of development. Little can be known for certain about this, the earliest and most basic phase of life, but much can be reconstructed from our awareness of the infantile and childlike within us.

In my introduction I discuss Melanie Klein's concept of reparation, and how it can help us to understand the way people deal with the destructiveness bound up with living. Theorists tend to ignore the vital role of reparation, or simply assume it. For instance, they agree on the importance of "working through," of a patient overcoming his tendency to repeat neurotic conflicts from the past. Freud defines psychoanalytic therapy as a process of "remembering, repeating, and working through," yet acknowledges how difficult it is for patients to change old habits and create new ways of living. I can find only one writer who helps to show how this rather mysterious process works. To do so he introduces a fourth step: "making good," which "allows the patient to see in present reality a chance to make restitution for what he believes the past has failed to provide and for his own failures."[1] He does not cite Melanie Klein (who is not especially well known in this country, and on some issues unorthodox). Klein's theory of reparation, however, places such restitution in the largest human context. Without reparation, everyone—and not just patients—would wallow in guilt and unresolved conflict.

I think that being reparative requires that our healthy narcissism, our self-esteem, be engaged. (In the introduction I give an example from the scene between the Duke and Isabella in 3.1 of *Measure for Measure*.) Recently, narcissism has begun to attract psychoanalytic interest, and not simply in its pathological aspects. Narcissism is also a healthy, universal part of human beings, as Freud first suggested. Heinz Kohut spells this out, as does Béla Grunberger. I defer the issue until roughly halfway into my book. It is relevant in plays earlier than *Twelfth Night*—say in *Much Ado about Nothing*—but becomes of central importance only when the characters become more self-absorbed, and the plays more skeptical about the kind of idealization which results from problems of self-esteem.

Healthy narcissism also serves as a motive or driving force for reparation—including the kind which takes place in us as we view these comedies. People are demonstrably guilt ridden, destructive, and conflicted; and yet they often seem to want to make good what they feel they have spoiled or lost. Guilt makes us feel worthless; being reparative, on the other hand, can create in us something like narcissistic elation. Grunberger argues that a similar tone characterizes the very start of all psychoanalytic therapy; this initial sense of heightened self-esteem provides the force which carries people through the process of frustrating old habits and creating new ones. The theoretical relationship between narcissism and reparation has not received much attention, but certainly looks well worth it—especially since the relationship involves

1. David M. Gottesman, "Working Through: A Process of Restitution," *Psychoanalytic Review* 62 (1975–76): 644.

crucial moments in an easily thwarted process.

This is not a book about psychoanalytic theory, or about the therapeutic effect of Shakespeare's plays. I address the sources of strength in these comedies, and try to explain the ways in which the characters can effect reparations for themselves and for us. One way in which all the comedies repair us is that they tempt us with the narcissistic elation of experiencing a near-perfect world— the kind of world which at some deep level we feel that we deserve. This is true of most art, however, and so I examine this idea only when looking at the last three plays which I consider: *Twelfth Night, All's Well that Ends Well,* and *Measure for Measure.* In these plays, happy, festive elation begins to grow suspect, and the fact that it does contributes to their achieving a different, and more profound, effect.

Several people have kindly assisted me in the preparation of this book. I especially want to thank the following: Janet Adelman, Jonas Barish, Sylvan Barnet, Irene R. Fairley, and Norman Rabkin. The late Ruth Sullivan gently persuaded me to give psychoanalytic criticism a try.

Note on the Text

All quotations from Shakespeare are from the Arden Shakespeare, published by Methuen, general editors Harold F. Brooks, Harold Jenkins, and Brian Morris: *All's Well that Ends Well,* ed. G. K. Hunter (1959); *As You Like It,* ed. Agnes Latham (1975); *Measure for Measure,* ed. J. W. Lever (1965); *The Merchant of Venice,* ed. John Russell Brown (1955); *Much Ado about Nothing,* ed. A. R. Humphreys (1981); *Twelfth Night,* ed. J. M. Lothian and T. W. Craik (1975). Reference numbers in the text indicate act, scene, and line. Occasional italicization in the quotations from Shakespeare has been done by the author.

~1~
Introduction

Psychoanalytic criticism heavily focuses upon conflict.[1] The plays which I consider in this book, however, are comic by virtue of their ability to contain and transcend conflict within their own worlds, and by their ability to instill in us some sense of worth or happiness. I want to look at the psychological processes by means of which these plays strike us as comic. I explore various strategies by which they overcome actual or potential stress and repair our sense of ourselves and life so that they help to make living, at least for the moment, rich and benign.

The festive plays from *The Merchant of Venice* through *Twelfth Night* may seem an odd choice for a psychoanalytic study; they rarely deal with overt destructive emotions. Yet in making members of an audience feel better reconciled to our own tough world, these plays must negotiate with the anger and guilt which we bring along with us, as part of our human nature. *All's Well* and *Mea-*

1. Frederick Crews vividly shows the limits of such an approach in "Reductionism and Its Discontents," in *Out of My System: Psychoanalysis, Ideology, and Critical Method* (New York: Oxford University Press, 1975). In "Anesthetic Criticism," also reprinted in this collection, Crews argues that "psychoanalysis offers no means of studying the transcendence of conflict" (p. 175). Frank Kermode maintains that these serious misgivings tend to disappear in the light of significant, and not so very recent, advances in psychoanalytic theory—especially Melanie Klein's theory of reparation. See Kermode's review entitled, "Fighting Freud," *New York Review* 23 (29 April 1976): 39–41. For excellent examples of nonreductive (and non-Kleinian) criticism, see *Representing Shakespeare: New Psychoanalytic Essays,* ed. Murray M. Schwartz and Coppélia Kahn (Baltimore: Johns Hopkins University Press, 1980).

sure for Measure, with their heated emotions and distress, more clearly call for a psychoanalytic approach; but here, too, critics overemphasize the unresolved and the problematic. The problem comedies encourage us to overcome the turmoil which we may feel when confronted with characters in such states (say, in watching Isabella, Angelo, and Claudio attack one another). All the comedies help us to surmount elusive but persistent anxieties which we bring with us.

Let us look, briefly, at Shakespeare's impulse to ground comedy in potentially tragic circumstances in order to deepen the reparative effect. I cite a very early play so that my discussion can begin on a simple, almost schematic level. In *The Comedy of Errors* numerous deft touches completely alter the hardheaded, hardhearted Roman source. The wandering brother in Shakespeare actively seeks his lost twin, rather than merely finds him by accident. Antipholus of Syracuse, like his father, hazards all in an effort to repair the damage done by fate. Shakespeare adds the plight of Egeon, condemned to death during the first scene. Rather than simply rejoin the brothers, Shakespeare expands their reunion: they find their father, save him from death, and reunite him with his wife. The play sublimates sibling and oedipal aggression in the presence of a loving and authoritative mother-Abbess, whose identification of her long-lost husband helps to unravel the confusions and persuade the Duke to save him.

Shakespeare creates female figures—three of them not in Plautus—who help to transmute Roman aggressiveness, greed, and predatory sexuality. He drops the Courtesan's maid (who is willing to bed with the citizen for a present). He makes the Courtesan much more sympathetic: she thinks the citizen mad and goes off to tell his wife so, rather than act selfishly. Nell, a female cook replaces the male cook in Plautus; her offstage sexual advances are comic, not very sexy, and link her with her homey counterpart, the resident Dromio. In Shakespeare even the shrew transcends her type: he makes it clear that her possessiveness is due to an excess of love. He gives her a sister, Luciana, who idealizes the role of wife as subordinate and has romantic sentiments; she serves as a perfect mate for the traveler brother. Finally, Shakespeare adds a mother to reunite the whole family. In a marvellous stroke of tact, the mother first scolds the shrew for not having reprehended her wayward husband—which validates the shrew's possessive instincts—and then scolds her for having been too possessive. In a nice touch, the scolding comes before anyone knows she is behaving just like a mother-in-law. The effect of these female figures, and of the reunion of the brothers with each other and with their father, emphasizes the family as a means of containing and sublimating the aggressiveness revealed during the error-induced conflict at the center of the play.

Shakespeare alters the ending in similar fashion. In Plautus the brothers proclaim an auction to sell off the resident-twin's belongings (and, were it only possible, his wife). In Shakespeare there are no plans for breaking up the home; instead all troop off for a "gossips' feast," a celebration of repaired losses. Even the twin servants catch the spirit, and transform their comic aggression; they reunite with gestures of gentilesse unimaginable in the *Menaechmi*. The servant brothers politely, humorously, defer to one another about who has precedence. They delicately overcome the issue of who may be the elder: "Nay then, thus: / We came into the world like brother and brother, / And now let's go hand in hand, not one before another."

Shakespeare de-emphasizes sexuality and greed, tempers sibling rivalry with the search of brother for brother, and diminishes potential oedipal rivalry by having the father seek his son and find his wife. Most of the aggression is transformed into love contained within family relations, and these benign effects take place under the watchful eye of two controlling figures who will prove dear to him throughout his career: the strong, protective woman (variants of whom are in all the female characters, from Courtesan to Abbess), and the enigmatic yet reasonable ruler. This, Shakespeare's first venture into the form, shows how skillfully he manages potential destructiveness so that it can be transcended, and introduces loss so that it can be repaired.

II

In this book I concentrate upon two kinds of reparative strategy. The more important is the way in which each comedy as a whole encourages an audience to transcend the inner conflict which they bring to their experience of the work. However, this larger process depends upon the way characters interact among themselves, and I begin here.

In *Measure for Measure,* to choose an especially troublesome instance, the Duke, disguised as a Friar, intervenes between a furious sister and her condemned brother (3.1.150). Most critics

find the scene faulty, and for numerous reasons.[2] Vincentio's tactics seem irresponsible, even spiteful and hypocritical; for instance, why does he force Claudio to resolve to die when he knows
that this must not, and need not, be allowed? Shakespeare is said
to have failed to make the best of an awkward plot shift; many
deplore the falling off of tragic excitement once the Duke takes
charge. One school of critics tries to explain Vincentio's intervention by making him a divine figure. God moves in mysterious
ways; but the bed trick is seamy, and the Duke quirky, improvisa-
tory, and even comic. The scene causes misgivings which
Kenneth Muir sums up: when the Duke enters "theatrical intrigue
takes the place of psychological profundity and great poetry."
Muir defends the loss: "the intervention of the divine in human
affairs . . . transforms the style. . . . The characters become puppets . . . and manipulated so that they all find either judgment or
salvation."[3] The defense seems every bit as damning as the charge.
    Psychoanalytic critics find similar problems. Richard P. Wheeler,
speculating with wonderful effect about Shakespeare's development as a dramatist, thinks his "idealization of Vincentio's manhood is the most significant indication of the intensity of conflict
that qualifies the comic action."[4] He bases this on his conclusion
that "in order to present Vincentio as the ideal ruler of Vienna,
Shakespeare displaces conflict away from the central figure and
into the world around him. Angelo, Claudio, Isabella, and other
characters come to experience life within scenarios the Duke has
arranged and which he closely observes" (p. 133). With characters
other than the Duke, psychoanalytic critics are on home territory,
for they can help us understand "Shakespeare's illumination of
the darker regions of the soul."[5]
    I want to explore these darker regions, but in order to show how
Shakespeare's characters, and plays, help us to get to lighter ones.
In doing so, I rely upon Melanie Klein's theory of reparation. She
has no illusions about man's conflicted and destructive inner

    2. See Rosalind Miles, *The Problem of "Measure for Measure": A Historical
Investigation* (London: Vision Press, 1976).
    3. Kenneth Muir, *The Sources of Shakespeare's Plays* (New Haven: Yale Uni-
versity Press, 1978), 181–82.
    4. Richard P. Wheeler, *Shakespeare's Development and the Problem Come-
dies: Turn and Counter-Turn* (Berkeley: University of California Press, 1981), 139.
    5. Harriet Hawkins, " 'The Devil's Party': Virtues and Vices in *Measure for
Measure*," *Shakespeare Survey* 31 (1978): 113. She rightly emphasizes that "what
remain pertinent are the problems posed," rather than critics' "solutions" of them.

world, but sees us as capable of moving from this ("the paranoid-schizoid position") to another in which we feel guilt for our real or imagined destructiveness, and attempt to repair the damage ("the depressive position").[6] This process can recur over and over as we move through life. Her formulation of the depressive position, and the reparation which it then allows for, helps to account for virtue, such as charity, without giving it a pathological taint. "Reaction formation" such as Angelo's strict adherence to justice is by nature unstable, as his actions show. "Reparation," on the other hand, works: it accomplishes its goal more readily and without drawing so much attention to the doer.[7]

Let us turn to the Duke's puzzling response to the predicament of Claudio and Isabella and see how he manages to turn a potentially tragic confrontation into one which leads to constructive feelings and deeds—and without turning Claudio and Isabella into puppets, or himself becoming a divinity. The Duke tells Claudio that he has heard what he and Isabella just said, and that "Angelo had never the purpose to corrupt her" (3.1.160–61). Angelo, he says, was only testing Isabella's virtue: "therefore prepare yourself to death. Do not satisfy your resolution with hopes that are fallible; tomorrow you must die; go to your knees and make ready." Vincentio's lie about Angelo's test comforts Claudio, for

6. Melanie Klein's earliest statement is in "Love, Guilt and Reparation," reprinted in *Love, Guilt and Reparation And Other Works, 1921–1945,* (London: Hogarth Press, 1975), ed. R.E. Money-Kyrle 306–43. The essay was originally published in *Love, Hate and Reparation* by Melanie Klein and Joan Riviere (London: Hogarth Press, 1937). Also see Hanna Segal, *Introduction to the Work of Melanie Klein,* The International Psycho-Analytical Library no. 91 (New York: Basic Books, 1973).

D. W. Winnicott points out the need for theorists and clinicians to try to account for the good in people in his "Morals and Education" (1963), reprinted in *The Maturational Processes and the Facilitating Environment* (London: Hogarth Press, 1965), 94. He evaluates Klein's work, which influenced his: "On the Kleinian Contribution" (1962), also reprinted in *The Maturational Processes* ; I quote from this below.

7. When Angelo insists upon "justice," for example, he shows no sense of reality—either the nature of Claudio's crime, or the precedent for ignoring it, or his own criminality. In reaction formation the benefits are confused and uncertain because colored by the impulse defended against (here, sadism), and because of the rigidity of the doer and his need for rewards for what he does (and does not do). In reparation, on the other hand, the emphasis is more on others whose needs are separate concerns—not merely an occasion for calling attention to oneself. Vincentio's deeds are reparative in this sense (although he, too, draws attention to himself: it is part of his character).

it no longer matters so much that he behaved badly. By lying, the Duke reduces his guilt about asking her, and also dampens his rage and frustration in thinking that she could have saved him if only she had wanted to. Now Claudio can repair his cruelty and face death again: "Let me ask my sister pardon; I am so out of love with life that I will sue to be rid of it." The Duke puts him in a position to assert his own integrity, to regain the self-respect which he lost when he thought only of himself. The audience does not hear the exchange between brother and sister, but we see him ask her pardon when the Duke draws the Provost aside. That Claudio becomes calm and whole again after the harrowing confrontation vindicates the Duke, who departs saying: "Hold you there: farewell." What little we see of Claudio before the final scene indicates that he remains steadfast.

When the Duke speaks to Isabella he employs a similar strategy. As she begins to leave the stage and furiously tells Claudio " 'Tis best that thou diest quickly," the Duke advances to ask a word with her. Although she angrily protests that "I have no superfluous leisure," the Duke first turns to Claudio, and then leaves brother and sister together while he talks to the Provost. Finally he turns to her, having forced her to wait and calm down. When he speaks to Isabella he makes an apparently fatuous compliment, given her cruel outburst:

> The hand that hath made you fair hath made you good.
> The goodness that is cheap in beauty makes beauty brief
> in goodness; but grace, being the soul of your complexion,
> shall keep the body of it ever fair.
>
> (3.1.179–83)

Why does he dwell upon her goodness and grace? As with Claudio, the Duke refuses to respond to weakness and failing; instead he addresses the character's basic strength, here Isabella's sorely tried sense of her own goodness. He tells her that he knows about Angelo's demand, "and, but that frailty hath examples for his falling, I should wonder at Angelo." The Duke feels more dismayed than he says; his deceptive equanimity about Angelo's "frailty" helps to calm her. He then encourages a positive response by diverting her attention from herself (where it has centered for too long): "How will you do to content this substitute, and to save your brother?" It never occurred to her that she could do either, let alone both, so she retorts: "I am now going to resolve him. I had rather my brother die by the law, than my son should be unlawfully born." The Duke now tactfully diverts her from destructive to reparative action. He points out that even if the Duke were to return, Angelo would simply say: "he made trial of you only. Therefore fasten your ear on my advisings, to the love I have in doing good; a remedy presents itself." He simply ignores the revenge Isabella hopes for:

> I do make myself believe that you may most uprighteously do a poor wronged lady a merited benefit; redeem your brother from the angry law; do no stain to your own gracious person; and much please the absent Duke, if peradventure he shall ever return to have hearing of this business.
>
> (3.1.198-204)

He shifts attention to a possible remedy, but only after agreeing that her discovery of Angelo to the Duke if he returns "shall not be much amiss. Yet, as the matter now stands . . ." His maneuver is just right: faced with an outraged Isabella, he never confronts her the way Angelo and Claudio do; nor, and this is just as crucial, does he deny what she feels. Instead he diverts her thoughts from anger to reparation, away from herself to concern for others, and with assurance that no stain will come to her "own gracious person." The latter estimate, along with his compliment on her goodness, confirms her sense of integrity, one which she almost lost in her rage at Angelo and Claudio—and at herself, because of her cruelty to her doomed brother.

An audience's response to this scene tends to be more untroubled than that of many critics; perhaps viewers are simply pleased that pain is avoided, or that a new plot is afoot. Muir allows that "the last two acts are highly successful in the theatre." Clifford Leech, more positively, describes a production in which Isabella's "relief when the Duke brought out his apparent ace in the hole was one of the most poignant moments in the play."[8] She once more sounds like the sister who at the start of the play assumed that Claudio could redress Juliet's wrong by marrying her, and

8. Clifford Leech, " 'More than our brother is our chastity,' " *Critical Quarterly* 12 (1970): 74.

who left the convent to argue his case. She responds to the Friar's plan by saying: "Let me hear you speak farther. I have spirit to do anything that appears not foul in the truth of my spirit" (3.1.205–7). The Duke replies to her guarded statement by addressing himself, as always, not to weakness but to strength. He picks up the way she uses "spirit" as "will," and then as "virtue or soul": "Virtue *is* bold, and goodness never fearful." The story about Mariana allows Isabella to feel the pity and compassion which she had to numb during her scene with Claudio: "Can this be so? Did Angelo so leave her?" Here is a new, fresh sympathy rather than the fury or cynicism which hearing about another instance of Angelo's corruption might have produced. Her brief questions suggest an air of open-eyed surprise, as in her poignant repetition of "so."

When Isabella learns of Mariana's long endurance in a painful situation, she momentarily reverts to rigid intolerance: "What corruption in this life, that it will let this man live! But how out of this can she avail?" We see Isabella in a transitional state: first she thinks in terms of absolutes (Mariana and Angelo, like Claudio—and like herself—would be better off dead); then she thinks imaginatively and with a sense of curiosity. The Duke seizes her question, picks up her abstract use of "corruption," and turns it into an idea with physical connotations: the situation is "a rupture that you may easily heal: and the cure of it not only saves your brother, but keeps you from dishonour in doing it." She can heal and even cure the "rupture" (not simply a "breach of agreement," but a "breach of body"). He continually perceives human, physical meanings within apparently abstract legal terms. He raises the issue of how Claudio might live, and ignores her rumination that Mariana and Angelo ought to be dead. We can see how the Duke transfigures her destructive anger. The cure will be at no cost to her honor; indeed to heal the rupture "keeps *you* from dishonour in doing it"—rather than, the Duke may imply, allowing your brother to be executed.

Critics often complain that her acceptance of the plan is inconsistent, even a sign of turpitude. To Quiller-Couch, who found "something rancid in her chastity," it was a sign that she is less a saint than she appears: "to put it nakedly, she is all for saving her own soul, and she saves it by turning, of a sudden, into a bare procuress."[9] Critics tend to split Isabella into opposites, saint or

9. Arthur Quiller-Couch, *New Cambridge Shakespeare* (Cambridge, England, 1922), xxx.

sinner; they either idealize or degrade, as they do in their response
to the Duke, Angelo, and Claudio. Her goodness is, admittedly,
too rigid and thus suspect; but now that she begins to be flexible
it seems odd that her willingness to help should be thought such
a problem. Isabella followed Lucio's advice and tried to persuade
Angelo, which creates precedent for her change. But then critics
also find it troublesome that Angelo is reprieved when he insists
upon his guilt. A rapid shift to wicked behavior somehow seems
more believable than one to good behavior. Isabella's lapse from
sisterly affection to deadly anger, like Angelo's lapse into sadistic
lust, calls forth no censure on grounds of credibility. The major
problem may not be consistency, but the fact that Isabella and
Angelo—like the Duke—implicate us in their grandiose idealizations. The characters fail to live up to their standards as completely as they—or we—think they ought to. We seem prone to be
destructive even of the characters'—and the play's—attempts to
be positive. Nevertheless, even so problematic a work as *Measure
for Measure* can, in moments such as the Duke's shifting of attitudes toward a comic rather than a tragic mood, offer the possibility of reparation not only within the play but within our own
worlds.

III

What particularly interests me is how these plays help to repair
our inner worlds. How do the comedies encourage us in ways
analogous to Vincentio's benign effect on the characters? We bring
our own actual or potential anger and guilt with us to the theater,
and need to be encouraged in our reparative tendencies. The scene
from *Measure for Measure* shows characters in whom both ferocious emotions and positive, constructive ones are awakened.
The force of my assumption may be blunted by the example itself.
If my reading is plausible, the shift from intense rage and guilt to
positive adaptations may seem easy; but it is not. As even Prospero must admit, "the rarer action is / In virtue than in ven-
geance." The intense discomfort of many critics validates my
assertion; many simply cannot accept the success which the Duke
(and Shakespeare) achieve.

Before I turn to the comedies I want to look at *King Lear,* for
it tellingly reveals both potential destructiveness and heart-felt
attempts to repair the damage. The first scene demonstrates
the terrible ease with which figures can be split into all good

and all bad, and the terrible effect of such splitting, especially in heightening paranoia. Absolutely good Cordelia fails to give her father exactly what he demands and so, in his disordered fantasy, she turns into a wicked daughter worthy only of dishonor. The startling change of mood in this scene can be difficult for actors and directors, yet it rings true when we watch it; we sense its validity as an exaggeration of how rapidly our own moods can alter.

Lear finds treason even in loyal Kent, and plunges into an increasingly chaotic situation. The need for reparation immediately forces itself upon the audience and the good characters. Kent, the Fool, and Gloucester try to help Lear—as does Edgar, who also tries to help his blind father. Cordelia, unlike the others, has political and martial power, and by her immediate forgiveness can save Lear from his overwhelming sense of guilt; her entrance, like Vincentio's, marks a momentous shift to reparative action. She begins to succeed, but her army loses the battle. Edgar's own attempt to redress wrongs makes him forget Lear and Cordelia, who die as a result. The play thwarts reparation by adverse events. More interesting, for our purposes, is that the play not only fails to heal splits, it avoids trying. We are left with two perfectly good children. Cordelia gives no sign of guilt for humoring Lear only when he has gone mad. Edgar seems oblivious that he could be to blame for delaying so long in revealing himself to his father, or for distracting attention from the royal prisoners.[10] The good children also seem to feel no ambivalence about their cruel, impetuous parents. The reparative efforts take on a slightly unreal air by being at odds with human psychology. This, in addition to the events, undermines the potential for restoration and assures that the play remains tragic.

We need to make a careful distinction. The plot defeats reparative actions, but the play's effect on the audience can, paradoxically, be reparative. One reason is that *King Lear* shows so much love in the good characters; positive and constructive actions are initiated by Kent, Cordelia, Gloucester, the Fool, Edgar, Albany (and even Edmund, at the very end). Also, the fathers begin to see—and want to repair—the wrong they did; this gives greater dignity, and perhaps meaning, to their suffering. Lear begins to

10. For a clear, stern view of deception in this and other plays, see Philip Edwards, "Shakespeare and the Healing Power of Deceit," *Shakespeare Survey* 31 (1978): 115–25.

make up for his deeds through his reconciliation with Cordelia and his compassion toward the Fool and poor Tom. Gloucester has less chance, largely because of Edgar's disguise, to do anything: "Better I were distract" (4.6.283). Fate emerges as the principal villain. Yet somehow—and for some members of an audience—*Lear* can reinforce a desire to believe that human goodness might have prevailed, might have succeeded in healing this great breach in nature.

Tragedy itself can be reparative in uncharted ways; otherwise it would only confirm our sense of conflict and destruction (which may be a reason why we like it, although Dr. Johnson, for one, had to forego whatever pleasure that brings in *Lear*). Speculation on this matter would lead to a different book, so I make only brief observations here. We may be reassured by the very survival of the play's world after the eruption and florid acting out of the states which the characters depict. Not many characters survive in *Lear*, but the world somehow limps along, relying on three worn-out but exemplary good figures. In a play such as *Macbeth* more good figures survive the onslaught; in *Coriolanus* only the hero among the central characters is destroyed. Perhaps the end result of tragedy may be to bring us to something like a depressive position, more thoroughly in touch with the destructiveness bound up with living and with our aggression. Tragedy confronts us with the fundamental opposition between destructive states and constructive ones.

IV

For a moment I want to belabor the obvious; most of us need assistance from various sources—family, work, friends, art—in order to maintain a positive sense of ourselves and of the world. And we especially need this assistance whenever destructive fantasies interact with real-life demands. We feel some profound similarities between ourselves and tragic heroes. In part this is self-dramatization or self-aggrandizement, and bolsters our feeling of importance. At times we feel as deprived and entitled as Lear: tell me how much you love me. And our rage, like his, can be titanic and omnipotent: "Strike flat the thick rotundity o' th' world! / Crack Nature's moulds, all germens spill at once / That makes ungrateful man" (3.2.7–9). Hamlet's paralyzing ambivalence strikes such a responsive chord that critics have a great deal of trouble seeing the character, rather than the Hamlet within themselves. Tragedy is an extreme view of our inner and outer worlds; such plays present us with a heightened and distilled version of what we more or less clearly perceive in ourselves and others. We sense the validity of such feelings: we are neither mad nor isolated, for others in the audience evidently find that they, too, have something in common with tragic figures. Yet we can also exorcise such feelings: despite similarities we really are not Othello or Hamlet; instead, we are more constructive, reasonable, and in control of our destiny.

Classic psychoanalytic theory takes an essentially tragic view of life, one which needs to be modified by Melanie Klein's theory of reparation. She shows how feeling guilt for our destructiveness allows us to repair what we fear we have destroyed. She illuminates this process in describing "the relation to ourselves":

> This is a relation to all that we cherish and love and to all that we hate in ourselves. I have tried to make clear that one part of ourselves that we cherish is the wealth we have accumulated through our relations to external people, for these relations and also the emotions that are bound up with them have become an inner possession. We hate in ourselves the harsh and stern figures who are also part of our inner world, and are to a large extent the result of our own aggression towards our parents. At the bottom our strongest hatred, however, is directed against the hatred within ourselves. We so much dread the hatred in ourselves that we are driven to employ one of our strongest measures of defense by putting it on to other people—to project it. But we also displace love into the outer world; and we can do so genuinely only if we have established good relations with the friendly figures within our minds. Here is a benign circle, for in the first place we gain trust and love in relation to our parents, next we take them, with all this love and trust, as it were, into ourselves; and then we can give from this wealth of loving feelings to the outer world again.[11]

Although this benign state often seems precarious to Klein (which is why she refers to "positions" rather than "states" in describing the paranoid-schizoid and depressive phases), she see numerous

11. Klein, "Love, Guilt and Reparation," 340. J. O. Wisdom brilliantly compares these views in "Freud and Melanie Klein: Psychology, Ontology, and *Weltanschauung*," in *Psycho-Analysis and Philosophy,* ed. C. Hanly and M. Lazerowitz (New York: International Universities Press, 1970), 327–61.

opportunities for reparation. Concern for others often becomes the usual response, a way of life. This is what D. W. Winnicott assumes when he affirms the significance of the depressive position. It is a crucial step in development during childhood, one which recurs as a necessary phase during psychoanalytic treatment. There is a point, he writes when

> being depressed is an achievement, and implies a high degree of personal integration, and an acceptance of responsibility for all the destructiveness that is bound up with living, with the instinctual life, and with anger at frustration. Klein was able to make it clear to me from the material my patients presented, how the capacity for concern and [feeling] guilty is an achievement.... Arrival at this stage is associated with ideas of restitution and reparation, and indeed the human individual cannot accept the destructive and aggressive ideas in his or her own nature without experience of reparation, and for this reason the continued presence of the love object is necessary at this stage since only in this way is there opportunity for reparation. This is Klein's most important contribution, in my opinion, and I think it ranks with Freud's concept of the Oedipus complex.[12]

From this perspective we can begin to account for literary works where conflict is minimal, or surmountable. Shakespeare's festive comedy presents a special challenge because it so thoroughly avoids open clashes—with the exception of some carefully limited ones such as Shylock's attempt, or Claudio's slander of Hero. Overt oedipal conflict, basic to most comedies other than Shakespeare's, drops out of sight after its pale appearance in *A Midsummer Night's Dream*.[13] Sibling rivalry appears in *Much Ado* (in minor characters), and then again in *As You Like It*, but the matter is ignored in Arden. Struggle and contention begin to prevail in the problem comedies, but are largely kept under control (as we saw in the Duke's intervention).

Shakespeare's comedies stir up reparative impulses in us by awakening potential fears—say, of manipulation in *Much Ado* —and then showing us various ways in which they can be tran-

12. Winnicott, "On the Kleinian Contribution," 176.
13. It reappears in the romances. See Wheeler, *Shakespeare's Development*, 45–47; he finds the first significant disruption between generations in *All's Well*.

scended: through the plot's outcome, the characters' reactions and moods, and the large process of interaction between the play and our inner world. Our response can be disrupted by what we bring to our experience of the play; comedy seems especially vulnerable. At times I feel that people regard these plays as out of touch with life as they know it. This rarely happens when we talk about, say, *Hamlet* or *Lear*. One reason for this difference is that we acutely feel conflict; thus we grasp the pertinence of plays which treat anger and splitting. Reparative attitudes and deeds, on the other hand, seem rarer ; and when they appear they are subject to being easily defeated. In addition, the positive attitudes in everyday life are often not clearly visible or accessible; members of a family can display a wide range of reparative feelings without anyone paying particular attention to them.[14]

One especially subterranean source of distorted perceptions about comedy is that this genre by its very nature can awaken in us feelings of envy and deprivation. Why, after all, should we like *The Merchant of Venice*? The idle rich get everything that they want—love, friendship, more money, a pliable legal code, and an excellent chance for salvation—whereas Shylock loses his daughter, his ducats, his livelihood, his self-respect, and even his religion. The play as a whole strongly favors the gentiles and their world of venture, but Shylock has captured people's attention for at least two centuries. He is so convincingly drawn, and his moments of pathos as well as vindictiveness are so striking, that he must have been designed to be a disturbing force deeper than what can be accounted for by modern Jewish or anti-Jewish sentiment.

I use "deprived" in a psychological sense: the world can never again be as supportive and undemanding as it was in the womb— or, when we were first born. Erikson speaks of "basic trust" which many see as the central issue in *The Merchant*—as an encounter "of mutual trustworthiness and mutual recognition" between mother and infant, and which "in all its infantile simplicity, is the first appearance of what in later reoccurrences in love and admiration can only be called a sense of 'hallowed presence,' the need for which remains basic in man."[15] Yet growing up ensures, as he puts

14. Melanie Klein discusses the reparative aspects of parenthood, love relationships, friendship, and wider areas of repair and creation in "Love, Guilt and Reparation," 313–38.

15. Erik H. Erikson, *Identity, Youth, and Crisis* (New York: W. W. Norton, 1968), 105. The second quotation is from Erikson's *Insight and Responsibility*

it, "an inescapable alienation . . . bequeathed to life by the first stage, namely a sense of threatening separation from the matrix, a possible loss of hope, and the uncertainty whether the 'face darkly' will brighten again with recognition and charity." Margaret S. Mahler argues that separation and individuation, the essential process whereby infants grow out of the symbiotic phase, become "the mainspring of man's eternal struggle against fusion on the one hand and isolation on the other."[16] Still another way of trying to grasp our tendency to feel deprived is to remember that childhood, despite its real or imagined drawbacks, often seems to have been better than adulthood: we were dependent, yet people usually took care of us, or if they failed—or failed to do so adequately, consistently, and over a long period—we can at least blame them. Many of us do so, consciously or unconsciously, and if we can feel guilt for our real or imagined attacks on those who failed, we can try to make better lives for our children (and others we see as needy and dependent).

Given our vulnerability, I think that comedy may by its very nature subject us to conflict between wish fulfillment (such as our vicarious pleasure in finding the world of *The Merchant* so consistently supportive of trust and venture) and a sense of deprivation caused by these deep wishes being fulfilled out there in the play, but not inside us. To prevent such feelings from becoming disruptive, the play needs to manage our responses; for instance, the ring plot introduces some sense of limitation to trust and venture, for the perennial risk-takers must temper their generosity and begin to worry about giving away their wedding rings and what that risk implies. The festive comedies usually avoid ferocious emotions in their plots and characters. The problem comedies prevent the tragic consequences of characters' turbulent feelings.

(New York: W. W. Norton, 1964), 154. Wheeler cites these passages in his discussion of the difference between the role of women in the festive comedies and in the romances. Part of the purpose of Portia and Rosalind "is to see to it that crisis does not develop into catastrophe. In the late romances catastrophic loss reenacts the loss in infancy of the maternal presence. The recognition scenes in the late romances dramatize the recovery of a lost sense of what Erikson calls 'hallowed presence'" (*Shakespeare's Development*, 83).

16. Margaret S. Mahler, "On the First Three Subphases of the Separation-Individuation Process," *Psychoanalysis and Contemporary Science* 3 (1974): 305. Wheeler cites this passage and discusses her theories (*Shakespeare's Development*, 157, 204). Mahler's major works are: *On Human Symbiosis and the Vicissitudes of Individuation* (London: Hogarth Press, 1969), and *The Psychological Birth of the Human Infant* (New York: Basic Books, 1975). Also see my chap. 2, n. 1.

However, the success of these plays is largely due to the various strategies whereby potentially destructive feelings in us—the viewer—are anticipated, contained, and transcended.

~ 2 ~
The Merchant of Venice
Merging with a Perfect World

The reparative effect of *The Merchant of Venice* is often diluted. Many viewers tend to "fuse" with its world, to merge with it so intensely that they cannot distinguish between what is in the play and what they wish, or fear, to find.[1] A. D. Moody chastises critics

1. This process can be normal or pathological. Although the terms are briefly explained in my text, I will for convenience relate them to one another here. *Fusion* is losing oneself, and one's limitations and imperfections, through merging with something omnipotent and perfect—say, God, or art, or the ideal mother. We seek to merge with what we *idealize* as a source of excellence in which we can partake, and which reflects our own perfection. Ultimately, if carried far enough, this is a regression to an infant's narcissistic bliss, a state free from the frustration and impotence which limit us in the real world. However, we cannot tolerate coming close to complete fusion, for we would lose our identity by merging in such a union. The prototype of fusion is our relation to mother before we separate and become individuals (on this see my reference to Margaret S. Mahler in chap. 1, n. 16). To approach such fusion with people is terrifying: it causes a sharp reaction toward an opposite state of *isolation* from others—and concurrently, the *degradation* of them and of what they could offer. The shift is between two poles (and I simplify here): the one, fusion, idealization, and trust; the other, isolation, degradation, and mistrust.

I concentrate upon the shift between these poles—and the play's effect in reducing such fluctuation—in my chapters on the three earlier plays. *The Merchant* encourages fusion; *Much Ado* (except for Beatrice and Benedick) encourages isolation; and *As You Like It* seems the first of these comedies to convey a serene sense of autonomy. Richard P. Wheeler nicely summarizes the psychological process which I concentrate upon in these chapters: "The longing for merger threatens to destroy precariously achieved autonomy; the longing for complete autonomy threatens to isolate the self from its base of trust in actual and internalized relations to others"; *Shakespeare's Development*, 206.

for romanticizing, for giving way to "a wish to find in the play an assurance that the world may be simple and good, in spite of its evidence to the contrary."[2] The impulse is especially noticeable among Christian interpreters: Portia becomes a figure of mercy or the new law, and the play takes on a strong religious tone.[3] Interpreters begin to ignore details such as the play's secular extravagance, bawdy jokes, and sexual romance. Psychoanalytic critics also idealize: they see Portia as benign and maternal, and view the drama as a contest "between a loving mother, Portia, and a castrating father, Shylock."[4] Such an interpretation ignores Portia's trickiness about the law and the rings; it also underestimates her ability to provoke the terrifying fantasy of a maternal figure who deceives, manipulates, and always wins.

Other critics go to the opposite extreme and "isolate" the play by degrading or limiting its effect. They keep the work at arm's length by concentrating on its unrealistic attitude toward trust and money, and its antisemitism; Shylock turns out to be something of a hero, and the Christians hypocrites. This impulse is the opposite extreme, a reaction against the impulse to fuse. Other festive comedies are less seductive, for they continually touch base with a realistic world. *As You Like It,* for example, reminds us that fantasies about ideal love and the golden world need to be brought down to earth. *The Merchant* can provoke extreme wariness. Moody sees the play as thoroughly amoral, although somehow

2. A.D. Moody, *Shakespeare: The Merchant of Venice* (Woodbury, N.Y.: Barron's Educational Series, 1964), 15. This is an excellent, if too antiromantic, reading.

3. See, for example: Barbara K. Lewalski, "Biblical Allusion and Allegory in *The Merchant of Venice,*" *SQ* 13 (1962): 327–43; Nevil Coghill, "The Basis of Shakespearean Comedy," *Essays and Studies* 3 (1950): 1–28; and René E. Fortin, Launcelot and the Uses of Allegory in *The Merchant of Venice,*" *SEL* 14 (1974): 259–70. John S. Coolidge in "Law and Love in *The Merchant of Venice,*" *SQ* 27 (1976):243, argues that "the play is in fact a kind of hermeneutic drama, reflecting the contest between Christian and Jew for the possession of Hebrew scriptures."

4. Norman Holland, *Psychoanalysis and Shakespeare* (1964; reprint New York: Farrar, Straus & Giroux, 1976), 236. Wheeler argues that "the triumph over Shylock protects *Merchant* from the threat of the vengeful, possessive father," and with this play masculine values based on competition and conquest (such as found in Shakespeare's histories) disappear from the festive comedies. In these plays he sees, "more than the release of sexual desire . . . a rhythm of frustration and fulfillment grounded in trust, focused specifically through the presence of a trustworthy woman" (*Shakespeare's Development,* 175).

instructively ironic: we see *through* the Christians' hypocrisy. Marilyn L. Williamson takes a detached look at the romantic heroine, and finds that in the ring plot she "exercises a last petty tyranny on her open, unsuspecting bridegroom," and contrives a situation in which she will have to reveal her central role in saving Antonio.[5] Vera M. Jiji seeks to present an unidealized account of Portia, but instead degrades her by dwelling on the bad side, by finding her acerbic, mocking, tormenting, and even "the agent of death—her weapon, the genital trap."[6] We are far from Holland's comfortable sense of the play working "with the feeling of trust a child needs to have toward his mother" (p. 330).

As Norman Rabkin demonstrates, intelligent critics offer "interpretations opposed so diametrically that they seem to have been provoked by different plays."[7] Unlike Rabkin, I think that *The Merchant* triggers peculiarly unsettling emotions. In the process, crucial aspects drop out of sight; for instance, critics wary of the play's idealism forget that Shylock attempts murder, Portia is largely benign, and the romantic and Christian values which infuse the play are not all touched with irony. Wheeler remarks that "psychologically, *Merchant* is inhabited by helpless, dependent children, whose fates turn on the contest" between Portia and Shylock (p. 172). This is true, and since we identify with the characters, in varying degrees, the play must negotiate with our unconscious fear and rage at finding ourselves in such a spot. Here is one reason for the extreme responses to *The Merchant*. Most critics seem to deal with this fear by finding either Portia *or* Shylock estimable, or by damning both of them; however, I think that they both stand for something which we value.

Many think Portia stands for trust; they often refer to Erik Erikson's idea of "basic trust," but not to his qualification of this term. Trust is not an achievement, but the principal one of two

5. Marilyn L. Williamson, "The Ring Episode in *The Merchant of Venice*," *South Atlantic Quarterly* 71 (1972): 591.

6. Vera M. Jiji, "Portia Revisited: The Influence of Unconscious Factors Upon Theme and Characterization in *The Merchant of Venice*," *Literature and Psychology* 26 (1976): 11. Jiji wisely observes that the need "to keep Portia divine, or to delight in her surrender to Bassanio, may betray some distortion of their [romanticizing critics'] vision of women rather than an understanding of Shakespeare's" (p. 6).

7. Norman Rabkin, *Shakespeare and the Problem of Meaning* (Chicago: University of Chicago Press, 1981), 5.

potentials: "a person devoid of the capacity to mistrust would be as unable to live as one without trust."[8] The play strongly conveys both potentials. Mistrust can be a positive attitude; it is, for instance, a useful way to assert autonomy, as in Portia's complaints about the lottery and her behavior in the trial. On the other hand, mistrust can be negative and lead to isolation such as Shylock's. Since the play can encourage too much trust, to the point where viewers fuse or isolate, Shylock must be convincingly drawn to serve as a counterweight.

Because of his arresting nature, we are faced with two compelling characters; what they represent becomes polar. An unsettling situation readily develops: characters seem split into all good or all bad. Critics debate, however, about who is which; this probably indicates that we are meant to be ambivalent about Portia and Shylock—as, say, we are about the Duke in *Measure for Measure*. If we could feel of two minds about Shylock, the play would seem realistic, rather than a possibly frightening fantasy: we could respect his mistrust as an outsider in a hostile world, and yet perceive its self-destructive nature. If we could feel ambivalent about him, the comedy would prove less disturbing. This would also be the case if we were able to admire Portia for her deep trust *and* for her wariness. However, such even-tempered responses are rare, as critics bear witness. Shakespeare's characterization is more complex than in the earlier comedies, more ambitiously detailed, yet the mixture of traits fails to coalesce. This distorts the reparative effect. The central characters rarely temper basic trust with mistrust, or convince us that their actions are believable. Since the characters are either not very consistent (the gentiles) or seem fragmented (Shylock in his isolation and rage) it is difficult to identify with them, to use them as models. The fantasies awakened by *The Merchant* can be potent, and viewers seem distressed to find none of the characters able to contain and transcend them.

II

Before going into this further, let us look at the first scene of the play, for here Shakespeare sets up contrasting attitudes in an analogous attempt to offer alternatives and to temper extremes. Antonio has no fear of losing his ships—just as he later has no qualms about losing a second loan to Bassanio, or signing Shy-

8. Erikson, *Identity, Youth, and Crisis,* 325, n. 8. He specifically addresses what he sees as a common misunderstanding of his idea about basic trust.

lock's bond, or dying at Shylock's hands. Such wondrous poise can encourage us to follow suit, as can the whole play. Yet we know better, so it would help if we sensed that the play, and significant characters, were not so out-of-touch with the danger— or "so very very far above money."[9] Salerio and Solanio protest *they* would worry had they so many ships at sea:

> should I go to church
> And see the holy edifice of stone
> And not bethink me straight of dangerous rocks,
> Which touching but my gentle vessel's side
> Would scatter all her spices on the stream,
> Enrobe the roaring waters with my silks,
> And in a word, but even now worth this,
> And now worth nothing?
>
> (1.1.29–36)

Antonio replies to this poignant expression of loss not in a grandly venturesome but in a carefully down-to-earth manner:

> Believe me no, I thank my fortune for it—
> My ventures are not in one bottom trusted,
> Nor to one place; nor is my whole estate
> Upon the fortune of this present year:
> Therefore my merchandise makes me not sad.
>
> (1.1.41–45)

He sounds curiously prudent here, given his behavior during most of the play. His doggedly measured terms and their repeated negatives make him for a moment akin to Shylock (although the latter thinks him mad to take so many chances with crazed vessels). The scene gives a sense of possibilities other than the gentiles' extravagant trust. Salerio's account of the ship being engulfed conveys the danger of merchant enterprise. On a deeper level, it suggests that venturing in the larger sense is a going out of self which can result in being engulfed, lost, and destroyed: "but even now worth this, / And now worth nothing." Antonio's first appearance begins the play's series of contradictory impressions. He begins by being aloof, and ends the scene by being on intimate terms with Bassanio, almost to the point of fusing (or losing) himself with his friend.

9. C. L. Barber, *Shakespeare's Festive Comedy* (Princeton: Princeton University Press, 1959), 190.

At the outset he denies being melancholy because of love, yet by the scene's end we know his melancholy stems from the departure of his good friend. He begins by being prudent (1.1.41–45); he ends by contradicting what he claimed earlier: now "all my fortunes are at sea, / Neither have I money, nor commodity / To raise a present sum" (1.1.177–79).

Such details do not constitute a character about whom we can feel "ambivalent," for they hardly seem aspects of one psyche. Instead, the opposed aspects are simply contradictory. This also happens later when Antonio treats Shylock at first in a civil manner, then grows haughty and outraged: "The devil can cite Scripture for his purpose,— / An evil soul producing holy witness / Is like a villain" (1.3.93–95). Antonio sounds self-righteously vigorous, whereas during the trial he sounds pathologically passive: "I am a tainted wether of the flock, / Meetest for death" (4.1.114–15). He seems not so much a well-rounded character as one composed of minor contradictions which give us a sense of his being imperfect, hard to understand completely, and thus vaguely realistic. He shows that he knows about evil, tries to prevent the consequences of Shylock's usury, and yet trusts that things will work out. This can quiet some of our fears about being caught up in a fictional world which denies the validity of mistrust. Still, Antonio signs the bond. And Bassanio uses the money to woo Portia. Most of the characters pay no attention to danger and live in a never-never land.

III

Portia bears the burden of making us feel that reality has not been totally ignored, and that trust is not a dangerous fantasy. Unusually powerful for a heroine in a festive comedy, she runs the risk of being felt too much in charge. At first she has too little power, for she must rely on the lottery, and this momentarily troubles her. But during the trial she has too much control as both lawyer and judge; also, she would not need to assert herself so much if she were actually as trusting as the play would have us believe. She becomes progressively more assertive and prudent as the potential for danger increases.

As we look at her behavior during the play, we find a curious situation: her trusting and mistrusting attitudes remain contradictory rather than cohere into some comprehensible unity. We logically assume that an important character in Shakespeare is most likely a unified one, but this may not be the case with Portia (or Antonio). William Empson argues that at times, for instance in the song sung while Bassanio chooses a casket, "We are concerned ... with a sort of dramatic ambiguity of judgment which does not consider the character so much as the audience."[10] Still, as we experience a play we probably expect a character's actions and words to become more than a bundle of facts and traits. With Portia and Antonio, though, the viewer has to create the unity, to labor in a vain attempt to conceive of the character as *being* ambivalent. Since Portia seems not to integrate her feelings—unlike, say Beatrice or Rosalind—critics find it almost impossible to do so. Moody, for example, notes that she is "a warmly and resourcefully human person" (p. 37), but he continually finds her deeply suspect—and, perhaps as a result, makes her a larger and more disturbing figure than warranted. Shakespeare has introduced canny mistrust into a highly romanticized heroine, a fairytale princess.

Portia chafes at the potential risk when she discusses the lottery. Unlike Antonio, who blithely signs Shylock's bond, and Bassanio, who lets him do so and proceeds to hazard for her, she momentarily finds taking a chance irritating and irrational: "I may neither choose who I would, nor refuse who I dislike, so is the will of a living daughter curb'd by the will of a dead father" (1.2.22–25). Nerissa easily—too easily—persuades her that the right man will reveal himself by his choice, for it will indicate his attitude toward her and toward life: he will have to be willing to give and hazard all, to venture out of himself to love her. Still, when Bassanio appears and she falls in love, Portia tries to postpone the test, fearing that he might lose. For a moment we find someone in the play realistic about taking chances. Later, this fear grows pronounced: we can wonder if she cheats by giving him a hint in the song sung "the whilst Bassanio comments on the caskets to himself" (3.2.63). Whether the song is a clue or not remains contested by critics (Arden edition, p. 80). And rightly so, for we are not supposed to be sure, but to wonder if her mistrust has overwhelmed her. Here is a conflict such as we ourselves might feel. We know that Bassanio probably needs no clue, but Portia does not. He hazards all the time: taking another loan, he draws an analogy to shooting a second arrow to find the first; he seems

10. William Empson, *Seven Types of Ambiguity* (1930; reprint London: Chatto and Windus, 1947), 43.

perfectly at home in the Venetian world of venturers. She says that she will not cheat, but the song's rhymes on "lead" could serve as a clue. It would be very odd, though, if she cheated, for she seems loyal to her father's will. Perhaps Shakespeare directs the clue to the audience: we are allowed to wonder if it is Portia's trick, but never to be sure.

The practical and mercantile terms which the lovers use during their love scene also help to bring it down-to-earth. Bassanio says "I come by note to give, and to receive" (as if a bill or note of dues prompted him), and he doubts "whether what I see be true, / Until confirm'd, sign'd, ratified by you" (3.2.140,147–48). She says: "Myself, and what is mine, to you and yours / Is now converted" (3.2.166–67). All ventures out of the self, especially in love, are ones which can entail a fear of fusion—which is why people often either avoid them, or recoil once they make them. The mercantile and legal terms help to make the lovers' venture less threatening: such terms indicate that some control is available, as it more often is in daily business and legal relationships than in highly romantic situations.[11]

IV

In the minor love plot involving Jessica and Lorenzo we find lovers who are pitted against a more formidable obstacle than the lottery set up by Portia's father (a test we know must be benign). Latent anxieties about love emerge more openly here. Unlike Portia, Jessica must throw off parental restraint, for she knows Shylock would prevent her marriage. Nor does Jessica bravely, foolishly, leave herself open to adversity. She firmly takes matters into her own hands, disobeys her father, and steals money from

11. The love scene can be read differently, and in a way which gives Portia's character greater coherence. The intensity of her speech when she gives Bassanio everything may indicate why she takes such delight in controlling him by means of the ring plot:

> But now I was the lord
> Of this fair mansion, master of my servants,
> Queen o'er myself: and even now, but now,
> This house, these servants, and this same myself
> Are yours,—my lord's!—I give them with this ring.
>   (3.2.167–71)

She tries to get back the control which of necessity she gave up in marrying, and this can be disturbing to us. (The insight is Janet Adelman's and not published.)

him. We are in the world of conventional comedy, which is unusual for Shakespeare: a miserly father would prevent the marriage of true lovers. To judge from critical commentary, Shakespeare
may have avoided such situations because the consequences can
be disruptive.[12] Viewers are disturbed in unexpected ways. For
instance, the psychoanalyst Theodore Reik identifies himself so
completely with Shylock that he sees himself, and his own daughter and her suitor locked in a painful relationship which he finds
in the play itself (by projection, I think).[13] We can to some extent
sympathize with a badly deceived father. However, that Shylock
should wish Jessica dead and the ducats in her coffin should keep
us at a distance from such grotesque love. Many people try to
sympathize with Shylock by wishing away his clear lack of affection. Spedding, for example, would like to excise Jessica's theft so
that "the secret that [Shylock] really cared more for the ducats
than the daughter would not be forced upon the knowledge of his
admirers, who regard paternal tenderness as one of his most con-
spicuous virtues" (Variorum edition, p. 99). Critics seem to deny
the guilt which Shylock can stir up in us—in that we identify with
his destructive response to being deprived. Others seem to deny
the guilt which Jessica can stir up—in that we identify with her
rebellion against her father. The scene often leaves a bad taste, or
gets explained in evasive ways.

That Jessica steals money is a strongly potent issue (one Reik
took very much to heart). Why she does so is not clear, especially
in a world where Antonio and Portia dispense money so lavishly.
The play instills a deeper sense of mistrust by using such details:
Jessica cannot be sure of how to get along once she elopes. In
addition, her theft makes us suspicious about her: can a daughter
who steals from her father be good? It seems not, for she squan-
ders the money—and her mother Leah's ring. Shylock's sense of

12. On this see Rabkin, *Problem of Meaning,* 17–19; the Arden edition, xlv; and
Leonard Tennenhouse, "The Counterfeit Order of *The Merchant of Venice,*" in
Representing Shakespeare, 58. Jessica's betrayal, Tennenhouse argues, "is presented in such a way as to *deny* that it is in fact a betrayal, an illusion that those who
are disturbed by Jessica's behavior find reassuring to accept. And yet the justificat-
ions that Shakespeare has built into this plot seem to reflect a real ambivalence
on his part." Also see my chap. 2, n. 19.

13. Theodore Reik, "Jessica, My child," in *The Secret Self* (New York: Farrar,
Straus & Giroux, 1952); reprinted in *The Design Within: Psychoanalytic Approaches to Shakespeare,* ed. M. D. Faber (New York: Science House, 1970),
441–62.

loss grows credible and our sympathy turns to him, and away from the otherwise ideal young lovers. At the very moment she goes off to gild herself with more of Shylock's ducats, Lorenzo idealizes her (without meaning to be ironic): "wise, fair, and true, / Shall she be placed in my constant soul" (2.6.56–57). Alexander Leggatt notes that "metaphorically, Jessica is taking love from her father and transferring it to her husband; but the throwing of the casket and the extra detail of her disappearing to get more ducats put the focus on the literal wealth she is stealing."[14] Jessica is possessive and mistrustful like her father. This love plot is more realistic, less idealized; we begin for the first time to find the conflict about trust out in the open. This minor love plot can have unexpected effects: viewers are unsettled by the theft, by Shylock's destructive anger, and, ultimately, by the reverberations we may feel when faced with an outraged parent and an abusive child.

V

Greed and possessiveness taint Jessica and Lorenzo, but form Shylock's center of being. He can easily dominate the play and overwhelm us with his sense of mistrust. Viewers have seen Shylock in strikingly different ways; it is impossible to know the original intention or best reading. He was played by comedians very early in the eighteenth century (although Rowe was sure that he was "design'd Tragically by the Author"); by the middle of the century more serious actors played the role. In 1814 he was given a "terrible energy" in Kean's innovative interpretation, one which led Hazlitt to find Shylock "honest in his vices; [the Christians] are hypocrites in their virtues." (As early as 1796 the idea was recorded that he is not wholly malignant.) Sir Henry Irving, who in 1879 produced an immensely successful *Merchant*, pronounced Shylock "a bloody-minded monster,—but you mustn't play him so, if you wish to succeed; you must get some sympathy with him" (for this summary, see the Arden edition, pp. xxxiii–xxxv). Irving's view seems closest to what the text suggests (although he made much of Shylock as a member of a despised race).

We can make Shylock's contradictory aspects cohere more readily than we can Portia's. Perhaps we more easily comprehend evil characters who display a few sympathetic traits than we do good characters with bad ones (as in the case of Isabella). And yet,

14. Alexander Leggatt, *Shakespeare's Comedy of Love* (London: Methuen, 1974), 125.

Shylock's sympathetic traits are difficult to find. He has no obvious virtues. His love for Jessica is possessive and selfish. He even seems to have little of the pride often ascribed to him; for instance, he readily backs down once defeated by the law, and then leaves without even complaining about being misled. (If he did so, of course, the play might grind to a halt.) Monstrous, and at times comically so, he holds values not entirely bad: they are ours, in part, and this contributes to our sense of his dignity. Harold C. Goddard acutely suggests that the Christians "project on him what they have dismissed from their own consciousness as too disturbing."[15] Rather than attribute this to projection by the characters, who seem too thinly drawn for such activity, I think that *viewers* project on Shylock what they have dismissed from their own consciousness as too disturbing. Then he can be damned for their feelings. Viewers can also project good traits (prudence, dignity, honesty) onto Shylock, and value them.[16]

Ever alert to risks, Shylock tries to anticipate and prevent bad consequences. When he goes out he locks up his daughter. He gladly rids himself of a servant who allegedly eats too much. When Skylock sees a chance to get rid of Antonio, his competitor (as he sees it), he tries to catch him with his merry jest. In court Shylock relentlessly insists upon his "rights," and when they vanish he tries to get his money back. Even his sense of religion has a self-sufficient and narrowly prudent quality: he takes no chances on mercy (although a good Jew should), for he thinks that he can justify himself. These traits, odd though it seems, are basically congenial to a part of many of us; we, too, profoundly hope that to "fast bind" is to "fast find." His profession is unsavory to us—and was even more so to Shakespeare's audience—but has its

15. Harold C. Goddard, *The Meaning of Shakespeare* (Chicago: University of Chicago Press, 1951), 85. Moody quotes this (*Shakespeare*, 32); he remarks that "in condemning Shylock they [the Christians] are condemning their own sins" of worldliness and inhuman behavior.

16. On "projective identification" see Melanie Klein, "Notes on Some Schizoid Mechanisms" (1946), and "On Identification" (1955), in *Envy and Gratitude and Other Works, 1946–1963*, ed. R. E. Money-Kyrle (London: Hogarth Press, 1975). Also see Segal, *Introduction to the Work of Melanie Klein*, 126. Projective identification is "the result of the projection of parts of the self into an object. It may result in the object being perceived as having acquired the characteristics of the projected part of the self but it can also result in the self becoming identified with the object of its projection." This basic, complex process seems to account for viewers unconsciously seeing themselves as Shylock—and then reacting with unconscious and extreme scorn, or admiration.

own inner logic: he minimizes risks as, say, a banker, or insurance agent, or doctor should. We sympathize with his loss of his daughter (who really seems dead to him), and of his ducats, because we grieve for our own losses. In seeking to ward off adversity, he isolates himself so thoroughly that it can be terrible to see— especially if the viewer sometimes errs in this direction.

The play gives a hearing to Shylock's feelings, but since its predominant attitude encourages trust, and since we need the capacity for both trust and mistrust, the reparative strategy is to try to manage our identification. Some ways of distancing Shylock from viewers have vanished, or so we like to think: especially the assumption that Jews are exotic, alien, subhuman creatures. We may not understand the moral outrage against usurers in the way Shakespeare's audience did, but we still know the evil of usurious rates and the lender's cold malice—"I will feed fat." That Shylock is a comic miser, too, and a ridiculously inept and callous father, continue to keep us at a distance. We prefer to imagine that Shylock is not our sort.

Nonetheless, many try to excuse Shylock. Perhaps it is simply because he is Jewish: gentiles feel guilt, and Jews outraged sympathy. Or perhaps he points out the hypocrisy and complacency of the predominant group in his society, and that cannot be all bad. On the deepest level, however, I suspect that Shylock's wish to control his world overstimulates our identification with him. To some degree we must feel as he does: the world is full of dangerous possibilities. He adduces many reasons why Antonio is not "sufficient" as a potential debtor:

> ventures he hath squand'red abroad,—but ships are but
> boards, sailors but men, there be land-rats, and water-
> rats, water-thieves, and land-thieves, (I mean pirates), and
> then there is the peril of waters, winds, and rocks.
> (1.3.19–23)

Unlike Salerio and Solanio, who also foresee trouble, Shylock concentrates upon the probable failings of people (sailors are but men), or a paranoid view of them (as water-thieves and land-thieves). Even the land-rats and water-rats worry him. Then he briefly mentions what *no one* can control: "waters, winds, and rocks." Only the latter inanimate forces beyond man's control capture the imagination of the trusting Salerio and Solanio in their lyrical account of shipwreck.

Shylock does not even take much of a chance in loaning money to Antonio (he thinks), for he wins either way if Antonio cannot discharge the debt. The loss of money would be well worth it: "I will have the heart of him if he forfeit, for were he out of Venice I can make what merchandise I will"—that is, drive usurious bargains (3.1.116–18). If Antonio can pay, then Shylock merely loses his chance. Everything is legal, he thinks, and thus he should be safe.

VI

Shylock's attempt to control the outcome of events reaches its high point during the trial. Now we find the two principal characters both exercising control: the issue becomes central, yet critics rarely agree about the resolution. Some praise the trial as an allegory of "Justice and Mercy, of the Old Law and the New" (Coghill, p. 21). But Shylock cannot represent justice or the old law, for he is a comic, murderous figure; nor can we feel comfortable that Portia's theatrical interpretation is allegorically related to the workings of mercy or the new law. Other critics find her conduct reprehensible: she sings "the praises of mercy when she is about to insist that the Jew shall have the full rigours of justice according to the strict letter of the law."[17]

The trial has a number of theatrical surprises. Just before it, Shylock seems certain to win, for "the duke cannot deny the course of law." Antonio begins to behave oddly, and becomes baroquely coercive: "pray God Bassanio come / To see me pay his debt, and then I care not" (3.3.35–36). This remark anticipates the gentiles' covertly manipulative approach during the trial. Shylock, on the other hand, is perfectly open about his need to control, and grandiosely omnipotent: "What judgment shall I dread doing no wrong?" Antonio's inability to do anything makes him degrade himself:

> I am a tainted wether of the flock,
> Meetest for death,—the weakest kind of fruit
> Drops earliest to the ground, and so let me;

17. John Palmer, *Comic Characters of Shakespeare* (1946; reprint London: Macmillan, 1961), 87. Palmer and Coghill ("The Basis of Shakespearean Comedy"), are cited in the concise summary in the Arden edition, l–lii.

You cannot better be employ'd Bassanio,
Than to live still and write mine epitaph.
(4.1.114–18)

Antonio's impotence sounds pathological, and makes us eager for someone who can take charge. Shylock's omnipotence also disturbs us: he fuses with the law—"I crave the law" (4.1.202). When Portia enters we are ready to put up with a great deal in order to repair the damage which is being done. She talks about mercy, and although we know that Shylock will render none, it helps to have the issue of control deflected from human affairs to a higher level: mercy drops from heaven and is beyond our control, for it is "an attribute to God himself" (4.1.191). The religious frame of reference helps to make her discovery of a way out seem providential—even though we may upon reflection find her tactics distressing. Before setting to work she acknowledges human fallibility, something which we can forget because of Shylock's omnipotence and his seemingly airtight case:

in the course of justice, none of us
Should see salvation: we do pray for mercy,
And that same prayer, doth teach us all to render
The deeds of mercy.
(4.1.195–98)

Soon we see how she might catch Shylock, for he questions the need for a surgeon to staunch the blood: "Is it so nominated in the bond?" His reliance on the bond as a magical entity—it has all the answers—may suggest the solution to Portia, who replies, "It is not so express'd, but what of that?" Before she exerts the control we have been waiting for, Antonio has a final disconcerting speech, one which makes his impotence almost as odious as Shylock's grandiosity:

Give me your hand Bassanio, fare you well,
Grieve not that I am fall'n to this for you:
. . . .
Repent but you that you shall lose your friend
And he repents not that he pays your debt.
(4.1.261–62,274–75)

Some of this is noble sentiment—"bid her [Portia] be judge /

Whether Bassanio had not once a love" (4.1.272-73); but most of it is passive-aggressive. He puts the blame on Bassanio, not himself: "grieve not that I am fall'n to this for you." If Antonio really wants to assuage his friend's guilt, he should not at the same time say that it is his fault. Again, we are tempted to find an inner logic to Antonio's remarks, but if we do he turns out to be far too troubling for his role—and for the approbation of his community. I think that Shakespeare has a limited goal in mind, but the effect can be unsettling. Antonio's loss of self-esteem is supposed to make us long even more for someone who will resolve this painful situation. Characters now seem so helpless before Shylock that we are ready to accept almost anything. Even Bassanio and Gratiano make oddly unreal statements: they would be willing to sacrifice themselves, or their wives. Portia and Nerissa greet this with wry disbelief, which confirms that at last such high-minded sentimentalizing must be set aside.

Portia's intervention—"Tarry a little, there is something else"— strikes just the right note: calm, controlled, reasonable. She works out her bold deed in legalistic terms. Some critics think the outcome demonstrates that "the vicious circle of the bond's law can be transformed into the ring of love ... through a literal and unreserved submission to the bond as absolutely binding."[18] This seems too extreme, and makes it difficult to see how an ordinary, sensible person would react to the scene if under pressure to feel this. Portia says that the law is absolutely binding; but she interprets it in a way which many find suspiciously creative; lawyers find it downright illegal (Arden edition, p. li). Her emphasis on legal points and quibbles, along with her delay in discovering them, discourages fusion with an idealized law. The Venetians discover that they can trust the law because it anticipates danger, hedges itself about with mistrust, and leaves itself open to the interpretation along lines which it helps to delimit. In a word, the law is not, as it seems to Shylock, a magically perfect entity. For instance, the law apparently discriminates against an alien who seeks to take the life of any citizen (whether it protects an alien against a citizen we do not know, for we need not know here). The trust which the trial scene encourages in a viewer is not merely in the law, or in Portia, or in society—but in all of them working together under providence. Insofar as the power is spread out, the

18. Sigurd Burckhardt, *Shakespearean Meanings* (Princeton: Princeton University Press, 1968), 210.

play helps to establish a clear relation to reality—with the law's quibbles, the judge's rather arbitrary interpretation, and the prevalence of common sense in deciding matters of life and death. To the degree that the trial keeps us *away from* fantasy, it works well. Unfortunately, some of this "reality" can be interpreted differently. On a conscious level, Portia is tricky and the law readily manipulated to serve powerful members of society. On an unconscious level, one that is influenced by the apparent tricks and manipulation, fantasy destroys the reparative sense that life can be trusted to be benevolent and supportive. Portia seems a powerful, arbitrary, deceptive female who endangers Antonio, briefly, and then Shylock. Society appears hypocritical and prejudiced against anyone different from the norm. Life can seem out to get us. Viewers who strongly respond to the details of plot and characterization along these lines—many critics do in various degrees—will find that the reparative effect of *The Merchant* has derailed. Since such viewers are already prone to be mistrustful, the fact that Shylock voices such feelings, and then is punished, will add to their discomfort. Perhaps such derailment occurs more often now than when the play was first presented—because, say, we now suspect the *status quo* more readily, or are more sensitive to persecution of Jews, or simply think too much about what is, first of all, a theatrical experience in which a man's life is saved. Or, Shakespeare may not yet be fully in control of what he writes.

VII

The remainder of *The Merchant* at last begins to confront the need for prudence. The deep mistrust which Shylock raises begins to subside when he leaves the stage; but it lingers on, as it must. At this point mistrust becomes respectable, not an easily repudiated trait tied to Shylock. So far, reservations about giving and hazarding have surfaced only fitfully. For the first time, the lovers seriously entertain the need to be possessive. The ladies stress the outward signs of love, the rings, just as Portia and others stressed the exact proscriptions of the bond and lottery. As I noted in discussing the odd responses of Bassanio and Gratiano during the trial, the husbands' characteristic generosity appears for the first time excessive—ridiculous even for a romantic and theatrical moment. When Bassanio says that to save Antonio he would give my "life itself, my wife, and all the world" (4.1.280), Portia wryly dashes cold water on the notion: "Your wife would give you little thanks for that." To Gratiano's similar gesture, Nerissa trenchantly remarks " 'Tis well you offer it behind her back, / The wish would make else an unquiet house." When Portia has defeated Shylock, Bassanio gratefully presses her (that is, Balthazar) to "take some remembrance of us as a tribute, / Not as a fee." She asks for his ring, with the result that for the first time in the entire play the unbelievably generous Venetians find themselves in a dilemma: "Good sir, this ring was given me by my wife, / And when she put it on, she made me vow / That I should neither sell, nor give, nor lose it" (4.1.437–39). The wedding ring stands for fidelity and chastity, and serves, in effect, as a contractual bond; it cannot be given away as ships and money can. Unlike other ventures—going out of oneself to be loving, friendly, and altruistic—giving up the rings entails more than the possibility of losing oneself. Someone in addition to the venturer has a stake in the risk. Thus the need for prudence here is clearer and not contaminated with selfishness; here to give and hazard would be to betray the trust placed in one by another person. In the back of our minds we may remember Jessica's willful, distressing act of giving away Leah's ring. Our unease at Bassanio risking Antonio's life by accepting and spending the money may lurk about. If we think Bassanio sufficiently developed as a character who could feel guilt, we might see his gift of the ring as an attempt to repair the almost fatal damage to Antonio. Still, Bassanio has no right to give the ring no matter how good the cause. We find a real conflict here. It differs from the previous stylized conflict between attitudes identified with different figures: now conflict is *within* individuals.

In the last act, Jessica and Lorenzo (who are far from being ideal) talk about famous lovers (all ill-fated), and heavenly music (which they cannot hear). Portia and Nerissa talk about light, music, and song (all perceived in relative terms). Bassanio and Gratiano enter and are closely questioned about their fidelity (which they cannot prove, having given away the rings). The play separates ideal from actual with a clarity unknown before. The wives mock their husbands and threaten to be as liberal with their own bodies as the men were with the wedding rings. Now mistrust has explicitly religious overtones: although God must be trusted absolutely, the rings remind the husband and wife that they must be careful and possessive in marriage. Mistrust becomes a virtue, not a passing fear such as Portia's about the lottery or the potential subversion of the state—as it would be if acted upon by the friends of Antonio with regard to observing the bond. Portia tells Bassanio that it was his "own honour to contain the ring" (5.1.201). The playful squabbling can be reparative for viewers in that the wives' retentiveness is legitimate, as is the husbands' demand that their wives not play around with other men. Shylock's mistrust— "fast bind, fast find"—now emerges as the counterpart of trust. The poesy on Gratiano's ring, "love me, and leave me not" is a version of Shylock's motto. Without a bit of mistrust, of fear that the partner may be too liberal, the trusting relationship would have little chance to survive the potential unkindness of real circumstances.

More than elsewhere Portia now behaves like the controlling characters of the other comedies; her power is limited, which was not true during the trial. She and Nerissa "manage," rather than manipulate. Like the Duke in *Measure for Measure*, the ladies offer an occasion for characters to rise to the task of controlling themselves and assisting in the creation of a happy outcome. This, I think, can be reassuring to an audience. Bassanio and Gratiano always knew that they should not give away the rings, and are ready to agree with their wives. In contrast, Shylock could not be brought to be merciful. The husbands and wives can face mistrust because it has been safely contained by the situation. Bassanio and Gratiano, and Antonio as well, find that they were too generous; but since Portia and Nerissa themselves received the rings, there are no serious consequences such as those which face Antonio about the bond. Since the husbands are ready to match their inner sense of what they ought to do with what their wives insist upon, they can take the trick in good humor and without fear of being manipulated. The need for prudence arises within the context of an underlying trust in one another. The ring episode creates a situation similar to the one in *Much Ado* where Beatrice and Benedick find themselves tricked into admitting what they already know to be true.

In *The Merchant of Venice* trust comes a little too easily, and never to Shylock: the play's numerous qualifications prove too slight to quiet possible objections to such an expansive view. In *Much Ado about Nothing,* probably the next comedy Shakespeare wrote, we find nearly the opposite pattern: instead of moving from trust to some reservations about it, *Much Ado* begins with such strong reservations that the possibility only gradually, fitfully, emerges. It is located almost exclusively in Beatrice and Benedick rather than in an entire society. The note of constriction on which *The Merchant* ends, and which assists in making the play's world somewhat more like our own, becomes the predominant tone in the next comedy.[19]

19. Tennenhouse ("The Counterfeit Order of *The Merchant of Venice,*" 63), and many others feel this note of constriction in Antonio being left without a mate at the end; nothing has changed for him except that he is restored to his riches by Portia's mysterious message. If we take his isolation during the trial seriously, and relate it to his melancholy at the beginning and his being without a wife at the end, we may be troubled for him. However, at the end of *Much Ado* Benedick tells Don Pedro: "thou art sad; get thee a wife, get thee a wife"; at the end of *As You Like It* the converted Duke and Jaques are to be left in Arden; and Malvolio leaves in fury at the end of *Twelfth Night.* All are solitary, outside the community, and not married. Perhaps this is a gesture to indicate that the demands of reality have not been completely overlooked.

~3~
Much Ado about Nothing
The Temptation to Isolate

Unlike *The Merchant of Venice, Much Ado about Nothing* is not a seductive play; it invites us into no world of wish fulfillment, but instead seems to hold us at arm's length. *Much Ado about Nothing* "has never provoked elaborate critical appraisal"; some, like Dr. Johnson and C. L. Barber, decline to interpret it.[1] Although Bea-

1. David L. Stevenson, "Introduction," to *Much Ado about Nothing,* Signet ed. (New York: New American Library, 1964), xxii. C. L. Barber enigmatically declines to discuss the comedy in his excellent book: "what I would have to say . . . can largely be inferred from the discussion of the other festive plays" (*Shakespeare's Festive Comedy,* 222). Samuel Johnson offers a general assessment of every one of the plays which I discuss but *Much Ado.* A. R. Humphreys, the Arden editor, says of the play: "Some critics have thought it discomfiting, hard-edged in its confrontations whether of wit or of malice, and even to those more sympathetic it shows little of the romantic (as distinguished from the good-hearted), if by that one means the generous effusion of idealizing sentiment" (p. 74). His own sense of the play is that the characters "show a lively concern to catch others out; they walk, as it were, among benevolent or malevolent minefields. Within the general air of enjoyment there is a tingling vitality, even a sense of hazard; . . . to be outmanoeuvred is to incur penalty" (p. 75). I sense some strain here, although I agree with his—with everyone's—appreciation of Beatrice and Benedick. What are "benevolent minefields," for instance? It also seems important that Humphreys, unlike other Arden editors, cites little criticism in his long introduction. Interpreters often emphasize motifs such as "noting" and misapprehension, which seem quite general; see Graham Storey, "The Success of *Much Ado about Nothing,*" in *More Talking of Shakespeare,* ed. John Garrett (New York: Theatre Arts Books, 1959); reprinted in *Discussions of Shakespeare's Romantic Comedy,* ed. Herbert Weil, Jr. (Boston: D. C. Heath, 1966); see also, A. P. Rossiter, *Angel with Horns,* ed. Graham Storey (London: Longmans, Green, 1961).

trice and Benedick win everyone's praise, the play as a whole
seems to make critics rather uncomfortable, and yet uncertain
why this should be so. For instance, Humphreys writes of the
stage history: "Messina's world has not struck everyone as essentially good-natured. Yet essentially good-natured is surely what
it is" (Arden edition, p. 50). G. K. Hunter remarks that "the whole
work is more bitter than is usually allowed; the world of Messina
buys its elegance dearly; it is a world . . . where the comic vision
of happiness is available only to those with enough poise to remain balanced and adaptive throughout conflict and deception."[2]
On the other hand, the relationship between Beatrice and Benedick conveys a depth of love quite new to these plays—a classic
instance of reparation based on acknowledgment of guilt and a
chance to repair the wrong.

Part of *Much Ado* suggests that control is good, and another part
suggests that it is bad: a manipulation which deprives characters
of their autonomy. We need to clarify the issue. There is so much
deception that the play easily awakens fear in the characters, and
in us, about being small, helpless, and controlled by others. These
fears live on in us from childhood; as Erik Erikson puts it:

> the unavoidable imposition on the child of outer controls
> which are not in sufficient accord with his inner control at
> the time, is apt to produce in him a cycle of anger and
> anxiety. This leaves a residue of an *intolerance of being
> manipulated* and coerced beyond the point at which outer
> control can be experienced as self-control.[3]

Because Beatrice and Benedick can experience outer control—the
tricks played on them—as self-control, they achieve a positive
advance: they rise above their defensive isolation and convincingly fall in love before our very eyes. However, Claudio and Hero
are subjected to outer controls which they can only experience as
impositions: they feel pushed about, and so do we insofar as we
identify with them. We may unconsciously feel discomfited by
their world, and even by the play's maneuvering them into a
happy solution at the end—one which, unlike Beatrice and Benedick's, robs them of autonomy because it has so little basis in

2. G.K. Hunter, *Shakespeare: The Late Comedies,* Writers and Their Work
no. 143 (London: Longmans, Green, 1962), 31.
3. Eric Erikson, *Childhood and Society* (New York: W. W. Norton, 1963), 409.

their changed perception of each other or of the numerous deceits. Messina is at once a world with too much control and too little—the worst of all possibilities since it causes confusion and anger, as well as the feeling of being manipulated. Numerous characters intrude on one another, yet the ones who ought to be in control, the protectors, are bungling. First let us glance at the endemic control. Pedro benignly fools Beatrice and Benedick; John malevolently plots against his brother by deceiving him and Claudio; the Friar ineffectually tries to make all end well by setting up a ruse about Hero's death. The play begins with a rehearsal of this consistent pattern: Pedro woos Hero for Claudio and thereby sets off a series of misunderstandings. Since everyone expects some sort of trickery, everyone's perception of reality grows warped. Such a pattern can make us feel rather like the characters: open to anxiety about being manipulated. What makes the effect more intense is that *Much Ado* lacks a central controlling figure—such as Portia, Rosalind, or Viola—under whose benign protection events turn out well. All the guardians in *Much Ado* fail to be sufficiently protective. In Shakespeare's comedies the law and its representatives usually have things firmly in hand. Here we find an intrusive Prince, a hasty and ineffectual governor and father (Leonato), a bungling constable, and a rather ineffectual Friar. As Prince, Don Pedro might be expected to stand for paternal and social order; he means well, but continually interferes and proves disconcertingly credulous. In *All's Well*, the King turns matchmaker, like Don Pedro, but only because of a clear need: he must reward Helena and make his decision stick. Don Pedro does not come across as a ruler at all. He might be expected to speak to Hero and to her father on behalf of his courtier's desire to wed, but he goes beyond the call of duty in pretending to be Claudio and woo her in disguise. Pedro's behavior during the entire play suggests a compulsive need to intervene in others' affairs.

In this he and his brother Don John have much in common, although John intervenes for evil ends. John's friends advise him not to show his true colors until he "may do it without control-ment" by Pedro (1.3.19). He bridles at finding himself in such a position:

I am trusted with a muzzle and enfranchised with a clog; therefore I have decreed not to sing in my cage. If I had my mouth I would bite; if I had my liberty I would do

my liking: in the meantime, let me be that I am, and seek not
to alter me.

(1.3.30–35)

Don John automatically takes even Conrade's sound advice as an
attempt to infringe upon his liberty. The sentiment reverberates
through the play: "let me be that I am, and seek not to alter me."
Although critics find John's character two dimensional, his slander of Hero can make sense as an attempt to control others rather
than himself be subject to manipulation. John plots against Hero,
just as he rebelled against his brother before the play began, because he resents and fears "controlment." This version varies
from its source in a way which underscores the point: John tries
to harm his brother because he has just defeated and "muzzled"
him, not because of an unsuccessful love affair.[4] The issue for
John is anger at manipulation, not love. The two brothers, one
good, one bad, color the world of the play so that it seems a
peacetime version of the battlefield from which the men have just
returned.

Like the Prince and his brother, Hero's father meddles; worse,
he either undercontrols or overcontrols: he fails to protect his
daughter, and later forces her slanderer to marry "another Hero."
This tendency is disturbing. The Prince, Hero's father, and her
suitor give no sign of being able to assume the protective role
which we expect of them. Perhaps Shakespeare dropped the mysterious Innogen of the Quarto because it would be too painful for
us to watch Hero's mother also stand by idly.

It is unusual for a Shakespearean comedy that so much anger
pervades the play; Don John's rage seems surprising largely because of its unvarying intensity. Pedro, Claudio, Leonato, and
Antonio lapse into moments of fury; even Beatrice and Benedick
seal their bond of affection with a pact to kill Claudio. When the
characters feel pushed about, or feel that someone dear to them
has been pushed about, they grow testy. Those who intrude, or
merely seem to intrude, are regarded as wholly bad. Many characters find it impossible at one time or another to tolerate mixed
feelings; instead, they split their views of one another in a defense
against intolerable ambivalence. (Benedick, in contrast, can tolerate being of two minds about Claudio's guilt—unlike Beatrice—
and is reluctant to pledge to kill him.) The prevalence of manipu-

4. Muir, *The Sources of Shakespeare's Plays,* 113.

lation, anger, and splitting makes for an extraordinary sort of
world for a festive comedy (and I suspect this is why C. L. Barber
avoids the play). Such attitudes are largely confined to Shylock in
The Merchant; when they flare up in *As You Like It* they do so
only briefly, and are kept to a minimum in *Twelfth Night*.

II

Critics note the dissimilarity between the two love plots—what E.
K. Chambers refers to as a "clashing of dramatic planes."[5] Nevertheless, until the middle of the play when Beatrice and Benedick
lower their defenses, suspicion characterizes their relationship
just as much as it does Claudio and Hero's. First, let us consider
Claudio's wooing, for it sets the mood in Messina. Some allege
that the problems which critics find in his behavior are not there;
he is not a rounded character, not psychologically consistent, and
so we ought not to expect that he be (Storey, pp. 38–39). Not every
Shakespearean character is psychologically consistent (as I argue
in the previous chapter); but Claudio's behavior becomes comprehensible in the context of a world in which almost everyone
expects to be manipulated, and behaves accordingly.

Even before Claudio appears we learn to expect a sentimental
figure, one in whom aggression and tenderness are at odds: a
young man who, during the recent war, excelled in "doing, in the
figure of a lamb, the feats of a lion" (1.1.13–14). The euphuistic
terms emphasize the courtly artifice which surrounds him, and
prepare us for an apparently conventional emotion. When Claudio
sees Hero he falls in love at first sight, but says nothing to her—
nor does she say anything to him. Once she leaves, however, he
interrupts Benedick's resolute and defensive banter:

Claudio.	Thou thinkest I am in sport: I pray thee tell me truly how thou lik'st her.
Benedick.	Would you buy her, that you inquire after her?
Claudio.	Can the world buy such a jewel?
Benedick.	Yea, and a case to put it into. But speak you this with a sad brow? ...

5. E.K. Chambers, *Shakespeare: A Survey* (London: Sidgwick and Jackson, 1925), 128; cited by Humphreys, who reminds us that Elizabethans worried little about dramatic consistency (Arden edition, 51).

Claudio.   In mine eye, she is the sweetest lady that
                    ever I looked on.
                                        (1.1.165–75)

Some people think his attitude businesslike.[6] Instead, it strikes me
as highly, dangerously, idealized. Hero rarely speaks, so that
Claudio, and we, can imagine her as perfect: "a jewel," "the
sweetest lady." Claudio seems conventional, not a hard-nosed
participant in an arranged marriage, but an overly sentimental
lover. As such, he exposes himself to manipulation almost at
once. Don Pedro's busybody intervention nearly makes Claudio
give up Hero; then Don John's slanderous intervention makes
him radically degrade her.

In Freudian terms these polar responses, idealization and degradation, are defenses against anxiety caused by sexual impulses.
Arthur Kirsch, following Freud, says that "the heated carnal fantasies that emerge in [Claudio's] charges against Hero suggest the
repression of his own sensuality, and his idealistic interest in her
tends from the start to be overly self-centered."[7] Kirsch finds
Claudio's psychology not developed, his characterization largely
muted. We can better understand Claudio's character if we slightly shift the terms in a direction which Melanie Klein mapped out.
Freud thought of sexual impulses as existing apart from relationships to others and love as sublimated surplus libido. Klein thought
of sexuality and love as implicated from the start in relationships
to "objects" (persons, or aspects of persons). As J. O. Wisdom
concludes: "According to Freud, the problem [of neurosis, of guilt
and anxiety] arises over sexuality imperfectly directed toward the
sexual object, whereas in Melanie Klein it concerns aggressiveness
ambivalently directed toward the sexual object." Klein gives more
adequate emphasis to aggression in relation to sex and love.[8]

Claudio is easier to understand from Klein's perspective, for we
need not postulate "heated carnal fantasies." They are not clearly

6. Charles T. Prouty argues that the match is largely a business arrangement,
as was common in Shakespeare's time; see Prouty's *The Sources of "Much Ado
About Nothing"* (New Haven: Yale University Press, 1950), esp. 41 and 50. Muir
(*Sources,* 115–16), argues that although a convenient alliance for both parties, this
is not just a marriage of convenience; T. W. Craik, *"Much Ado about Nothing,"*
Scrutiny 19 (1953): 299, sees Claudio as a romantic lover.

7. Arthur Kirsch, *Shakespeare and the Experience of Love* (Cambridge: Cambridge University Press, 1981), 45.

8. Wisdom, "Freud and Melanie Klein," 337. Klein's view is adequate at this
point. A recent view of narcissism suggests that Freud was partly right in his rather

present in any of the lovers in the festive comedies. Instead, we can focus on Claudio's anger and aggression, which are overt and stirred up by his finding himself at the center of a court intrigue after having just returned from war. His "conventional" romantic sentiments result more from repressed aggression than from repressed sexuality. Claudio preserves Hero, "the sweetest lady," in an isolated state—one uncontaminated and safe from angry attacks. He idealizes her, and in doing so he denies her sexuality. When her sexuality emerges, it proves intolerable and persecutory. He feels deceived and manipulated by her. He cannot bring these splits closer together so as to conceive of Hero as a whole person, someone about whom he might have mixed feelings which he could tolerate. He seems unable to feel guilt about the aggression he directs toward her. G. K. Hunter remarks that "a relationship which, like that of Hero and Claudio, omits to notice the self-will, suspiciousness and acerbity of the individual [which Beatrice and Benedick notice] is incomplete and riding for a fall" (p. 28). Claudio first comes to life when he vents his rage during the church scene. Of course, sexual aggression is transformed into wit in *Much Ado,* but the continual jokes about cuckoldry indicate as much aggression as sexuality. Being cuckolded makes the man feel intensely manipulated: by the spouse, by the lover, and by the public at large. To make the joke is both an attack and a defense. Because of the brittle defensiveness which prevails at court, Claudio does not know how to take the Prince's remark about Hero: "Amen, if you love her, for the lady is very well worthy" (1.1.205). To this unambiguous and unambivalent statement, Claudio replies in the guarded way which characterizes him and Messina: "You speak this to fetch me in, my lord".

Up to this point Claudio seems about to embark upon a tender, uneventful love quest:

> war-thoughts
> Have left their places vacant, in their rooms

---

confusing account of nonobject-related ("primary") narcissism; on this see Béla Grunberger, whose work I discuss in chap. 5, n. 10 and 11.

Unlike Orsino and others in *Twelfth Night,* Claudio's character is simply sketched in—but with great accuracy. His precarious self-esteem distorts his ability to love others—to repair his destructiveness—and opens him to severe fluctuation between feeling impotent ("poor Claudio," as he refers to himself at the end) and omnipotent in his self-righteous slander of Hero at the altar.

Come thronging soft and delicate desires,
All prompting me how fair young Hero is,
Saying I lik'd her ere I went to wars.
(1.1.281–85)

The complication which immediately ensues gives us our first
fleeting glimpse of his vulnerability to overcontrol. Don Pedro
appropriately offers to negotiate, to "break with her, and with her
father, / And thou shalt have her" (1.1.289–90). He alters his plan:
"I will assume thy part in some disguise, / And tell fair Hero I am
Claudio, / And in her bosom I'll unclasp my heart" (1.1.301–3).
Strangely, Claudio says nothing about this unnecessarily fanciful
scheme. Why Pedro suggests it, and why Claudio acquiesces are
inexplicable unless we refer to the pattern of manipulation.
Within twenty lines this intrusive scheme becomes secondhand
and distorted news. Antonio reports that Pedro himself loves
Hero (1.2.10–12). In the next scene, Borachio says that he "heard
it agreed upon that the Prince should woo Hero for himself, and
having obtained her, give her to Count Claudio" (1.3.57–60). But
what was agreed upon was that Pedro would break with Hero and
her father, and would woo her as if he were Claudio, not "woo
Hero for himself." Borachio, like most of the play's eavesdrop-
pers, hears what he expects to hear: some deception. Similarly,
Antonio and Leonato readily believe what they hear. Even though
John has been clearly told about Pedro's plan to give Hero to
Claudio, he jumps to the conclusion that "Sure my brother is
amorous on Hero" (2.1.145). He expects treachery from his brother,
and hence cannot believe what his own spy has told him. Like
everyone else, Benedick believes the false report. Beneath the
comic confusion, and beneath the rehearsal of a pattern of good
deception defeating bad deception, we glimpse a troubling world
in which everyone readily suspects everyone else. Even the supposedly plain-dealing villain can trust neither the report nor his own
eyes.

Characters are so isolated that they lose their basis of trust in
actual and internalized relations to others. Claudio accepts the
Prince's apparent deception so readily that his love seems hollow,
perhaps just a businesslike wish to wed as well as possible. Yet
what he says is startling:

Let every eye negotiate for itself,

And trust no agent; for beauty is a witch
Against whose charms faith melteth into blood.
(2.1.166–68)

Such acquiescence is suspect not because pallid, but because of the barely concealed rage. No wise courtier would challenge his Prince, but the tone is unsettling. If Claudio will "trust no agent," why does he persist in such reliance throughout the play? He continually lets others do what he could be expected to do for himself, yet readily fears that they trick him. There is a passive-aggressive quality here, and it seems a defense against the longing to trust others—and, indeed, to fuse with them (as he longs to merge with an idealized Hero). He "trusts" Pedro again, instantly believes the slander—and then the Friar's scheme, and finally Leonato's offer of another Hero. Claudio continually gets just what he expects: some deception.

I hesitate to make Claudio so complex, but the psychological consistency is there and contributes to the play's effect: he voices fear of manipulation and reveals the self-fulfilling nature of paranoia. Beatrice and Benedick, for instance, are in much the same state for a large part of the play, yet they are ready and able to stand on their own two feet. Claudio's more precarious independence results in more potent and diffuse anger. For instance, his philosophical acceptance of Don Pedro's apparent deceit is a sham; its petulance flares out when he vows to "trust no agent." Then he focuses his anger on Hero: "beauty is a witch / Against whose charms faith melteth into blood." Kirsch draws a parallel to Othello, which indicates, rightly, that the lines are far from businesslike or vapid. Claudio disturbs viewers in subterranean ways: they find him a cad, or deny that he is furious, or find him conventional (which does not get one very far). In the most thorough indication of how unsettling he is, they deny him psychological consistency. Claudio, however, is all too consistent for comfort. When Pedro ends the confusion and hands over Hero, Claudio reverts to his (by now suspicious) tenderness; he resorts to an idealization of Hero that can make us uneasy after his condemnation of beauty as a witch: "Silence is the perfectest herald of joy. . . . I give away myself for you and dote upon the exchange" (2.1.288–91).

III

We may well want to hear more of what these lovers have to say, but Shakespeare shifts our attention to Don Pedro's intervention in the relationship of Beatrice and Benedick. In doing so he reveals what is missing in the romance of Hero and Claudio, and helps to make Beatrice and Benedick more engaging and admirable. In both instances, Shakespeare presents love in a novel way: he begins to explore defenses caused by aggression ambivalently directed to the sexual object. In his earlier comedies we find either less ambivalence or less aggression; the lovers seem simply to be "in love." One possible exception is the glimpse we get of Portia's attempt to regain control over Bassanio by means of the ring plot. And in *The Taming of the Shrew* we find Kate and Petrucchio resolutely aggressive; the degree of ambivalence, however, is not so extensively explored or resolved as it is with Beatrice and Benedick, and expresses itself in farcical violence.

When Don Pedro intrudes upon Beatrice and Benedick we find a clearly benevolent effect: control in this situation proves constructive. He momentarily becomes a male version of the trustworthy controlling figure we find in other festive comedy. Virtually all interpreters, crusty George Bernard Shaw aside, find Beatrice and Benedick and the nature of their love unusually satisfying. The reason, I think, is that we find them not only convincingly drawn as characters, but also because their newly achieved concern for each other comes as a relief in the context of Claudio's failure to love Hero. Don Pedro's maneuver is a classic instance of a reparative strategy.

Claudio exists throughout the play in what Klein calls a paranoid-schizoid position; the term, ponderous though it is, captures the flavor of his precarious independence in the face of persistent manipulation. He expects to be done wrong and barely suppresses his anger; and he resorts to splits of the most thorough sort in order to defend himself. So far we have seen him regard Hero as "the sweetest lady," refer to her supposed enticement of Don Pedro by saying "beauty is a witch," and then veer back to seeing her as someone he gladly "dotes" upon. He repeats this pattern later in the play. Hero's own feelings about Claudio are never revealed; she cannot be allowed an inner life lest we never forgive those who hurt her.

Don Pedro, in a hubristic and not very considered way, accomplishes something roughly similar to what Vincentio does in *Measure for Measure*: he breaks up the cycle of anger and isolation by making Beatrice and Benedick feel guilt for being destructively defensive and selfishly isolated. Pedro suggests a way to repair the real—or in this case, partly imagined—harm which they have done. He succeeds precisely because everyone in Messina is so wary of being tricked. When Benedick spots him and Claudio, Benedick at once hides in the arbor—just as Beatrice will when she spots the ladies bent on tricking her. So automatic and predictable a response ceases to be effective. Instead of protecting the characters it opens them to the very deception which they seek to avoid by eavesdropping. The expectation that they will be manipulated becomes self-fulfilling.

As a prelude to the trick on Benedick, Pedro asks for the song "sigh no more, ladies, sigh no more." The song has now taken on a life of its own, so that we need to see it in context. At first the song seems out of place, for it presents feelings of mistrust suitable to Beatrice, not to Benedick: "men were deceivers ever: / One foot in sea, and one on shore, / To one thing constant never" (2.3.63–65). Critics even use the song as a gloss on Beatrice's feelings; but she does not hear it, Benedick does. The song forces him to hear what women feel about deceptive men: it confronts him with men's inconstancy, a trait he prefers to project onto women—as do the other male characters. Benedick claims not to like the song, or the singer, but what he really must not like is its unwelcome sense that men are fickle: not victims but villains. The word "villain" is too strong, as the song tactfully suggests by its refrain with its consolation to deceived ladies. They need not feel overwhelmed or resort to manipulation, or even be bitter:

> Then sigh not so, but let them go,
> And be you blithe and bonny,
> Converting all your sounds of woe
> Into Hey nonny, nonny.
>
> (2.3.66–69)

Brilliantly appropriate here, the refrain counsels the ladies to accept things as they are. Rather than try to do anything about deceivers—or even to dwell upon their deceit—simply "let them go." And do not take it all too much to heart, for "the fraud of men was ever so, / Since summer first was leavy." This worldly tone suits Benedick, and all Messinans. The calm acceptance acknowledges what Benedick, Beatrice, and others in this play so much want acknowledged: their autonomy. The song mollifies those who worry about being deceived and manipulated: they at least have it in their power to accept their state: "be you blithe and bonny."

Benedick—and the viewer who identifies with him, say as a lover—can interpret the song as a confirmation of his fears of deception: it *is* prevalent. This strikes me as crucially tactful, much in the way Vincentio had to confirm Isabella's anger at Angelo and her desire to tell the absent Duke: "That shall not be much amiss. Yet, as the matter now stands . . ." Just as Vincentio then gets Isabella to consider how she herself will redress wrongs, so the tricksters in *Much Ado* encourage Benedick to consider how he will set things right for Beatrice.

Let us look at the manner in which Benedick is deceived. Leonato conveys the exact tone of Beatrice: "she loves him with an enraged affection" (2.3.101). Pedro adds: "I would have thought her spirit had been invincible against all assaults of affection." And the men report just what she would be likely to say: " 'I measure him [Benedick] . . . by my own spirit, for I should flout him, if he writ to me, yea, though I love him, I should.' " Here and elsewhere the lords' version of Beatrice accurately reflects her ambivalence and aggression, but makes it less daunting: "Then down upon her knees she falls, weeps, sobs, beats her heart, tears her hair, prays, curses—'O sweet Benedick! God give me patience!' " They report that Beatrice is thought ready to "do a desperate outrage to herself." So far they have presented Benedick with a Beatrice who sounds like the real one, yet is less likely to put him on the defensive. Her ambivalence seems comic, and she turns her aggression on herself. The tricksters also help Benedick to tolerate his own ambivalence about what he feels. First they chide him for his scorn: "the man, as you know all, hath a contemptible spirit"; then they bolster his sense of self-worth: he is handsome, "hath indeed a good outward happiness," is "very wise," and has sparks of wit. The lords deny his overassertiveness by joking that he is "wise; for he either avoids them [quarrels] with great discretion, or undertakes them with a most Christian-like fear." Benedick, eavesdropping, can see himself as someone less formidable than he presents himself—as quite likeable, and indeed, to Beatrice, loveable. Still, he has one flaw which he can easily remedy. The tactic is excellent, for he might balk if he heard only charges of his scorn—or of Beatrice's languishing. Instead, he hears a positively slanted account of her and of himself. The lords leave him with an affectionate, nonthreatening injunction: "I love Benedick well, and I could wish he would modestly examine himself, to see how much he is unworthy so good a lady."

Although we know this is a trick, Benedick is not a victim of deceit but someone managed with kindly intent. He overhears a largely truthful assessment of himself, one which presents him with an opportunity easy to seize. Because of this deception, he need not fear being the victim of Beatrice, as he always imagines he might be if he let himself go. The lords present him as a man in charge of his own destiny; he can be autonomous, as he insists, without remaining an isolated wit. They present his love not as a danger to the self, but as an opportunity to assist someone reticent and vulnerable. Beatrice is alleged to be dying of love for him; this might seem an imposition, but the lords show she is still her old, feisty self.

Until Benedick's—and Beatrice's—defenses are lowered they really cannot see each other as a person in his or her own right. All that they saw previously was their armor, their mutual scorn. Benedick's soliloquy at the end of the trick marks (as Jonas A. Barish nicely observes) the collapse of his "stylistic cunning"; this serves as "the outward sign of an enlarged conscience . . . a newly tentative attitude toward his own relations with the rest of the world."[9] Benedick says:

> They seem to pity the lady: it seems her affections have
> their full bent. Love me? Why it must be requited. I hear
> how I am censured: they say I will bear myself
> proudly. . . . They say the lady is fair—'tis a truth, I can
> bear them witness; and virtuous—'tis so, I cannot reprove
> it; and wise, but for loving me—by my troth, it is no ad-
> dition to her wit, nor no great argument of her folly, for I
> will be horribly in love with her.
>
> (2.3.214–27)

His ambivalence toward himself and Beatrice is both comic and touching, and entirely in keeping with the way his friends have assessed him.

During the following scene the ladies play a similar trick on Beatrice, but it differs in tone and strategy. Perhaps this simply adds variety, but I think Shakespeare keeps the victim's different

9. Jonas A. Barish, "Pattern and Purpose in the Prose of *Much Ado About Nothing*," *Rice University Studies* 60 (1974): 26.

character and gender in mind. The lords present Benedick with
a fictional view of his beloved and himself colored with positively
weighted ambivalence. The ladies present Beatrice with a view of
herself and Benedick which almost entirely lacks ambivalence.
She is "too disdainful ... her spirits are as coy and wild / As
haggards of the rock" (3.1.34–36). On the other hand, the ladies
continually praise Benedick as a deserving gentleman for whom
she is not the right woman: "Nature never fram'd a woman's heart
/ Of prouder stuff"; "She cannot love, / Nor take no shape nor
project of affection, / She is so self-endeared." Hero (of all characters) even offers to protect Benedick by devising "some honest
slanders / To stain my cousin with." The one positive remark, in
contrast to many made by the men in Benedick's hearing, is that
Beatrice "cannot be so much without true judgement— / Having
so swift and excellent a wit / As she is priz'd to have—as to refuse
/ So rare a gentleman as Signior Benedick." They then continue
to sing his praises. They point out that she is so aggressive that
he ought to resign himself, to "wrestle with affection," or "like
cover'd fire, / Consume away in sighs, waste inwardly," or "fight
against his passion." They make Benedick seem rather feminine
in the view which they present for Beatrice's edification. Thus she
gets the point that she ought to be less aggressive in order to allow
the poor man to be appropriately assertive and to keep him from
turning against himself and love. Perhaps the men were not able
to be as tough-minded about one of their own kind as the women
are. Or perhaps Shakespeare could not so readily admit male
aggression even in a fictive, deceptive view of Benedick. The
ladies may also be thought to assess Beatrice accurately as too
tough to be managed by half-measures, by evaluations which give
their due to her ambivalence about herself and about Benedick.
The result, whatever the reason, is that Beatrice sounds much less
tentative in her response to the trick. She presents a very direct
and unqualified assessment (unlike Benedick's), and waxes romantic. Prodded on by the stern view of herself with which she
has been presented, she concludes:

> What fire is in mine ears? Can this be true?
> Stand I condemn'd for pride and scorn so much?
> Contempt, farewell, and maiden pride, adieu!
> No glory lives behind the back of such.
> And, Benedick, love on, I will requite thee,

Taming my wild heart to thy loving hand.
If thou dost love, my kindness shall incite thee
To bind our loves up in a holy band;
For others say thou dost deserve, and I
Believe it better than reportingly.

(3.1.107–16)

Beatrice and Benedick readily admit the justice of their censure
by others; aware of their own guilt, they resolve to redress their
wrongs. This is a classic instance of Klein's postulate about the
dynamic relation between guilt and reparation. They experience
depression, and try to repair their wrongdoing, at virtually the
same moment. They admit the damage they have done only when
they see a way to repair it. (Klein points out that until one can
imagine reparation possible, a true sense of guilt is intolerable.)
Since they can save each other from pain, they can easily "re-
quite" or recompense the victim (a verb both use). Instead of
being brazenly witty yet vulnerable, each is alleged to be in a
position of control. Not only are they safe from being hurt, but
they can help each other. Thus their romantic love is altruistic, as
well as beneficial to the self; before this powerful combination,
their previous defenses crumble.

IV

Unlike Beatrice and Benedick, the rest of the characters remain
very much the same, despite a near disaster and the accumulation
of much guilt. We shift from a deep level of development in one
plot, to a superficial level in the other. Still, there is a psychological point to be derived from the joining of the plots. That Beatrice
and Benedick confront their faults makes us value their love all
the more, especially in contrast to Claudio's love. The play presents him, and Don Pedro and Leonato, as simply the victims of
trickery; the very circumstances which extenuate their faults prevent them from being faced adequately. In a word, they fail to
come to terms with their aggression. This makes us aware of how
far Beatrice and Benedick have come in breaking out of the isolation prevalent in Messina.

Claudio accuses Hero in a tone of childish anger. He vows to
"lock up all the gates of love, / And on my eyelids shall conjecture
hang, / To turn all beauty into thoughts of harm" (4.1.105–7). He
will be an active agent: he will suspect all beauty, transform it into
thoughts of harm. Thus his paranoid sense that "beauty is a witch"

now becomes destructive spoiling, a sadistic defense. As early as 1710 Charles Gildon felt that

> the imposition on the Prince and Claudio seems very
> lame, and Claudio's conduct to the woman he loved
> highly contrary to the very nature of love, to expose her
> in so barbarous a manner and with so little concern and
> struggle, and on such weak grounds without a farther ex-
> amination into the matter.[10]

Some modern critics try to defend Claudio and the Prince; for Gildon and others there is no excuse.[11] Claudio behaves in a peculiarly childish and nasty manner. When he says to Leonato, "Give not this rotten orange to your friend" (4.1.31), he sounds not only cruel but petulant: a tricked schoolboy or an irate customer at a greengrocer's.

Claudio is not alone in his attitude, which indicates that he is not just a callow youth, but a typical member of the world in which he lives. Hero's own father offers not a word in her defense, and shows no faith in her. When he says, "Hath no man's dagger here a point for me?" (4.1.109), his daughter immediately faints in reaction to his having abandoned all trust in her. He luxuriates in a passive, self-aggrandizing attitude similar to Claudio's. When she swoons, Leonato devotes thirty lines to his own grief and to the wish that she might die. Were Hero not so shadowy and undefined a character, it would probably be impossible to recon- cile ourselves to Leonato or to Claudio. So unkind a father even helps to make the suitor and the Prince seem less outrageous.

Like Beatrice and Benedick, the Friar pities Hero; all three believe in her innocence. He appropriately dwells upon the need

10. Charles Gildon, "The Argument of *Much Ado About Nothing*," in *The Works of Mr William Shakespear*, ed. Rowe, vol. 10 (1710). I quote from the Signet edition of *Much Ado*; "The Argument" also appears in the Variorum edition.

11. Those who excuse Claudio and the Prince are, for example: Prouty (*The Sources of "Much Ado"*), with his emphasis on the business arrangement; J. R. Mulryne, who would not have us dwell on their "callousness" in *Shakespeare: "Much Ado About Nothing"* (Woodbury, N.Y.: Barron's Educational Series, 1965), 35. Among those who condemn him, Bertrand Evans states in *Shakespeare's Comedies* (Oxford: Clarendon Press, 1960), 81–82, that "Though we are made to remember that Claudio speaks in ignorance, the excessiveness of his outburst destroys the mitigating effect of our awareness: ignorance cannot excuse so much zeal"—"an exuberance that borders sadism."

for trust:

> Call me a fool;
> Trust not my reading nor my observations,
> . . . .
> My reverence, calling, nor divinity,
> If this sweet lady lie not guiltless here.
> (4.1.164–65, 168–69)

He finds in her blushes the kind of proof which Claudio denies, and appeals not to reason but to an instinctive sense of faith. The Friar links his trust to his religious vocation, thereby strengthening the case. Like the Duke in *Measure for Measure,* he diverts attention from specific charges and avoids challenging the characters for their cruelty; instead he offers a positive move designed to lessen anger. Leonato agrees to the Friar's proposal in a way which reveals the infantile nature of his rage: "Being that I flow in grief, / The smallest twine may lead me" (4.1.249–50).

The Friar proposes that they pretend Hero died; this will "change slander to remorse; that is some good." Feelings of guilt might bring Claudio to his senses. The Friar's external control of the accusers might be met with internal guilt and lead to change—as it just has for Beatrice and Benedick. He senses the crucial need for a "good object" or internalized benign and trustworthy figure:

> Th' idea of her life shall sweetly creep
> Into his study of imagination,
> And every lovely organ of her life
> Shall come apparell'd in more precious habit,
> More moving-delicate and full of life,
> Into the eye and prospect of his soul
> Than when she liv'd indeed.
> (4.1.224–30)

By gaining such a loving internal figure, Claudio will, the Friar thinks, "mourn— / If ever love had interest in his liver— / And wish he had not so accused her: / No, though he thought his accusation true."

Claudio always dwells on Hero's beauty in the abstract: a sign of how he idealizes her. When he thinks her unchaste, he says "beauty is a witch," and when he accuses her in church, he vows "to turn all beauty into thoughts of harm" (to destroy it by his

suspicion). The Friar conceives of her differently; he emphasizes
her goodness, and describes the "idea of her life" in a way which
makes her seem alive and potentially sexual: "every lovely organ
of her life / Shall come apparell'd in more precious habit, / More
moving-delicate and full of life." The Friar's view makes Hero
more complete and human than she is in Claudio's view of her
static "beauty" (which seems to have nothing to do with her other
traits, for she has it even when he sees her as persecutory).

The Friar's plan fits into the play's long series of manipulations,
but with a highly important difference: it lacks the omnipotence
which characterizes other maneuvers:

> But if all aim but this be levell'd false,
> The supposition of the lady's death
> Will quench the wonder of her infamy:
> And if it sort not well, you may conceal her,
> As best befits her wounded reputation
> In some reclusive and religious life.
>
>   (4.1.237–42)

Pedro never entertained the idea that he might not be able to get
Hero for Claudio, or that Beatrice and Benedick might not fall for
his trick—or that any of his attempts might be officious. Nor does
Don John consider that his slander might backfire and lead to
further muzzling, let alone that he has no right to hurt Claudio
and Hero. Neither brother has a good sense of reality, an awareness that others exist separately from what he wishes and that they
lie outside his control. An air of "manic," inauthentic reparation
pervades Messina: an attitude of control, triumph, and contempt.[12] This tone may be muted, certainly, by Pedro's good
results. Still, Claudio's and Pedro's cruelty, Leonato's wish that

12. Hanna Segal summarizes Klein's view in *Introduction to the Work of Melanie
Klein,* 83–84. Such feelings are defenses against the depression which would arise
from valuing someone and thus depending on him; if we value and depend on
someone, we open ourselves to fear of loss and guilt. Manipulative "*control* is a
way of denying dependence, of not acknowledging it"; instead, we compel people
to depend upon us. Someone "wholly controlled is, up to a point, [someone who]
can be depended on. *Triumph* is a denial of depressive feelings of valuing and
caring; it is linked with omnipotence. . . . *Contempt* for [people] is again a direct
denial of valuing [them, a feeling] which is so important in the depressive position." Contempt "acts as a defense against the experience of loss and guilt. An
object of contempt is not an object worthy of guilt." (The italics are mine.)

his daughter were dead, and John's malice—all are manipulative in the worst sense. These characters defend themselves against valuing and depending upon others, and against feeling either guilt for hurting them or loss when they are destroyed. An audience's sense of this, however unconscious, accounts for what critics refer to as the play's bright hardness, "brittle" tone, and "flat" characters.[13] The Claudio plot is not defective or tragic—or psychologically inconsistent. What can make it disconcerting is the implication that one must isolate oneself to avoid being manipulated beyond endurance.

V

Only the Friar, Beatrice, and Benedick transcend this brittle, defensive approach to life. The lovers' awakened sense of each other as individuals draws them into a real world beyond their fantasies—as strikingly revealed by their remarkable exchange at the end of the church scene. Benedick first shows concern, appropriately, for the woman he loves: "Lady Beatrice, have you wept all this while?"

Benedick.	Surely I do believe your fair cousin is wronged.
Beatrice.	Ah, how much might the man deserve of me that would right her!
Benedick.	Is there any way to show such friendship?
Beatrice.	A very even way, but no such friend.
Benedick.	May a man do it?
Beatrice.	It is a man's office, but not yours.
Benedick.	I do love nothing in the world so well as you—is not that strange?
Beatrice.	As strange as the thing I know not. It were as possible for me to say I loved nothing so well as you, but believe me not; and yet I lie not; I confess nothing, nor I deny nothing. I am sorry for my cousin.
Benedick.	By my sword, Beatrice, thou lovest me.

. . . .

Benedick.	What offense, sweet Beatrice?

13. Rossiter (*Angel with Horns,* 35), Hunter (*Shakespeare: The Late Comedies,* 31). Storey ("The Success of *Much Ado*," 38), refers to the characters' identities as "masks." Also see Humphreys, Arden edition, in n. 1 above.

Beatrice.	You have stayed me in a happy hour, I was about to protest I loved you.
Benedick.	And do it with all thy heart.
Beatrice.	I love you with so much of my heart that none is left to protest.

(4.1.259–73, 281–86)

Barish remarks that the lovers, "thinking as much of Hero for the moment as of themselves, absent-mindedly, as it were, confess their love to each other" (p. 26). Their concern for Hero at such a moment actually *accounts* for their sudden ability to confess their love; in each instance, Beatrice and Benedick think about someone other than themselves—not only their beloved, but also Hero. Now they channel the aggression which they devoted to self-protection through witty isolation, to a new concern for others: their beloved and the slandered bride. The confession of love comes at the very moment when they reach out to help Hero; this indicates that they have entered a reparative mood which extends beyond romantic love. This is the most carefully articulated instance of falling in love which Shakespeare depicts in his comedies up to this point in his career. In other plays we are simply told that characters fall in love; here we see resistance and how it is overcome.

One especially important aspect of Beatrice and Benedick's love is that their concern for others extends beyond themselves to Hero. Reparation becomes a way of life for them, and involves anxiety about the loss of a loved one. In *The Merchant* we find a similar link between romantic love and concern for others: as soon as Portia and Bassanio pledge their troth they must come to Antonio's aid. However, this is not a novel experience such as Beatrice and Benedick's, for the lovers in *The Merchant* seem loyal by habit—and, again, have to overcome no doubts, such as Benedick must in giving way to Beatrice's demand to attack Claudio. In *Romeo and Juliet,* so often thought a romantic comedy turned tragic, the two young lovers also undertake reparative attempts as soon as they fall in love—in the face of social pressure and with results which intensify Juliet's ambivalence toward Romeo. Shakespeare often links romantic love to altruism in his comedies; the fact that Beatrice and Benedick conceive of even falling in love as "requiting" their wrongs may be one reason why the couple, and the nature of their love, strike such a responsive chord. They

have an unspoken effect on us, a depth which we do not find in
Shakespeare's comic lovers previous to this play, but which helps
to give later characters such as Rosalind and Orlando, Viola,
Helena, and even Vincentio some of their resonance.
Klein's theory helps us to make more sense of such love. As
John Wisdom points out, "Freud's *Weltanschauung* is that, for
the most part and with not very far-reaching exceptions, man is
fundamentally a selfish pawn at the mercy of the pleasure princi-
ple. . . . the Kleinian *Weltanschauung* includes a measure of altruism as part of the nature of man, even from earliest childhood.
This is not an uplift picture (Melanie Klein had no illusions about
what people are like); it does not mean that man is predominantly
altruistic. . . . It means that selfishness and altruism exist side by
side, each a 'genuine' phenomenon" (p. 343). The depressive position is, he suggests, a theory of love, whereas Freud's libido theory
is a theory of sex (I oversimplify, of course; see pp. 345–48).
    Still, there is something unsettling about the exchange between
Beatrice and Benedick, for she coerces him:

Benedick.	Come, bid me do anything for thee.
Beatrice.	Kill Claudio!
Benedick.	Ha, not for the wide world!
Beatrice.	You kill me to deny it. Farewell.
Benedick.	Tarry, sweet Beatrice.
Beatrice.	I am gone, though I am here; there is no love in you; nay I pray you let me go.
Benedick.	Beatrice—
Beatrice.	In faith, I will go.
Benedick.	We'll be friends first.
Beatrice.	You dare easier be friends with me than fight with mine enemy.
Benedick.	Is Claudio thine enemy?
Beatrice.	Is a not approved in the height a villain, that hath slandered, scorned, dishonoured my kinswoman? O that I were a man!

(4.1.287–302)

In *Much Ado*, characters always respond at once to any threat by
attempting to control others. Beatrice forces Benedick to avenge
Hero, even though the Friar has just set up a ruse which might
make Claudio repent. Benedick agrees to challenge his friend

despite his better judgment, and despite knowing Hero still lives. Although the duel never takes place and the challenge can easily be set aside, we get a pungent whiff of control, triumph, and contempt.

This scene and the one following (where Leonato and Antonio indulge in furious outbursts) "employ deliberate ambiguities of tone and demand a double response" to what is heroic and sympathetic, yet also ironic and absurd (Storey, p. 45). We are fond of Beatrice and Benedick, yet find them doing something we may not like. The witty exchanges between Benedick and Claudio which later follow make both men seem unattractive: "Benedick is absurd, shackled, as it were, to the interests of Beatrice; and Claudio is repellent for his very lack of involvement" (Hunter, p. 31) Beatrice and Benedick no longer seem totally admirable when she demands that he challenge Claudio, and he acquiesces.

The viewer is now made to feel ambivalent about a wide range of characters, including the favorites, Beatrice and Benedick. This seems a crucial effect, one which adds depth and plausibility to *Much Ado*. It is another of the play's novel effects or devices. In *The Merchant* it is difficult to tolerate feeling of two minds about most characters. As I argued, Portia and Antonio seem bundles of contradictory traits, rather than psychologically coherent. Except for occasional moments, we tend not to unify the opposing elements — say, to relate the fact that Antonio is generous to Bassanio, but selfish in making him responsible for his own plight. From *Much Ado* onward, Shakespeare presents comic characters (but not all the characters in each play) as figures about whom some ambivalence can be felt. Usually it is easy to tolerate. Rosalind is manipulative, yet lets others live their own lives; she toys with Phebe, and takes pleasure in it, yet can hardly do otherwise. Viola finds herself in similar situations. In *Much Ado* the ambivalence we feel about Beatrice and Benedick is for a while intense. Still, we are not dealing with ambivalence of the sort we find in tragedy. Othello is plunged into a chaotic state: he loves Desdemona even as he kills her. Beatrice and Benedick only begin to split their views of Claudio, but they no longer see him as a tolerable mixture of good and bad traits (as, say, the too-ready victim of others, rather than a villain). Viewers often find it difficult to respond to Beatrice's hot-tempered aggression as merely a harmless trait in a love battle; nor can we entirely excuse Benedick, who knows better than to knuckle under. We need to face their faults without condemning or rejecting the character.

Shakespeare arranges this scene so that we can feel of two minds about Beatrice and Benedick, yet remain positive. The tone and situation are rather absurd in their excess; the duel never takes place, and proves uncalled for when Borachio confesses. In addition, the excesses of Beatrice here, and Benedick's challenge later, encourage us to remain positively inclined toward Claudio since he is the victim of their overreaction. The way that Shakespeare ends the near-tragic church scene encourages us, the viewers, to endure ambivalence toward characters. By virtue of their faults, Beatrice and Benedick help us to maintain our balance, our capacity for comedy. They validate our anger at the accusers, and yet show us that such a response is excessive and hasty.

VI

Before we consider Claudio's effect on the play as a whole, let us widen our perspective by attending to Dogberry and the Watch. They invariably please audiences and critics, but appear "loosely attached to the main plot" (aside from contributing to the pattern of distortions caused by overhearing).[14] The clown scenes place the main action in a new light. Dogberry's charge to the Watch enjoins them to withdraw from all situations in which they might exercise control. If any suspicious person refuses to halt, Dogberry advises the Watch to "take no note of him, but let him go" (3.3.28). A mad kind of logic prevails, a parody of the wisdom inherent in the song's wistful reasonableness in advising the beloved to forget the deceiver: "let them go, / And be you blithe and bonny." Dogberry's instructions turn all expectations on their head, for he wants the watch to avoid exercising any control at all. They are told "to offend no man, and it is an offence to stay a man against his will." The Watch, however, ought to observe and control citizens in so far as necessary for the preservation of the peace. Such action would differ from the intrusiveness so prevalent among the main characters: it would contribute to everyone's well-being. The long and wondrous charge can alert us to such a distinction, especially since the Watch at once wisely disobeys his instructions. As soon as Borachio and Conrade enter, the Watch

14. M. C. Bradbrook, *Shakespeare and Elizabethan Poetry* (London: Chatto and Windus, 1951), 187. Hunter (*Shakespeare: The Late Comedies,* 31), suggests that the watchmen's "sublime but also pathetic self-confidence, no less than their function in the intrigue," fits them into the play's structure.

behaves as it ought—albeit in a fashion typical of all Messinans: they hide, eavesdrop, and immediately suspect "some treason."

When Dogberry and Verges attempt to tell Leonato that villains have been apprehended, the governor meets his match. The clowns' random malapropisms and long-winded rambling reveal them to be as self-absorbed and self-important in their own bizarre way as the manipulators in the main plot. Dogberry so inflates self-assurance beyond what is usual in Shakespearean clowns that he seems a parody of characters such as Pedro, John, Leonato—and even Beatrice and Benedick (in their certainty about Claudio's being a villain to be challenged). This comic exaggeration becomes even more pronounced during Dogberry's final scene. When Conrade calls him an ass, Dogberry grows ponderously irate, just as Leonato and Antonio do in the scene which follows:

> Dost thou not suspect my years? O that he were here to write me down an ass! . . . I am a wise fellow, and which is more, an officer, and which is more, a householder, and which is more, as pretty a piece of flesh as any is in Messina, and one that knows the law, go to.
>
> (4.2.71–80)

Dogberry's fear of being small and vulnerable peeps out from behind this magnificently foolish bravado, as it does in his high-handed manner of examining Conrade and Borachio: "Masters, it is proved already that you are little better than false knaves, and it will go near to be thought so shortly. How answer you for yourselves?" (4.2.19–22). Since this scene immediately follows Beatrice and Benedick's reaction to the slander of Hero, we find an oddly similar—and totally comic—element of control. Dogberry proves the villains guilty even before he takes testimony, just as Beatrice, and then Benedick, demand revenge on Claudio without knowing the whole truth and without waiting for the Friar's plan to take effect. Also, Dogberry's anger when called an ass echoes Beatrice's excessive fury in the preceding scene, as well as Leonato and Antonio's justifiable yet ludicrous anger in the scene which immediately follows. The juxtaposition here helps to confirm a comic undertone in the two serious scenes.

More important, Dogberry implicates himself in the false sense of omnipotence which prevails in *Much Ado*. He runs like a steamroller over Conrade and Borachio—over their sensibilities (such as they are), over rational conduct itself, and over the premise that they must be assumed innocent until proven guilty. We are treated to a surreal version of the way the Prince and his brother ignore the autonomy of others. Dogberry and Verges, and the Watch itself, fit perfectly into the world of the play, but they arouse none of the anxieties which the others do. The crucial difference must be that the clowns, unlike other characters, are presented with a clear-cut need to do something and with an express authority to act. This is not so true of the Prince's maneuvers, and not at all true of John's. Perhaps even more important, Dogberry and the Watch almost fail to make things right; whatever control they exercise in bringing the truth to light and in saving the day becomes diluted by the fact that they nearly fail.

Dogberry's flawed ability to control becomes most obvious in his startling use of language as if it were his own magical creation. He and his companions cling to the language which they make up—mistakes, illogic, and all—just as a child does when learning to talk. The clowns, and perhaps children as well, invent their own language by a kind of hallucination (as a transitional object in Winnicott's sense); they then attempt to superimpose this creation on what already exists, the language as others speak it. That the clowns display their sense of magical omnipotence principally in their language, rather than in their relations with other characters, contributes to their agreeable effect in *Much Ado*. They blithely sail on, oblivious to the otherness of words and logic, and leave us behind trying to reconstruct what they have said—trying to bring it into line with the reality of words and thoughts as we know them. By doing this, they put the audience in a position which allows breathing space in the overly controlled world of Messina, a world which stresses ordered formality and symmetry in its rhetoric as well as in its plots and counterplots. We are forced to be on our own, to pull out some meaning for ourselves from the gallimaufry of familiar yet almost incomprehensible words and ideas which the clowns present to us.

This breathing space, this being put in a position in which we must be the responsible adult to their irresponsible language, provides relief from the regression back to infantile fears which the play might encourage. We can more easily see this process at work by considering the relation between Lear and the Fool; that is, my hypothesis about an audience's response can be tested against a character's response in a similar situation. When the truth about Lear's relation to his daughters begins to dawn on him, he fears going mad. The Fool, who prods him into such necessary realizations, continually tries to prevent the truth from becoming unbearable by making apparently inscrutable remarks which Lear must figure out for himself. In this, the Fool does not simply divert Lear from his pain, but forces him to function as an adult who can figure out the riddles and snatches of song; thus he can conceive of himself as not simply the victim of Goneril and Regan's manipulation, but as a man in his own right who can control—if not his daughters, as he falsely imagined—at least the meaning to be derived from his situation.

VII

The ending of *Much Ado* raises several problems for critics, although it seems less troublesome to viewers. I want to face some of the problems and suggest why an audience may not feel especially bothered by them. The central obstacle to the play's reparative effect, its success as a comedy, is that we—along with the characters themselves—find Messina too manipulative. In the case of Beatrice and Benedick the good results of their being tricked divert our attention and fears. In the case of Claudio the good results are flawed, for the Friar's plan fails in some ways. I think that we are meant to feel this. When Borachio confesses to his part in the slander of Hero, he sets a standard which Claudio—and Don Pedro and Leonato—never reach:

> My villainy they have upon record, which I had rather
> seal with my death than repeat over to my shame. The
> lady is dead upon mine and my master's false accusation;
> and briefly, I desire nothing but the reward of a villain.
>
> (5.1.234–38)

Borachio sounds truly contrite, and does not offer extenuating circumstances. Claudio says that he has "drunk poison" while hearing this confession. It is proof of Hero's innocence, and Claudio immediately says "Sweet Hero! Now thy image doth appear / In the rare semblance that I lov'd it first" (5.1.245–46). He asks Leonato's patience, when berated by him, and offers to submit to whatever penance he wishes: "yet sinn'd I not / But in mistaking" (5.1.268–69). This all falls short of what was hoped for. Proof of innocence, not news of her death—or, more crucial, a sense of the wrong he did her—makes Hero's image "appear / In the rare semblance that I lov'd it first." She does not, in this phrasing, even seem to be the *living* internalized image which the Friar so vividly portrayed. Claudio's choice of "rare semblance" is inadequate, unpleasing, coming as it does from a man who never gets beyond an abstract sense of external beauty and who accused her as being "but the sign and semblance of her honour" (4.1.32). His sense of trust remains stunted, as does his ability to feel guilt.

That he mourns Hero in a highly formal manner suits his character, and differs from the tentative soliloquies and probing exchanges of Beatrice and Benedick. Once again, Claudio is perfectly ready to do what others tell him to do: Leonato, not he, initiates this mourning rite. And Claudio's tone jars a bit: "I do embrace your offer," he tells Leonato when another bride is said to be ready for him, "and dispose / For henceforth of poor Claudio" (5.1.288–89). The epitaph which he hangs on the tomb names no names, and assigns no guilt. He has a song to Diana: "Pardon, goddess of the night, / Those that slew thy virgin knight." He again links Hero to "dian in her orb," as she was in his earlier fragile and idealized view of her. In context this compliment hardly sets our minds to rest about his penchant for seeing her as either a perfect Diana far above him, or a degraded Venus far beneath him.

If viewers expect the transformation which the Friar predicted, one similar to Beatrice and Benedick's when confronted with their faults, Claudio's response is disconcerting. Critics explain away the discomfort—or do not acknowledge it—for no one in the play seems surprised or displeased.[15] There is a glimmer of trust in Claudio's willingness to take a masked lady to wife, but the fact that a man who has continually been the victim of manipulation should persist in doing only what others direct him to do strikes me as a weak indication that he has changed. Claudio still idealizes women, and remains passive-aggressive: "dispose / For henceforth of poor Claudio."

15. For example, Mulryne, *Shakespeare: "Much Ado,"* 43–45; also Humphreys, Arden edition, 57–58. Craik (*"Much Ado,"* 312), thinks the effect on Claudio is "exactly as Friar Francis prophesied." Philip Edwards ("Healing Power of Deceit," 123), on the other hand, writes that the Friar's deception "has absolutely no effect upon Claudio"; "the big build-up of this deceit-therapy . . . and the attention given to its failure to affect Claudio, mean that there is a special importance in this part of the play."

I think that many viewers find themselves ambivalent about Claudio; critics seem roughly divided into those who find his supposed reformation satisfying, and those who do not. The Friar himself warned of the possible failure of his plan to make Claudio feel guilt, loss, and a more profound love for Hero. Perhaps at this point in his career, Shakespeare had trouble dealing with the aggressiveness of Claudio—and of other comic heroes. Benedick's aggression is more easily channeled than Claudio's, in part because he is witty and has a more equal mate in Beatrice. However, Claudio's partial and unconvincing change fits nicely into the comedy's larger pattern. Perhaps *Much Ado* would be less satisfying if Claudio *did* perfectly fulfill the Friar's and our expectations. Here at long last we find a trick which does not succeed. Viewers can regard this as a welcome relief in a world replete with well-intentioned control. The Friar joins a long line of benevolent, and usually central, figures in these plays who lack omnipotence; he told us that he knows the limits to his power, and the play bears this out.

The tone of the last fifty lines of *Much Ado* differs from that of other festive comedies—or even problem comedies. The wonder at the beginning of the scene is low-key: Hero is alive, married to Claudio, and we will hear more later (the Friar says, 5.4.69–71). Instead, what we hear about is the response of Beatrice and Benedick to their being tricked:

Benedick.	They swore that you were almost sick for me.
Beatrice.	They swore that you were well-nigh dead for me.
Benedick.	'Tis no such matter. Then you do not love me?
Beatrice.	No, truly, but in friendly recompense.
	(5.4.80–83)

Her phrase "friendly recompense" (restitution for some misdeed) affectionately softens "no"; we sense her enduring, but nicely underplayed, interest in him. That they were deceived bothers them not at all. Indeed, they gladly submit to another controlling gesture when their sonnets are produced as proof:

Benedick.	A miracle! Here's our own hands against our hearts. Come, I will have thee; but by

	this light, I take thee for pity.
Beatrice.	I would not deny you, but by this good day I yield upon great persuasion, and partly to save your life, for I was told you were in a consumption.

(5.4.91–96)

Such self-control indicates its congruence with outer control; the sonnets introduced as evidence get them to admit their love: "Here's our own hands against our hearts." He takes her "for pity," and she yields "partly to save your life, for I was told you were in a consumption." The irony here does not alter the fact that each of them could get out of the match if he or she wanted; they playfully yield to what they choose to regard as inevitable.[16] As lovers, Beatrice and Benedick are far from being an instance of Freud's early formulation that love consists of the ego emptying itself out in favor of the beloved.[17]

They approach each other as loving individuals, insistent on a measure of self-sufficiency, on a mild ironic detachment. From this moment Benedick himself begins to manage the situation and to lend a positive, forthright tone to the conclusion of the play. He becomes a forceful, yet tactful, lover. When Pedro jokingly refers to him as "the married man," Benedick asserts:

In brief, since I do purpose to marry, I will think nothing
to any purpose that the world can say against it; and
therefore never flout at me for what I have said against it;
for man is a giddy thing, and this is my conclusion.

(5.4.103–7)

16. Edwards ("Healing Power of Deceit," 123), nicely demonstrates the fear of over-control which a viewer can introduce even here: "we should be wary of too cheery a view of what happens in the minds of these two people when they realize that they have been tricked." Edwards sees many of the patterns I do, but finds "deceit-therapy" here and elsewhere in Shakespeare quite suspect.

17. Sigmund Freud, in, of all places, "Humor" (1927), in the *Standard Edition of the Complete Psychological Works of Sigmund Freud*, ed. James Strachey (London: Hogarth Press, 1966–74) 21:164. Also see *Group Psychology* (1921), in the *Standard Edition*, 18:112–13; and "On Narcissism: An Introduction" (1914), in the *Standard Edition*, 14:76. In the latter study, Freud laid the basis for recent work on how narcissism is implicated with sexual instincts; on this, see Béla Grunberger, *Narcissism: Psychoanalytic Essays*, trans. Joyce S. Diamanti (New York: International Universities Press, 1979), 1–26.

Some critics stress Benedick's idea of man as a giddy thing, but his composure is superb. He ends this speech by putting Claudio on the defensive: "I did think to have beaten thee, but in that thou art like to be my kinsman, live unbruised, and love my cousin." Although he jests, and the terms are still aggressive here, he clearly means to be affectionate to both Claudio and Hero. Claudio, defensive as usual, but with a rare sense of tact, alters the joke about the male's fear of being cuckolded—a fear which played a role in his believing John's accusation—to one about the female's fear of an unfaithful husband: "I had well hoped thou wouldst have denied Beatrice, that I might have cudgelled thee out of thy single life, to make thee a double-dealer; which out of question thou wilt be, if my cousin do not look exceeding narrowly to thee." That the man might be unfaithful seems a delicate touch under the circumstances. It might also be taken as a slight indication that Claudio, like Benedick, no longer fears being cuckolded. Rather than tediously project unfaithfulness onto the woman, Claudio accepts some of the responsibility himself. Benedick diverts the horn joke from his marriage to the Prince's, and adds a positive valence: "there is no staff more reverend than one tipped with horn."

Benedick now becomes a central figure, and significantly reduces fear of control by the way he manages others. He is the only major character except Hero who has never tried to control anyone—although he briefly, and with ambivalence, tried to challenge Claudio. Benedick behaves so benignly in directing others that he sets a new tone. The need for such a change in atmosphere accounts for an otherwise puzzling minor disagreement. He wants a "dance ere we are married, that we may lighten our own hearts and our wives' heels"; but Leonato intervenes: "We'll have dancing afterward." Benedick insists on the dance and prevails, thereby defeating Leonato's gesture, one so reminiscent of everyone's attempt to force others to do what he thinks best. Benedict also intervenes when a message about John comes to Don Pedro: "Think not on him till tomorrow; I'll devise thee brave punishments for him. Strike up, pipers!" Simply by interposing here, Benedick breaks into the brothers' cycle of enmity. Also, in both instances Benedick asserts himself, rather than defer to his superiors and their whims or troubles.

Much Ado concludes in a manner different from that of the other comedies by underplaying all sense of wonder; the tone remains stubbornly down-to-earth. *The Merchant of Venice* ends with suggestions that providence guides all. *As You Like It* concludes with Hymen speaking of "mirth in heaven"; the wicked are converted; and the dance at the end is followed by Rosalind's dazzling, paradoxical epilogue. In *Twelfth Night,* providence proves kind and Feste concludes with a mysterious and sweeping account of life in a song whose refrain later finds a home in *Lear.* In *All's Well,* Diana presents Helena as the mysterious answer to her riddle; even Bertram's troubling couplet haunts us with its never-to-be-explained import. *Measure for Measure* ends in an astonishing tour de force, and we are brought up short by the Duke's sudden, unanswered proposal to Isabella. Of all these endings, one might say with La Few at the end of *All's Well,* "Mine eyes smell onions." In such a context the wonder of Hero being found alive seems deliberately held in check. Instead, *Much Ado* rather prosaically clears things up and, unlike the other plays, concludes with a dance. This gives a visual sense of community, but rather than seem ideal or wonderful, it is familiar—and, in the formality of such a dance—still rather guarded.

~4~
As You Like It
Serene Autonomy

As You Like It is sane and wonderful, and it makes us feel that
we are too. The characters easily tolerate ambivalence about a
wide range of feelings and ideas, in part because they never experience fierce emotions like Claudio's (or like those merely implicit
in Antonio and Portia). Although *As You Like It* rarely treats
strong emotions, the serenity of the characters is a convincing
imitation of reality. One sign of this is that most critics feel at ease
with the play; although born to be contentious, they find nothing
much to quarrel about, and little to disturb them.

Here reparative impulses are integrated into a way of life.
Since conflict is so central to psychoanalytic theory, we might
wonder about the plausibility of a state of unconflicted ambivalence and ready concern for others. Melanie Klein describes how
this can come about as an infant or adult reaches a more integrated emotional state during the depressive position.[1] Three of
her points are especially relevant for understanding *As You Like
It.* First, a person's sense of omnipotence diminishes as he gains
greater confidence both in his objects and in his reparative powers. In this play, for example, major characters do not grasp at
simple, manipulative solutions such as Beatrice's demand that
Benedick kill Claudio. Second, as a person's sense of reality increases, he becomes more capable of distinguishing between frustration imposed from without and fantastic internal dangers; thus

1. Melanie Klein, "Some Theoretical Conclusions Regarding the Emotional
Life of the Infant" (1952), in *Envy and Gratitude and Other Works*, 75–76.

hatred and aggression become more closely related to actual frustration from the external world and arouse less guilt. In *As You Like It,* characters keep the Duke's and Oliver's cruelty in perspective (whereas Antonio's fantasy of being worthless heightens Shylock's apparent omnipotence; nor could Claudio differentiate between what was said about Hero and distorting fantasies of his own). Third, as a person grows more adaptive he develops a more secure relation between the external and the internal world: this "leads to a lessening of ambivalence and aggression which makes it possible for the drive for reparation to play its full part." The characters in *As You Like It* show ready concern for one another despite the frustrations of sibling rivalry and exile. From this perspective the world presented by *As You Like It* is a kind of wish fulfillment: would that we could be so serene in the face of distressing situations. The play presents this wish along with an encouraging model of how reparation can be a way of life, rather than simply a response to guilt. As Brooks Atkinson puts it: "the limpid sentiment" and the gentleness of the way characters speak to one another make the play "a triumph of good-will toward men."[2]

First, let us look at the way conflicts emerge in the first few scenes. The plot turns on sibling rivalry, but Shakespeare limits the anxiety which might be awakened in a viewer. For one thing, the evil is real, clear, and kept in the open. Orlando resents being badly treated and poor; unlike the younger brother in the source, *Rosalynde,* he is not left the most money. Orlando pointedly remarks: "Shall I keep your hogs and eat husks with them? What prodigal portion have I spent that I should come to such penury?" (1.1.37–39). Oliver also draws attention to the parable of the prodigal son by refusing Orlando money: "And what wilt thou do? Beg when that is spent?" The effect of these references is part of the play's strategy. Shakespeare brings the parable's hidden point—the hatred of the younger brother by the elder—into the open where it can be dealt with. This archetypal source of anger is so clear, and Orlando so unconflicted about the matter, that he can respond even to this with measure and ease: "The courtesy of nations allows you my better, in that you are first-born, but the same tradition takes not away my blood, were there twenty brothers betwixt us" (1.1.45–49). He then prods Oliver, and open phys-

2. Brooks Atkinson, "Kindness Being a Virtue," *New York Herald Tribune,* 2 Nov. 1937.

ical anger flares up—a rare event in these comedies. Oliver strikes
Orlando, who puts a grip on him. Still, this "frustration imposed
from without" stirs up no fantastic internal dangers in Orlando,
who straightforwardly tells his brother "I will no further offend
you than becomes me for my good."

The play immediately begins to counter this sibling rivalry by
drawing our attention to the sibling love between Rosalind and
Celia. We find that Rosalind remains at court; despite her father's
exile, she is "no less beloved of her uncle than his own daughter,
and never two ladies loved as they do" (1.1.110–12). Both ladies
soon leave the court because the Duke banishes Rosalind; however, Shakespeare postpones this development until Orlando and
Rosalind meet and fall in love. Until then—both for her sake and
for the viewer's—Shakespeare diminishes potential anxiety. The
Duke seems as friendly to Rosalind as Celia is; because the "sis-
ters" are safe and loved, they help diminish our anxiety about
Orlando.

The wrestling match brings the brothers' aggression into the
open, yet in sublimated form: Orlando fights in a game, albeit a
possibly fatal one. The match is fair. Oliver has persuaded Charles
to defeat and if possible kill his brother, but Orlando wins. Both
the danger of the wrestling and Orlando's bravery are heightened
because the wrestler, the Duke, and Rosalind and Celia all try to
dissuade him from fighting. We expect Orlando to be rewarded,
for in effect he has defeated his wicked brother; however, the other
wicked brother, the Duke, fails to do so because Sir Rowland was
a friend of the exiled Duke. Some critics see this doubling of sets
of good and bad brothers as indication of the literariness, the
unreality, of the situation.[3] Also, I think it is crucial that as soon
as a wicked brother does something bad, someone else does something good: the splitting becomes subordinated to widespread
general concern for others. The mean-spirited Duke refuses to
reward Orlando. Rather than become an occasion for anger, the
Duke's nastiness makes Celia and Rosalind determine to repair
the damage. Celia wants to make up for her father's "rough and
envious disposition." Rosalind, hearing that Orlando's father was
Sir Rowland, says she would have added tears to her entreaties
had she known, for "My father lov'd Sir Rowland as his soul"
(1.2.224). She gives him a prize to make up for what the Duke

3. Alexander Leggatt discusses such aspects at length in his chapter on the play
in *Shakespeare's Comedy of Love.*

failed to give. At this point Rosalind and Orlando fall in love, which neutralizes almost all the anger which has been stirred up: "Sir," Rosalind says, "you have wrestled well, and overthrown / More than your enemies" (1.2.244–45). Anger and aggression— channeled into the wrestling match by Oliver and Orlando, and expressed through withholding the prize by the Duke—pale in significance. Rosalind turns the fighting into a metaphor for being overthrown by love.

Orlando had just said something similar which she did not hear: "Can I not say, 'I thank you'? My better parts / Are all thrown down" (1.2.239–40). Most of the charm in this romance stems from the fact that the lovers never lose the capacity to think for themselves. Overthrown they may be, but they preserve their poise and ability to function. Orlando knows his own worth in relation to Oliver, and then to the Duke: he is proud to be his father's youngest son, and would not be heir to the Duke himself. Orlando is strong, assertive, and sure of himself despite setbacks; he is not likely to distort his real-life frustration by fantasies of worthlessness (unlike, say, Antonio and Claudio). Because others help Orlando, and because he meets every danger and defeat with self-assurance, it is difficult for the viewer to succumb to fantasies of anger and deprivation. For example, when told that the Duke now looks on him with disfavor and he had better leave, Orlando calmly listens. Instead of feeling persecuted (and by another wicked brother, this one the Duke senior's) he shifts attention to his new beloved: "I thank you sir; and pray you tell me this, / Which of the two was daughter of the Duke / That here was at wrestling?" (1.2.258–60). When Orlando then learns that Rosalind herself is in disfavor because of the Duke's malice, he remains unruffled:

> I rest much bounden to you. Fare you well.
> Thus must I from the smoke into the smother,
> From tyrant Duke unto a tyrant brother.
> But heavenly Rosalind!
>
> (1.2.276–79)

Orlando shows anger to be quite beside the point. Even though he must "from the smoke into the smother"—hardly an alarming prospect by the way he puts it—Rosalind remains the focus of his attention.

In the next scene the ladies refer back to the physical aggression of the wrestling match. Celia advises Rosalind: "wrestle with thy affections" (1.3.20). By referring to aggression so playfully they help to neutralize it and bind it up with affection, thus diminishing potential anxiety. Rosalind tries to explain that she fell in love with Orlando so readily because "The Duke my father loved his father dearly" (1.3.27). By this lame reasoning, Celia teases, *she* should hate Orlando, but does not. Rosalind concludes "Let me love him for that, and do you love him because I do. Look, here comes the Duke." And, Celia notes, "With his eyes full of anger" (1.3.34–36). Suddenly he accuses Rosalind of treason, and banishes her. Rather than allow us to feel much alienation, the play shifts once again to loving responses which repair the damage, as they did after the wrestling scene. Celia expresses dismay: "Wilt thou change fathers? I will give thee mine." She declares that she, too, will leave the court—having reminded her father that she and Rosalind are fast friends, "like Juno's swans . . . coupled and inseparable" (1.3.71–72).

They work out the details of their leaving without another reference to the Duke—or to the cruelty of exile. Instead they deal with the possible dangers in travelling. If this were real life, we might expect the ladies to be angry or overwhelmed; but they are not, which reminds us that some people actually respond as they do: "Now go we in content / To liberty, and not to banishment." The Duke senior at once seconds and amplifies this view—adding a more ambivalent sense of the loss and gain of banishment—in the first scene in Arden (2.1.1–17). The hue and cry raised by his brother at court confirms the bad side of the place (2.2). Adam's news of Oliver's wicked intention makes escape desirable: "he means / To burn the lodging where you use to lie, / And you within it"; "this house is but a butchery. / Abhor it, fear it, do not enter it" (2.3.22–24). Orlando asks:

> What, woulds't thou have me go and beg my food,
> Or with a base and boist'rous sword enforce
> A thievish living on the common road?
> This must I do, or know not what to do;
> Yet this I will not do, do how I can.
> I rather will subject me to the malice
> Of a diverted blood and bloody brother.
>
> (2.3.31–37)

Instead of joining in Adam's fear, Orlando stubbornly says that he has no option but to endure Oliver. He stood up to him before, and defeated the wrestler; he refuses to panic now. Orlando sounds almost too sure of himself, but under the circumstances that helps us to focus, as he focuses, on what he is to "do" (his repeated, appropriate verb). Instead of catching Adam's anxiety about danger and persecution, Orlando emphasizes reality: the external factors of his situation. This discourages us from paying much attention to fantasies which might surround so bad a brother. As always in *As You Like It,* good deeds immediately repair bad ones: Adam offers his life savings, companionship, and service. This exile, like Rosalind's, becomes an occasion for preserving loved ones and preventing damage.

Rosalind and Orlando's autonomy is impressive in relation to that of other lovers at the outset of their plays. In *The Merchant,* Bassanio relies on Antonio, who has to rely on Shylock—and finally Portia; she must submit to the lottery, and resist the temptation to cheat. In *Much Ado,* Claudio depends on a long series of figures from start to finish; Beatrice and Benedick assert themselves, but in a defensive manner. Orsino pines for Olivia and relies on Cesario-Viola, who longs for him; Olivia asserts herself, yet seems ridiculous. In *As You Like It,* Rosalind and Orlando stand on their own two feet. They test each reality as it comes up, which guards them, and us, from indulging in fantasies about persecution. Other festive comedies discourage reality testing at the outset, and often for most of the play. *The Merchant* never really faces the issue of why Portia should submit to a lottery, or why Antonio should sign the bond. In *Twelfth Night* reality testing would promptly force Orsino and Olivia to see Viola is a woman— or would make Viola unlikely to woo her rival for the Duke. At the start of *Much Ado* none of the lovers can face the outside world. The lovers in *As You Like It,* on the other hand, begin their play without illusions or rigid defenses.

II

There are two major achievements in Arden: easy ambivalence about the place in which characters find themselves, and easy ambivalence among the characters. In court they express little ambivalence, for this would legitimize conflicted love and hate (between Oliver and Orlando, Rosalind and the Duke, or the Duke and his daughter Celia). We could readily be pulled into such conflict. In Arden, however, there is virtually no actual frustration or harm derived from external factors, and thus less danger of triggering disruptive fantasies. For instance, Orlando enters the feast with drawn sword (in the source he is much more polite); he can safely be angry in Arden because there is no wicked brother to be attacked. Instead, the lords deftly transform his anger by kindly, and rather blandly, offering him whatever he wants.

Similarly, when Rosalind and Celia enter Arden—having been forced to leave the court—they for the first time in the play complain at some length, but about being weary, not about the deception and cruelty of uncles and fathers. Once the pressure is off, the ladies can begin to feel of two minds. This may seem escapist on their part, or evasive on Shakespeare's: he is reticent about presenting emotional conflict here. Instead of plumbing the depths as the problem comedies begin to do, *As You Like It* presents a different aspect of life, one in which "all difficulties are but easy when they are known." Vincentio has a few surprises in store for him when he says this in *Measure for Measure* (4.2.204–5), but in *As You Like It* problems barely exist for the characters—and for the viewers, as critics indicate. The play is a blessed relief. Characters who dwell on the problematic are shown to be excessive and hypocritical (Jaques), or silly and hysterical (Silvius). "Ambivalence" is so easily tolerated in *As You Like It* that it hardly seems the right word; "highly charged and opposed feelings" are simply "mixed feelings" here. The play gives us a glimpse of a world which we hear about, but experience less often than we would like. Or, and I think this more accurate, we get a glimpse of part of our life which we usually pay little attention to: times when we feel at ease with a variety of feelings which are not felt with much intensity and conflict, and when kind and generous responses make us feel part of a benign world. This is a time when reparation comes so effortlessly that we do not much notice it. No one knows what the play's title refers to, but certainly this is life as we like it. On the other hand, it is not what is dramatic in our lives; these effortless moments can escape notice: our relation to ourselves and to others can be so lacking in stress as to seem uneventful.

Life can be like this more often than we may realize. I turn to ambivalence about the place or world, for the pastoral itself encourages mixed feelings about a desired but not "real" state. Viewers now are less sophisticated about pastoral convention, but still have fantasies about a better, greener world. The characters talk about such expectations and how Arden measures up to them. Feelings about Arden are kept to a conscious, even intellectual, level. And rightly so, for on an unconscious level there lurks the potential of longing for a perfect world, or what Wheeler sees as "a trustworthy maternal environment" at the root of Orlando's relation to Rosalind.[4] I doubt that the play encourages us to look so deeply into what Orlando's love for Rosalind consists of, although Wheeler rightly observes that the mature heterosexual component in their love is largely absent (or, I think, assumed). What seems most important is that the play keeps us on a conscious level and discourages merger with a fantasy world: Arden exists somewhere between the ideal and the actual.

Belmont, in contrast, can easily be perceived by the characters and viewers as being a thoroughly supportive, maternal world: the home ruled by wise and powerful Portia, the place where she gives all to Bassanio and dispenses "manna" to Antonio in the form of recovered ships. As we saw, some critics get too close for comfort here—pulled so far into the fantasy that Belmont seems dangerous when Portia and Nerissa control their husbands. That characters continually talk about Arden in relation to conventional pastoral and to the real countryside, helps the viewer to conceive of it largely on a conscious level. Shakespeare reaps the advantage of dwelling on conscious ideas—one of the advantages of high culture, and appropriate, even inevitable, in using the pastoral mode.

Critics almost never deal with the play in terms of strong feelings. The general pattern, Beckman observes, is to see the play as "choosing either idealism or realism and then subordinating its opposite": Jenkins tends to dissolve "any hard opposition . . . into general approval of an idealistic love that is not uncomfortably extravagant"; Barber leans to the other side in concluding that Shakespeare "represents or evokes ideal life, and then makes fun of it because it does not square with life as it ordinarily is."[5] Beckman concludes that "many critics wish to dissolve opposi-

4. Wheeler, *Shakespeare's Development,* 175. Béla Grunberger (*Narcissism,* 12–26), sees this as a longing for the lost paradise of the womb (that is, before infancy, which is, after all, not a perfect state).

5. Margaret Boerner Beckman, "The Figure of Rosalind in *As You Like It,*" *SQ* 29 (1978): 44–45. I would not stress Rosalind's "extraordinary, seemingly impossible—and thus 'magical'—conjunctions between contrary things." The play makes such conjunctions seem easy and natural.

tion in *As You Like It* because they do not conceive of opposition
and ambivalence as offering a comedic resolution; to them, comedy is not an affirmation if it maintains alternative perspectives to
its very end" (p. 45). There is, she proposes, "no literary or dramatic reason why opposition, ambivalence, and alternative perspectives cannot work together to form an affirmative whole."
This affirmative whole is close to what I call a world where reparative impulses effortlessly prevail.

Critics always remark that the forest seems both homey and
exotic, a real place and yet no particular one. Some think this
novel, peculiar to the play or to Shakespeare's originality. However, as Patrick Cullen points out:

> While pastoral can portray an escape from reality, or a
> desire to escape reality, the pastoral *mode* itself from The-
> ocritus onward involved, implicitly or explicitly, a critical
> exploration and counterbalancing of attitudes, perspec-
> tives, and experiences.[6]

He continues: "if pastoral is ambivalent in its attitude toward the
world of greater things, it is ambivalent too in its attitude toward
the lowly rustic life" (p. 10). Pastoral serves as an ideal mode for
conveying the coexistence of opposites. It may be escapist, yet
often treats contemporary problems; it considers sophisticated
matters in a simplified world; and is contemplative, yet makes a
significant gesture toward the outside world of action. We find the
quintessence of this in *The Tempest,* where characters relive a
complex active life of courtly intrigue within the confines of a
contemplative, schematized world. Richard Cody sees the balanc-
ing of alternatives as so basic to pastoral that during the Renaissance the form partook of a sort of neo-Platonic mystery, ineffable
in and of itself. One particularly relevant aspect of Cody's argument is the insistent duality of pastoral; for example:

> Hercules embodies the shepherd as well as the warrior. . . .
> This duality is a counterpart to the logic of *discordia con-*

Beckman quotes C.L. Barber from his *Shakespeare's Festive Comedy,* 228. She
refers to Harold Jenkins's article, *"As You Like It," Shakespeare Survey* 8 (1955):
40–51. He very nicely concludes that ideals "do not delude the eye of reason, yet
faith in them is not extinguished in spite of all that reason can do" (p. 51).

6. Patrick Cullen, *Spenser, Marvell, and Renaissance Pastoral* (Cambridge:
Harvard University Press, 1970), 1.

cors, the "mutual entailment of the gods." If a myth fails
to include an episode in either mood, then the missing
one has to be invented, as in the case of a warrior Christ.[7]

This insistent duality pervades *As You Like It.* For instance, Arden
is no magical place like the wood outside Athens or Prospero's
island. Nevertheless, Rosalind plays with the idea: she invents
"magical" aspects and thereby offers an alternative to the prevalent naturalistic and logical mood. Supposedly an uncle taught her
magic, as in the source; Shakespeare encourages this notion by
having her present a godlike Hymen, as if by magic (a detail he
added). Still, when she deals with Orlando and others she relies
entirely on common sense. Without stirring up fears of omnipotence (as *A Midsummer Night's Dream* and *The Tempest* can), the
play introduces the possibility of magic so as to provide yet another occasion for harboring opposites.

Critics have so thoroughly explored Arden's various contradictory aspects, such as its hint of economic distress in Corin's relation
to his master, that I turn to a passage which appears not to have
been examined in any detail.[8] Corin and Touchstone debate the
nature of pastoral. To Corin's question "how like you this shepherd's life?" Touchstone answers in a way which parodies ambivalence:

> Truly shepherd, in respect of itself, it is a good life; but in
> respect that it is a shepherd's life, it is naught. In respect
> that it is solitary, I like it very well; but in respect that it
> is private, it is a very vile life.
>
> (3.2.13–17)

He pretends to be of two minds, and simply creates a rhetorical
stance. He concludes in the same manner: "As it is a spare life,
look you, it fits my humour well; but as there is no more plenty
in it, it goes much against my stomach." The terms which he
presents as opposites are equivalents, even identities. Corin calls
Touchstone's bluff by phrasing his ideas in ways which *preclude*

7. Richard Cody, *The Landscape of the Mind: Pastoralism and Platonic Theo-
ry in Tasso's "Aminta" and Shakespeare's Early Comedies* (Oxford: Clarendon
Press, 1969), 107. He quotes Edgar Wind, *Pagan Mysteries in the Renaissance*
(London: Faber and Faber, 1958), 163.

8. But see Brian Vickers, *The Artistry of Shakespeare's Prose* (London: Methuen, 1968), 205–6. He remarks on the "paired, symmetrical, antithetical, and
finally tautological clauses."

an opposite view—an extremely rare tactic in this play. For example, Corin's statement that "the more one sickens the worse at ease he is" admits no contradiction; nor does the rest of the sentence: "and he that wants money, means, and content is without three good friends." By including "content" Corin removes the possibility of a contrary view; he prevents us from entertaining the familiar idea that money and means are inimical to content. Thus he makes fun of Touchstone's parody of ambivalence, and even makes fun of his pseudo-oppositions: "he that hath learned no wit by nature nor art may complain of good breeding or comes of a very dull kindred." To lack, or be blunted by, good breeding can only momentarily be thought an alternative to coming of a very dull kindred. When Touchstone rather desperately pronounces Corin damned, he replies: "Nay, I hope"; that is, he hopes for salvation and can neither despair nor be certain of it (Arden edition). A true believer must endure such contrary feelings; the religious paradox partakes of the mystery which Cody finds so central to pastoral itself.

Having frustrated Touchstone's attempts, Corin launches into the valid oppositions we are accustomed to finding: "good manners at the court are as ridiculous in the country as the behaviour of the country is most mockable at the court." He forces Touchstone to deny these truths in order to prove his wit. Touchstone earlier tried to present identities as opposites; now he tries to prove that opposites are identities. Even his rhetorical posturings counterbalance one another. He pronounces the courtly kissing of hands appropriate to shepherds by denying that they have hard and dirty hands quite unsuited to such civility. His failure allows Corin to conclude the episode by describing what a shepherd's life truly consists of (3.2.71–75). At this point the audience can return to its accustomed role: we contrast his view of pastoral content ("the greatest of my pride is to see my ewes graze and my lambs suck") with the more idealized one of pastoral literature (including the play)—and also with the court.

Touchstone attempted a kind of fake ambivalence in his match with Corin; Jaques, in his speech on man's seven ages (2.7.139–66), attempts to deny all sense of it. *As You Like It* balances alternative views so relentlessly that we long to hear something reduced, oversimplified. That Touchstone and Jaques do so may explain why critics spend such disproportionate energy on them, and especially on Jaques's seven ages of man. For similar reasons

we may be drawn to Polonius's simplistic advice to Laertes, for
Hamlet confronts us with a world of intolerable ambivalence.[9]
Jaques draws upon ancient commonplaces; as Samuel C. Chew
points out, however, schemes other than his often have touches
which make their view less bleak. In Jaques's version we find:

> no toys in infancy; no playmates in boyhood; no hunting
> or hawking or jousting in youth; no commerce or industry
> in middle-life; no "honour, love, obedience, troops of
> friends" such as should accompany old age. There is no
> companion on the journey through the years.[10]

Jaques's scheme excludes elements which Shakespeare's audience
probably expected, and which we might expect if the speech had
not overwhelmed other versions. Even Jaques's concluding phrase
about man's "strange eventful history" is eccentric (Arden edition); he calls it a history, not a comedy or a tragedy. He flattens
out opposed views, turns the prevalent idea of life as comedy or
tragedy into the idea that it is simply history. Although the context puts his single-minded attitude in perspective, the speech
itself denies ambivalent feelings. The viewer, however, can supply
them for himself unless he has been conditioned—most likely by
Shakespeare's own speech—to accept it as the whole truth.

All these qualifications about pastoral minimize its seductive-
ness as a fantasy. The characters refuse to idealize it; economic
problems, bad weather, and limited emotional distress occur there.
In a way this seems mostly a literary game, Shakespeare's playful
version of convention. The effect, however, is to throw the characters onto themselves as individuals: they contradict established
sentiments by word or deed, and contradict each other (and sometimes themselves). They come to life largely insofar as they strike
out on their own from their—and our—expectations about "pastoral" behavior. Even Silvius and Phebe do so: he elevates the
pitiful state of the rejected swain to the sublimely ridiculous; she
unknowingly carries disdain to the point of literally giving up
men.

9. See, for example, Joseph Westlund, "Ambivalence in the Player's Speech
in *Hamlet*," *SEL* 18 (1978): 245–56.

10. Samuel C. Chew, "This Strange Eventful History," in *Joseph Quincy Adams
Memorial Studies,* ed. James G. McManaway (Washington: Folger Shakespeare
Library, 1948), 158.

III

The autonomy of Rosalind and Orlando is, paradoxically, an impressive aspect of their love for each other. Neither steps on the others toes, although she exercises some control by virtue of her disguise as Ganymede—and then as "Rosalind." In this she differs from Portia and Beatrice, both of whom seem to enjoy controlling others. None of the characters—or critics—objects to the way Rosalind employs the power which she gains by her disguises. The one exception seems to be Ralph Berry, who perceives the debates in the play as invariably a "struggle for mastery. . . . The constant human drive to dominate another is the underlying theme of much of the dialogue." Furthermore, he sees the play as centered on the "mating dance of a masterful female round her captive male."[11] From this response, we can see why Shakespeare is so careful to minimize Rosalind's control. She continually perceives mixed feelings within herself and others, and is extraordinarily alive to multiple meanings and self-contradictory responses. This helps to make her interventions palatable. Even her mastery of Phebe (which I discuss in the following section) depends upon her awareness that Phebe needs to be put in her place so that Silvius will not suffer.

As Ganymede, Rosalind first strikes up a conversation with Orlando on an abstract topic, time, which sets the tone of their detached yet heart-felt romance (3.2.295–327). In the source, Ganymede talks about Rosalynde. The exchange makes us see how alive she is to human nature in all its variety and particularity. This vitality makes her—as Ganymede—appealing to Orlando, who has just thwarted Jaques from engaging him in sterile railing "against our mistress the world and all our misery." Rosalind uses the unlikely subject to its greatest advantage: to convey not only her wit but her enjoyment of human complexity. Her first instance about "a young maid between the contract of her marriage and the day it is solemnized" can suggest her own need to endure the interim between having fallen in love and being able to marry her lover; yet she and Orlando never suffer the pain which she attributes to the young maid or to the sighing lover. She treats the other examples in her characteristically sympathetic manner: the unlearned priest "sleeps easily because he cannot study" (a sweet

11. Ralph Berry, *Shakespeare's Comedies: Explorations in Form* (Princeton: Princeton University Press, 1972), 176, 194. Also see Bertrand Evans, *Shakespeare's Comedies*, 97–98.

use of adversity); the rich man "that hath not the gout . . . lives
merrily" (a nice awareness of what might oppose his happiness);
a thief on route to the gallows feels that time gallops no matter
how slow the pace (a sympathetic imagining); and lawyers in
vacation term find that time stands still, for "they perceive not
how Time moves" (in this they are like the characters in Arden).
In contrast to Jaques's dry overview of man's life, his seven ages,
Rosalind presents a particularized and affectionate one: the person, his feelings, circumstances, health, learning, and even the
season of the year in which he finds himself—all determine not
just his role, or his age, but how he feels at any given moment.
Thus, she conceives of time in metaphorical terms as a horse who
ambles, trots, gallops, and stands still—not, as Jaques does, in
abstract terms. How the horse moves affects how the rider feels,
in the most basic physical sense.[12]

Rosalind struck Orlando's fancy from the start, and he seems
substantially the same at the end as at the beginning. They each
feel "overthrown" and "mastered" when they fall in love, but give
no sign of defensiveness. Remarkably secure in themselves, they
willingly acknowledge dependence on one another. They trust and
are trustworthy. There is therefore no need for control to get what
they want (unlike Beatrice and Benedick, or the wives at the end
of *The Merchant*). Rosalind needs no disguise, and this helps to
make her seem less manipulative. Orlando chooses to be captive:
"I would not be cured, youth," he tells Ganymede, yet he readily
agrees to woo "Rosalind." The reason must be that he *can* "live
by thinking" (since he complains at the end that this will no longer
suffice); he can imagine Ganymede to be "Rosalind."

12. For a different account, see Jay L. Halio, " 'No Clock in the Forest': Time
in *As You Like It*," *SEL* 2 (1962): 197–207.

Rosalind's choice of a topic has interesting psychological implications. One
reason why Béla Grunberger (*Narcissism*, 16, 26–34), thinks that we long for a
prenatal state is that his patients' narcissistic mode, like the prenatal one, is
timeless: time seems not to exist and wishes are to be met before they become
conscious. Being out of time clearly indicates that someone is not in touch with
reality—with the process of living as articulated in the movement from youth to
old age and death, and in the interaction with persons in the outside world (with
attendant frustration). A sense of timelessness, plus one of omnipotence, characterizes magical worlds such as pastoral. Thus, Rosalind's topic for her first conversation is peculiarly apt. It allows her, and Shakespeare, to insist that the world of
time and of real persons exists here, rather than the timeless mode of fantasy and
narcissistic detachment.

Shakespeare emphasizes timeliness in other of his plays which present magical

Orlando and Rosalind assert their independence while betray-
ing eagerness. They feel mild ambivalence: not simultaneous love
and hate, but mixed ideas and attitudes about what the beloved
is really like, and what love consists of. Their aplomb indicates
a secure relation to inner and external reality; they know whom
they love, and who loves them. It is largely the *roles* which give
them pause: can Orlando really be a lover if he has none of the
fashionable signs of one? Rosalind poses this not as a question
which gives her much anxiety, but as a way of teasing Orlando:
"you are rather point-device in your accoutrements, as loving
yourself than seeming the lover of any other" (3.2.372–74). She
asserts herself by getting him to woo her, Ganymede, as if Rosalind; but there is little she can do except play with the notion that
love may not be so ideal as he—and, we suspect, she—thinks.
There is little for him to do but entertain her objections to
idealization, while wondering if "Rosalind" is similar to the one
he loves.

Rosalind is both herself and what others imagine her to be.
Orlando sees her as Ganymede; but later on he describes the boy
to Oliver as looking like his own "ripe sister." He spots the feminine in Ganymede, and thus more easily imagines "Rosalind" to
be like the real one. This playful wooing allows Orlando to be
assertive (since Ganymede is not Rosalind), yet dependent (since
"Rosalind" seems close to being Rosalind herself). She can be
unusually bold and assertive as a saucy knave playing "Rosalind,"
and even get Orlando to marry her in a mock ceremony. Still, the
trait is present in her from the start when she gives Orlando the
chain and turns back to answer a question he did not ask. Rosalind's playfulness keeps a balanced view of love before his, and
our, eyes: "men have died from time to time and worms have

---

worlds. In *The Comedy of Errors* it gives direction to the multiple confusions of
the plot, the action of which transpires in roughly the same time as it takes to
perform the play itself. This is also the case in *The Tempest*. Despite the magical
nature of Ephesus and the enchanted isle, events are placed in the most realistic
of time frames: it takes just as long for them to occur on stage as it does for us to
watch them from our vantage point in the outside world. In *A Midsummer Night's
Dream* events occur over three or four days, a much looser time span; but everything is geared from the start toward the wedding feast of the Duke which ends
the play. By way of contrast, in *As You Like It* Shakespeare merely hints at the
world being magical, and thus can let events unfold with little sense of time; as in
so many instances here, time—like magic—becomes instead a topic for discussion.
sion.

eaten them, but not for love" (4.1.101–3). She makes the feeling
poignant by introducing the idea of death, but modifies this by the
phrase "from time to time" as though it were not a universal end.
She brings up the horror of "worms have eaten them," but counters it with the sensible, reassuring idea that love did not cause the
death. This is wit, but so serene is the tone that one hesitates to
pin it down.

We can be perplexed about just which role she assumes at any
given moment; she responds with various parts of herself to various situations. Critics often perceive a clear distinction between
her pose as Ganymede and the character behind the role, but
Shakespeare blurs the relationship. In an analysis of the mock
betrothal (4.1.116–33), John Russell Brown demonstrates her ambiguity and variety. Celia, playing the role of priest, asks: "Will
you Orlando have to wife this Rosalind?" and he replies, "I will."
Brown observes that:

> the charade begins to run smoothly: but Rosalind, who
> proposed it, now disturbs it, speaking in quick rhythm
> and with revealing directness: "Ay, but when?" This ques-
> tion could hardly come from Ganymede or from Gany-
> mede-Rosalind: this is Rosalind herself involuntarily
> expressing her doubt, impatience, helplessness, self-
> doubt.[13]

A few lines later Orlando says "I take thee Rosalind for wife." To
which she replies: "I might ask you for your commission; but I
do take thee Orlando for my husband. There's a girl goes before
the priest, and certainly a woman's thought runs before her actions." Brown suggests (p. 87) that she breaks the spell by running
ahead; yet her reference to "commission" implies:

> doubt or defensiveness, or is, possibly, a delighted, playful
> excuse. . . . Ganymede-Rosalind may say "I do take thee
> Orlando for my husband," and Ganymede the rest. Yet
> somewhere Rosalind is liable to speak for herself, since
> her voice has almost certainly been heard earlier with . . .
> "Ay, but when?"

We cannot be sure exactly whose voice we hear; Rosalind may be

13. John Russell Brown, *Shakespeare's Dramatic Style* (London: Heinemann,
1970), 86.

uncertain about her precise role and feelings, but not about whether she loves Orlando or he loves her (although the question intrigues her). She shifts between a multitude of feelings consonant with being in love: hope and despair, power and helplessness, patience and impatience, seriousness and mockery. The emphasis falls on how the principal lovers respond to being in love: not on the process, as with Beatrice and Benedick, but on the shades of ambivalence involved in a paradoxical state of dependence and independence. One thing is clear: we are not likely to feel the need to isolate ourselves from the sort of experience which Rosalind and Orlando articulate, nor tempted to merge with its carefully limited perfection.

IV

Autonomy becomes an issue only in the relation between Silvius and Phebe, and in Rosalind's intervention. Shakespeare links the two courtships tightly: while Rosalind impatiently awaits Orlando, she involves herself in their squabble (3.5); and while again waiting for him, she further intervenes (4.3). That she has to wait for him is itself pertinent: it shows his separateness from "Rosalind," yet her dependence on him. In her intrusion upon the romance of shepherd and shepherdess—which is partly thrust on her since Phebe takes a fancy for Ganymede—Rosalind opens herself to the charge of being manipulative. Silvius and Phebe take her pose at face value, without the ironic detachment which Ganymede's role as "Rosalind" instills in Orlando. Also, Orlando is not cured of love, but Phebe really seems to be.

Still, the shepherd and shepherdess were deluded before Rosalind intervened. Silvius sees in Phebe beauty which he puts there, and this makes Phebe overestimate herself; as Rosalind says, " 'Tis not her glass but you that flatters her" (3.5.54). Phebe sees masculinity in Ganymede because she wants to see it there: Ganymede has just what she misses in sentimental, meek Silvius: "I pray you chide a year together. / I had rather hear you chide than this man woo" (3.5.64–65). She imagines that she has at last found the man for whom she has been waiting: not someone sweet and eager to do her bidding, but someone hard to get and hard to control—like her. In a way Phebe falls in love with herself: she projects her traits onto Ganymede and falls in love with them.

Rosalind draws Phebe's hopeless quest, her idealizing fantasy, closer to real circumstances. This is the first time in the play that

we see a character endure ambivalence of a moderately painful
sort, and change because of it. Shakespeare lightly sketches in this
romance; still, we see more irrational and contrary oppositions in
this than in the main love plot—where they could be disconcerting, or could lead to a different sort of romance, such as that of
Beatrice and Benedick. Phebe says that she would rather be chided
by Ganymede than wooed by Silvius, which at first seems merely
another of her perverse whims. But after her first meeting with
Ganymede, she begins to change:

> Silvius, the time was that I hated thee;
> And yet it is not that I bear thee love,
> But since that thou canst talk of love so well,
> Thy company, which erst was irksome to me,
> I will endure; and I'll employ thee too.
>   (3.5.92–96)

She begins to sound human: she perceives some virtue in Silvius—and intends to use it to further her own ends. Phebe becomes explicitly ambivalent about Ganymede:

> It is a pretty youth—not very pretty—
> But sure he's proud, and yet his pride becomes him.
> . . . .
> I love him not, nor hate him not; and yet
> I have more cause to hate him than to love him.
>   (3.5.113–114, 127–28)

Even her tone changes; it grows halting, as in the way "and yet"
wavers at the very end of a line.

Rosalind defeats Phebe's sly, manipulative treatment of the
shepherd by her own openness: she refuses to hide the contents
of the letter; at the same time, she tries to soften the blow he
receives when hearing them. Phebe benefits from control and has
changed by the time we get to the last scene. When Ganymede
promises to bring in Rosalind, the principal characters speak ex-
pansively: the Duke will bestow her on Orlando "had I kingdoms
to give with her"; Orlando will have her "were I of all kingdoms
king" (5.4.8, 10). Phebe at first gets into the spirit of the others,
and pledges to marry Ganymede "should I die the hour after." In
context, Phebe's reply to Ganymede's question—"if you do refuse
to marry me, / You'll give yourself to this most faithful shepherd?"—proves stunningly simple and direct: "So is the bargain."

She sounds petulant, yet prepared to return to reality, to the place where bargains are made ("Sell when you can, you are not for all markets"). Phebe no longer indulges in lofty disdain. When Hymen enters with Rosalind, Phebe announces: "If sight and shape be true, / Why then my love adieu" (5.4.119–20). She wonders if her own perception of Rosalind is "true" to what she actually is. Phebe has to acknowledge Rosalind as separate from her fantasies about her. She must accord to Silvius's love "Or have a woman to your lord," and so she accepts him:

> I will not eat my word; now thou art mine,
> Thy faith my fancy to thee doth combine.
> (5.4.148–49)

Once more she speaks in a new, no-nonsense way; "I will not eat my word," like "So is the bargain," exudes none of the entitlement which formerly characterized her speeches. A note of wonder may enter: "Thy faith my fancy to thee doth combine" suggests that she now conceives of Silvius as someone in his own right and with his own virtues. She sees his faithfulness bound to him by her love. She connects his "faith" to his whole personality, rather than simply use the trait regardless of his feelings. We are now, given the rapid and schematic nature of this plot, led to believe that Phebe can feel love.

V

The only character Rosalind changes is Phebe. Silvius remains attached to his shepherdess, and Orlando to his Rosalind. The other couples—Celia and Oliver, Audrey and Touchstone—pair off on their own. At the end of the play a great deal happens in the plot, but Rosalind has no control over the events: Orlando saves Oliver, the wicked brothers convert, and Celia and Oliver fall in love. Rosalind prepares for the weddings and puts herself at the center of the denouement by being the only one who knows who she is, and therefore how Silvius, Phebe, and Orlando will fare. Simply by revealing her identity, she will solve the love problems; that is quite enough power. The wives manage their husbands at the end of *The Merchant,* and almost everyone is maneuvered right to the end of *Much Ado;* here, Rosalind has no need to manage others, yet by holding the key she does. Few critics, and no characters, object; yet they might very well do so.

As Bertrand Evans remarks, she has, "in effect, if not fact," as much control as Oberon and Prospero in their worlds; another sort of man than Orlando, "recalling the outlandish spectacle he had been tricked into making—would bide his time until fast married . . . and then beat her until she begged for mercy" (pp. 97–98). It would have to be quite another Orlando, and quite another play; yet the potential for anger exists. The play successfully manages the fantasy, the fear of being manipulated, as the rarity of the complaint testifies. All the characters respond with equanimity to discovering that Rosalind has deceived them all along. We might feel that stronger emotion is called for, but none of the characters even shows annoyance.

One final instance of the way *As You Like It* manages potential anger is Shakespeare's alteration of the tone at the end. In *Rosalynde,* violence intrudes: ruffians try to abduct Alinda, and are beaten off by Rosader and his brother; a brief report of battle between the Twelve Peers of France and the usurper concludes the story (with the usurper slain). Shakespeare drops all this. Instead we find the potential for violence emerge in Touchstone's digression on the seven steps in a fashionable quarrel (5.4.49–102). The anger is real enough, but readily contained within civil forms of expression: it can be controlled by gradually increasing the degree of insult. All but the seventh degree allows the duelist to vent just enough spleen to be insulting, but not so much as to make his opponent fight. For example: "I did dislike the cut of a certain courtier's beard; he sent me word, if I said his beard was not well cut, he was in the mind it was; this is called the Retort Courteous." The wranglers behave aggressively but civilly right up to the seventh cause, the Lie Direct: "and you may avoid that too, with an If. . . . Your If is the only peacemaker: much virtue in If." "If" acknowledges that the contrary may be true, and also signals that the duelist feels ambivalent about fighting. Much depends upon the willingness of the opponents to forebear, as in the blunt Countercheck Quarrelsome: "If [I sent him word] again it was not well cut, he would say I lie." This is a great insult, an ordinarily intolerable attack on a Renaissance courtier's honor. Touchstone presents a formal series of steps which allows the quarrelsome men to toy with the idea of fighting, yet also allows them to maintain the peace. Here, as in the play itself—and in the numerous formal one-line, antiphonal responses of the lovers in the fifth act—the tension caused by contradictory feelings yields pleasure and ends positively: "And so we measured swords," preliminary to dueling, "and parted."

Much of the pleasure for us is the sense of independence which characters feel throughout the scene even when their autonomy seems intruded upon. The freedom of Arden is the liberty to follow one's will within acceptable limits (which Jaques oversteps). This persists to the very end. Some characters decide to stay in Arden (the reformed usurper and Jaques, Celia and Oliver, and the country folk). That so many should remain in a world apart from that of the festive community which here goes off to the court is unique among the comedies, and adds to our sense that no one feels the need to give up his right of self-government. Nor do critics worry about the state of things at the end (as they do about the other plays). Even Dr. Johnson, who deplores Shakespeare's haste and carelessness in winding up his comedies, can merely lament that he "suppressed the dialogue between the usurper and the hermit, and lost an opportunity of exhibiting a moral lesson in which he might have found matter worthy of his highest powers."[14]

Rather than give us this dialogue, Shakespeare presents one of his most dazzling epilogues. Puck and Prospero maintain their fictional role while asking for applause, but the King in *All's Well* steps out of it: "The King's a beggar, now the play is done." Feste seems to refer to himself as a little tiny boy who grew to manhood; only at the end does he drop the pose: "But that's all one, our play is done, / And we'll strive to please you every day." Rosalind proves neither so blunt as Feste and the King, nor so consistent to her fictional role as Puck and Prospero. Instead, she draws attention to herself in a way which explores her independence: both a character and an actor, a woman and a boy player, an epilogist and one who will neither plead nor flatter. She asserts herself by working contrary to our expectations, a familiar device in this play: "It is not the fashion to see the lady the epilogue; but it is no more unhandsome than to see the lord the prologue." Contrary to custom, she seems not in the least concerned about the play being thought good, or even being well received: "a good play needs no epilogue. . . . and good plays prove the better by the help of good epilogues." None of Shakespeare's other epilogists is so utterly self-confident, yet she immediately protests that she

14. Samuel Johnson, *Yale Edition of the Works of Samuel Johnson,* ed. Arthur Sherbo (New Haven: Yale University Press, 1968), 7:265.

has no power to influence the audience: "I . . . am neither a good epilogue, nor cannot insinuate with you in the behalf of a good play." More punctilious and naturalistic than the King in *All's Well,* she draws attention to her splendid attire: "I am not furnished like a beggar, therefore to beg will not become me." Here we find her in a typical hardheaded and realistic mode, but on a whimsical issue. At once, and quite effortlessly, she shifts to her mode of fantasy and sentiment: "My way is to conjure you, and I'll begin with the women." As a magician, and in contradiction to her protests of being ineffectual or ill-suited to her role, she will "conjure" the audience.

As a woman, she first addresses them: "I charge you, O women, for the love you bear to men, to like as much of this play as please you." This is a sentimental ploy, but also a realistic one—after all, they need like only as much as pleases them. She then turns to the men: "for the love you bear to women . . . that between you and the women the play may please." By drawing attention to the sexual play between men and women, she prepares for her final assertion of personal freedom: "If I were a woman . . ." As Rosalind she is a woman, the character whom we know; but as an actor, she is a boy—and someone about whom we know nothing at all, someone whose liberty includes the right to exist beyond our reach or comprehension. Shakespeare does not shatter the illusion of Rosalind as a woman; he certifies it, deepens it by reminding us both of Rosalind's autonomy as a character in fiction and of the actor's as someone who creates the fiction.

As always, Rosalind insists upon fantasy *as* fantasy; and at the same time she draws it into a more secure relation to reality. "If I were a woman," she says, "I would kiss as many of you as had beards that pleased me, complexions that liked me, and breaths that I defied not." She clarifies the fantasy, and juxtaposes it against reality—as a woman she would kiss those who attracted her, provided that they had no defiable breath. Finally she shifts back, it seems, into her role as a woman, not a boy actor:

> And I am sure, as many as have good beards, or good
> faces, or sweet breaths, will for my kind offer, when I
> make curtsy, bid me farewell.
>
> (5.4.217–20)

The men in the audience will for her kind offer applaud, yet as soon as they do she no longer exists, for the play is over. Rosalind's playfulness and complex assertion of autonomy consolidate the assurance which she and the play offer: they mirror and confirm our own independence and self-esteem. *As You Like It* marks a high point in so doing. In the following comedies, the characters become less certain of themselves, and in defense create the sort of grandiose idealization which Rosalind and her world persist in tempering with reality.

~5~
Twelfth Night
Idealization as an Issue

In the previous comedies we believe characters when they say that they love each other, but in *Twelfth Night* the notion is often absurd. Orsino imagines that a lady whom he never sees will make an ideal wife; yet he offers to marry Viola, whom he has treated as a boy throughout the play. Olivia idolizes Cesario, and marries him—or thinks that she does; instead, she marries Sebastian, whom she does not know. Characters idealize, they lose touch with reality and imagine perfection where it does not exist. This is one of Shakespeare's best-loved comedies, which suggests that we must want to believe in the existence of a world where idealizations, however unrealistic, prove true. Only viewers of dormouse valor will object, it seems, to Olivia and Sebastian not knowing each other—or to Orsino marrying someone he always thought to be a boy, or to Viola idolizing so self-absorbed a man. The comedy sweeps aside common sense, apparently to our relief.

Many critics, though, get suspicious. The characters are convincingly drawn and resemble enigmatic, real human beings; but the shifts in affection seem caused by chance, rather than by changes in a character's nature and motivation. Many interpreters find that the lovers' shifts are too arbitrary. As Samuel Johnson puts it: "The marriage of Olivia, and the succeeding perplexity, though well enough contrived to divert upon the stage, wants credibility, and fails to produce the proper instruction required in the drama, as it exhibits no just picture of life."[1] Many agree.

1. Johnson, *Works of Samuel Johnson,* 7:326.

The outcome is said to be made possible "not by developing characters to a greater understanding, but simply by moving the plot around till the major characters each find themselves opposite a desirable partner and an escape hatch from absurdity."[2] Or: "it is not Viola but the accidents of the plot which make Olivia and Orsino come to terms with life."[3] Harold Jenkins, however, sees considerable change: "Orsino and Olivia come to their happy ending when they have learnt a new attitude to others and to themselves"; they are devoted to "an ideal of love while mistaking the direction in which it should be sought"; and they change in the presence of Viola, who "represents a genuineness of feeling against which the illusory can be measured."[4]

The issue is whether or not their shifts in affection are plausible (caused by "a new attitude to others and to themselves"), or arbitrary (and, in such lifelike characters, incredible). This central critical issue arises from the play's preoccupation with idealization. Most critics doubt that the characters have changed; for these viewers, the tension between the ideal and the actual persists at the end, and reminds us that most men live by error and delusion. *Twelfth Night* conveys this—along with a charming, warm sense of affection between characters. This leads the other school to believe that the ideal, the perfect beloved, is *attained* by major figures, who do not merely "attribute" excellence (by idealizing), but "actualize" it (by changing their attitudes and drawing closer to reality).

I think that Orsino and Olivia develop in Viola's presence, and that their love becomes plausible. Indeed, the characterization is unusually convincing *because* of Orsino's, Olivia's, and Malvolio's penchant for idealizing—for attributing excellence to themselves and others which is not really there. This emphasis is new

2. Hunter, *Shakespeare: The Late Comedies,* 47. Herschel Baker in his "Introduction," to *Twelfth Night,* Signet ed. (New York: New American Library, 1965), thinks that Orsino never changes during the play; nor does anyone learn from experience. C. L. Barber (*Shakespeare's Festive Comedy,* 242), thinks that characters "are caught up by delusions or misapprehensions which take them out of themselves, bringing out what they would keep hidden or did not know was there. *Madness* is a key word."

3. Clifford Leech, *"Twelfth Night" and Shakespearian Comedy* (Toronto: University of Toronto Press, 1965), 36.

4. Harold Jenkins, "Shakespeare's *Twelfth Night,*" *Rice Institute Pamphlet* 45 (1959); reprinted in *Shakespeare: The Comedies,* ed. Kenneth Muir (Englewood Cliffs, N.J.: Prentice-Hall, 1965), 73, 76, 79.

in Shakespeare's comedies. Portia and Bassanio were right to see one another as ideal mates, as were Beatrice and Benedick, and Rosalind and Orlando. The lovers in *Twelfth Night*—like the major characters in the problem comedies—long for, imagine, and pursue excellence which is not there. What makes these later comedies so moving is their exploration of this basic human trait. Melanie Klein, as usual, goes right back to what an infant may feel as a way of explaining what is true for adults:

> idealization derives from the innate feeling that an extremely good breast exists, a feeling which leads to the longing for a good object and for the capacity to love it. This appears to be a condition for life itself, that is to say, an expression of the life instinct. Since the need for a good object is universal, the distinction between an idealized and a good object cannot be considered absolute.[5]

The reparative effect of *Twelfth Night* is that it makes us feel this distinction because of the absurdity of the lovers' idealization. And yet we are reassured: such good objects exist; the lovers do find ideal mates in each other, and change enough to make this credible.

II

I begin with Orsino, and want to show that he is more lifelike and sympathetic than the usual portrait of him allows. Some see him as conventionally romantic, or comically self-indulgent, or rather mad (but then the whole play is alleged to be "with an exception or two ... an anthology of madnesses, sad and merry").[6] Some critics think that "only our own romanticism can blind us to the absurdities in [Orsino's] opening speech"; his madness has "the usual causes ... boredom, lack of physical love, and excessive imagination ... the victim is unaware that he is in love with love rather than with a person."[7] Or, "Orsino, the premier fantasist, merely switches faces in the image of the dream-woman."[8] The

5. Melanie Klein, *Envy and Gratitude* (1957), reprinted in *Envy and Gratitude and Other Works*, 193.
6. Goddard, *The Meaning of Shakespeare*, 299–300.
7. Joseph H. Summers, "The Masks of *Twelfth Night*," *University of Kansas City Review* 22 (1955), reprinted in *Shakespeare: Modern Essays in Criticism*, ed. Leonard F. Dean (New York: Oxford University Press, 1961), 129–30.
8. Berry, *Shakespeare's Comedies*, 209.

tone of such remarks is too dismissive, given the ultimately convincing effect of romance in this enchanting play. *Twelfth Night*
flagrantly ignores reality, but the notion of madness is vague.
Unlike similarly perplexed lovers in *A Midsummer Night's Dream,*
the lovers in *Twelfth Night* reveal through their characterization
just how they get themselves into their predicament. In discussing
them I may seem to assume too much psychological consistency;
it is there, I think, and created by an author who was, within
roughly the same year, hard at work on *Hamlet.*

Orsino's first speech strikes critics as a romantic apostrophe to
love, or an amusing instance of self-indulgence. They are right, as
are those who see something vaguely mad about him. I find the
speech disconcerting in ways which need to be sorted out. His
attitude toward love is both self-indulgent and dissatisfied:

> If music be the food of love, play on,
> Give me excess of it, that, surfeiting,
> The appetite may sicken, and so die.
> (1.1.1–3)

He wants to surfeit on music, to deaden his appetite for love itself.
The terms "surfeit," "appetite," and "die" do not, as we expect,
refer to sexual activity; this is odd, for it would be an obvious way
to sate his hunger. Nor does he refer to a beloved, or even to
women. Instead he obsessively concentrates on his dissatisfac-
tion:

> That strain again, it had a dying fall:
> O, it came o'er my ear like the sweet sound
> That breathes upon a bank of violets,
> Stealing and giving odour. Enough, no more;
> 'Tis not so sweet now as it was before.
> (1.1.4–8)

He grows sick of music; its action seems vaguely analogous to
some loving activity—yet he seems to have no person in mind,
nor does it seem to *mean* very much to him:

> O spirit of love, how quick and fresh art thou,
> That notwithstanding thy capacity
> Receiveth as the sea, nought enters there,
> Of what validity and pitch soe'er,

But falls into abatement and low price,
Even in a minute! So full of shapes is fancy,
That it alone is high fantastical.

                                                        (1.1.9–15)

Critics refer to Orsino as being in love with love, or with himself;
but this does not explain much. He likes to talk about himself and
love, yet seems curiously detached from the dismaying situation
which he describes: one in which love loses value either through
satiety or abatement. Anne Barton sees the speech as evidence of
an "essentially sterile and self-induced . . . state of mind dependent upon that very absence and lack of response from Olivia
which it affects to lament."[9]
  I want to define this state of mind. To begin with, let us look
at the way Shakespeare has one of his characters define a similar
state. Olivia says that Malvolio is "sick of self-love" when she
defends Feste, who has just made her realize how excessively she
mourns for her brother. Malvolio cannot endure Feste being praised,
and launches into a nasty attack; she halts it: "O, you are sick of
self-love, Malvolio, and taste with a distempered appetite" (1.5.89–
90). Malvolio's distempered appetite reveals itself throughout the
play: he attacks Cesario when the latter gains Olivia's favor; he
remonstrates with the entire household, including his mistress;
and he vows revenge at the end. Olivia indicates how he differs
from others:

  To be generous, guiltless, and of free disposition, is to
  take those things for bird-bolts that you deem cannon-
  bullets. There is no slander in an allowed fool, though he
  do nothing but rail.

                                                        (1.5.90–94)

She does not speak of his being "selfish" or "self-centered," although these are apposite terms which come to our mind. Instead,
she says that he lacks generosity, feels persecuted (taking bird-
bolts for cannon-bullets), and has no sense of reality (as in the
instance of bird-bolts, and in ignoring that fools have license to
point out folly). She employs (as Orsino does) metaphors of taste
and appetite: Malvolio cannot accurately taste or well digest what
he takes in, which is reality itself. He spoils Feste's success out of

  9. Anne Barton, "Introduction," to *Twelfth Night,* Riverside Shakespeare, ed.
G. Blakemore Evans (Boston: Houghton Mifflin, 1974), 405.

envy. Rather than join in the applause, he perceives it as dangerous to himself: "Infirmity, that decays the wise, doth ever make
the better fool" (1.5.74–75); "I marvel your ladyship takes delight
in such a barren rascal" (1.5.81–82). From what we know about
Malvolio in the play as a whole, it seems safe to conclude that he
projects onto Feste his own sense of being emptied—made barren
and decayed.

Orsino has much in common with his fellow contender for
Olivia. The Duke also is sick of self-love, and tastes with a distempered appetite. Either he sates himself on what he takes in:
"Enough, no more; / 'Tis not so sweet now as it was before"; or
he devalues it: "nought enters there . . . But falls into abatement."
Orsino claims that love and music do not satisfy, but the failure
really seems to lie within himself. It is due to what Barton calls
an "essentially sterile and self-induced . . . state of mind," but
does not depend upon Olivia's absence and lack of response.
Indeed, his mood has remarkably little to do with her. We cannot
be sure what he really wants, which leads critics to say that he is
in love with love; but we can be fairly sure that he does not want
Olivia, and the play bears this out. Nor does he seem to desire
sexual union, for he never plays with sexual implications of words
such as "dies," "dying fall," or of metaphors about appetite and
the sea. He longs for something extremely good, yet feels that it
will never satisfy him.

The problem seems to be—as for Malvolio—a precarious sense
of self-esteem. Healthy narcissism is love of oneself, without which
we cannot enter into a loving relation with others. Unhealthy
narcissism is fragile, defensive self-absorption; it results in being
unable to enter fully into relations with others. "Narcissism" has
recently become a central concern in psychoanalytic circles (Freud
offered profound, tentative insights on the subject). Heinz Kohut
emphasizes that narcissism can be normal as well as pathological,
and this has vital implications. He defines two essential require-
ments. First, we all need a healthy, grandiose self; but it must be
tempered by the frustrations of reality. We must feel our own
"innate sense of vigor, greatness, and perfection." As an infant we
initially derive this feeling from parents who mirror and confirm
our worth. Second, we also need a healthy, idealized "object"
(other person, external or internalized). This, too, must be tempered by the frustrations unavoidable in living—such as finding
the idealized object less than perfect. Such a person is initially

someone to whom an infant "can look up and with whom he can merge as an image of calmness, infallibility, and omnipotence." As infants we use this idealized object as a "self-object"—as something which is part of ourselves and under our absolute control (in analogy to the way adults treat parts of their bodies). This idealized object can eventually be internalized and felt to be an inner certainty (like one of Klein's friendly figures). Then we can expect, and search for, such a good object in the outer world of truly distinct other people.[10]

Rather than pursue this as theory, let us turn back to *Twelfth Night*. Orsino's self-esteem seems precarious, which is why he concentrates almost all his interest on himself (not others), and why he cannot endure the frustrations of reality. Whatever he idealizes in an effort to confirm his perfection—love, music, Olivia—eludes him. It never confirms his grandeur, because it is

10. I quote from a summary by Heinz Kohut and Ernest S. Wolf, "The Disorders of the Self and Their Treatment: An Outline," *International Journal of Psycho-Analysis* 59 (1978): 413–25. I also rely upon Kohut's *The Restoration of the Self* (New York: International Universities Press, 1977). Theorists differ on this matter. Otto F. Kernberg emphasizes the pathological, defensive, and regressive aspects of narcissism in *Borderline Conditions and Pathological Narcissism* (New York: Jason Aronson, 1976).

I find Béla Grunberger's work very useful; it predates that of Kohut and Kernberg, but since it was published in French—both in journals and then in the collection—it is hardly known to the English-speaking world. See his *Narcissism: Psychoanalytic Essays*, trans. Joyce S. Diamanti (New York: International Universities Press, 1979); this work was first published by Editions Payot, Paris, in 1971. I rely on Kohut, who is more familiar; but he is also more controversial because his "psychology of the self" seems not (as he thought) complementary to classic theory, but rather confusingly apart from it. Grunberger tries to integrate his speculation (and in ways sounds too orthodox, what with reifications and quantities of energy). At one point Grunberger conceives of narcissism as an "agency" in addition to id, ego, superego (pp. 107–9); at another, as a third force in addition to libido and aggression (p. 13). The latter seems to work better. He offers a detailed account of how a child's development follows a dual track: narcissistic and instinctive. As the stages (oral, anal, phallic, genital) unfold, each instinctual impulse will be invested narcissistically—that is, integrated into one's self-love. Conversely, each narcissistic striving will be augumented by instinctual drive, acting as a biological support (p. 174). Although one is aware of it only when the synthesis fails at some point (and leads to pathology), the two "realms" exist side by side: one unconflicted and narcissistic; the other conflicted and object-related.

As I suggest in my preface, Grunberger's view can clarify the vital role of narcissism in reparation. I think that reparation is colored and motivated by our attempt to restore "unconflicted, narcissistic" omnipotence—as well as (in Klein's theory) to assuage guilt in the "conflicted, object-related state." Grunberger relates his theory to Klein's in a more restricted way (pp. 75–76).

never as perfect as he demands that it be: "Enough, no more; / 'Tis not so sweet now as it was before." In addition, he idealizes himself in a grandiose way. Orsino's sense of his own excellence rings hollow to us (but not to Viola); he is so self-involved, so much a perfectionist, that he never engages himself in anything (hence the charge that he moons about). He courts an idealized lady at a distance by sending messengers, rather than pursue her more vigorously in person.

Another indication of Orsino's narcissistic imbalance is the wonderfully vitalizing effect which Viola has upon him. In her presence he becomes quite different. Kohut's psychological theory can help us to be more explicit about the way she provides (to quote Jenkins again) a "genuineness of feeling against which the illusory can be measured." Viola does something which Olivia could not do: as Cesario she confirms Orsino's innate sense of vigor, greatness, and perfection. Viola makes him feel rather elated: respected and loved for his own worth. But at the same time, she frustrates and tempers—but never tries to destroy—his illusory sense of omnipotence with regard to Olivia, to love, and to herself as Cesario. Using this perspective, we have a way of seeing the truth to nature which informs Shakespeare's apparently arbitrary treatment of the relationship between characters.[11]

Let us look back at the first scene. Immediately after Orsino's languorous speech, Curio asks if he will go hunt. "What, Curio?" Orsino replies, as if in a love-sick daze—or as if he had not thought of hunting anything or anyone. Olivia would be the likely object, if he is as smitten as he appears to be. Instead, he responds to Curio's suggestion, "the hart," by playing with it as a pun. Instead of hunting the hart—or Olivia—he *becomes* it:

11. Orsino is a romantic figure in a comedy, and thus I underplay the pathological aspects of narcissism. This is not a case history. Still, a clearer sense of these aspects can give us a better background. Significant disturbance in self-esteem makes a person pursue the chimera of perfection. Such pursuit is characterized by severe fluctuation between a sense of impotence (because unable to attain the desired excellence) and omnipotence (because able to imagine oneself capable of everything). Reality lies somewhere between these extremes. The cause of this disturbance seems to be the loss or unavailability of self-objects during infancy— and thus a feeling of worthlessness and impotence. The grandiose omnipotence of those so disturbed is an attempt to stanch this narcissistic wound. Since the loss occurred in the past, however, *no effort whatsoever* can change this fact. To "tame" such grandiosity means to frustrate the wish for perfection in objects, and omnipotence in oneself. I find Alice Miller unusually lucid on this in "Depression and

Why so I do, the noblest that I have.
O, when mine eyes did see Olivia first,
Methought she purg'd the air of pestilence;
That .instant was I turn'd into a hart,
And my desires, like fell and cruel hounds,
E'er since pursue me.

                                    (1.1.18–23)

He makes himself the center of attention, and in the idealized world of myth: she is Diana, he Acteon. The choice suggests two basic reasons for his ineffectual relation to Olivia. First, he idealizes her as Diana (who, by definition, will marry no one); she frustrates him in actuality, and persecutes him in fantasy (as revealed in the myth). Second, he reveals an ennervated sense of self-worth: Diana/Olivia is so perfect that Acteon/Orsino can never win her; pursuit can only be futile. Finally, Orsino, as the hart, becomes the object of his own desires—roughly the situation that Narcissus found himself in, and a classic instance of the sterile state of the narcissist.

Orsino's major failing is an inability to assess the world around him with any accuracy. When he learns that Olivia has vowed to mourn her brother for seven years, he ignores the excess, unlike Feste and Sir Toby; they see it as unrealistic and life-defeating, but Orsino has no sense of how it ruins his suit. To him, her mourning is solely a sign of her perfection. More important, it allows him to concentrate upon his own excellence:

O, she that hath a heart of that fine frame
To pay this debt of love but to a brother,
How will she love, when the rich golden shaft

Grandiosity as Related Forms of Narcissistic Disturbance," *International Review of Psycho-Analysis* 6 (1979): 61–76; a revised version appears in her excellent book *Prisoners of Childhood,* trans. Ruth Ward (New York: Basic Books, 1981). Grunberger would add, however, that—in less pathological ways—we all persist in this search; "one could regard all the manifestations of civilization as a kaleidoscope of different attempts by man to restore *narcissistic omnipotence*" (*Narcissism,* 78). On this, Kohut would largely agree.

How did Shakespeare know all this? I would opt for his acute observation of other people and of himself. However, Ben Jonson also seems to have been interested in some of the finer points of what we now call narcissism; see Judith Kegan Gardiner, " 'A Wither'd Daffodill' : Narcissism and *Cynthia's Revels,*" *Literature and Psychology* 30 (1980): 26–43.

Hath kill'd the flock of all affections else
That live in her; when liver, brain, and heart,
These sovereign thrones, are all supplied, and fill'd
Her sweet perfections with one self king!

                                        (1.1.33–39)

The "rich golden shaft" would in other contexts be a sign of sexual interest; but given Orsino's decided lack of such a drive, it serves here as an expression of his narcissistic grandeur. He will kill "the flock of all affections else / That live in her." The way he phrases this indicates that he sees her as having no life of her own, apart from what he bestows. If he supplies and fills her thrones of liver, brain, and heart "with one self king"—his literally aggrandized self—she will not exist in her own right. Orsino seeks to fuse with an idealized object—"her sweet perfections"—but in doing so, he invades and fills her up. He can no longer get what he wants, for the very good reason that, in his imagined fusion, it no longer exists. He has taken it over. The process is similar to the one at the start of the play: he longs for music or love, but spoils it because for him enough is never enough. Whatever he tries to merge with proves unsatisfying—like the music—and in reaction he immediately isolates himself and devalues what he sought. His goal is so unrealistic in itself—and so far beyond anyone's capacities—that he cannot pursue it. Instead, he relies upon messengers and never meets Olivia until the last scene. This allows him to preserve his idealization, and to avoid the frightening, painful acknowledgment that she is someone outside his control—an individual in her own right, rather than merely a gratifying extension of himself.

III

Viola helps to bring about changes in Orsino by her presence, by her personality. She plays no tricks like other disguised heroines. Instead, she inspires change simply by being receptive to the needs of others—to the point of seeming passive—yet without losing her own sense of worth.

This becomes clearer when we compare her to Olivia, who has more in common with Orsino than she thinks. Like him, Olivia reveals a mild exhibitionistic streak. Rather than mourn an acknowledged loss and try to internalize the person's memory, she draws attention to herself as someone who wants to preserve the "dead love":

> But like a cloistress she will veiled walk,
> And water once a day her chamber round
> With eye-offending brine: all this to season
> A brother's dead love, which she would keep fresh
> And lasting, in her sad remembrance.
>   (1.1.28–32)

Her brother's love actually seems dead to her in this account. Rather than try to bring it to life and use it—as Viola does by imitating her lost brother—Olivia concentrates on pickling it, keeping it immobile. She seems not to feel that her brother can, when internalized, be a living presence, a friendly figure. When Olivia first appears, Feste challenges her obsessive mourning: *no one* is constant to calamity—"there is no true cuckold but calamity" (1.5.49). Feste argues that if Olivia knows her brother's soul is in heaven, then she need not mourn so excessively. Her brother, or his soul, can take care of himself—and in any case lies outside her control. Like Orsino, she seems to find it difficult to believe that others exist (or existed), and that they can thus return love to her. And yet, like Orsino, she longs for a good object, inner and outer, and for the ability to love it.

Both characters need whatever Viola offers, which is why they so quickly make her central to their lives. Viola has a clear sense of herself, as we can see by the way she uses her brother as an internalized good object, a friendly figure. We can assume that she models her behavior on his, for she quite literally imitates him in her disguise:

> I my brother know
> Yet living in my glass; even such and so
> In favour was my brother, and he went
> Still in this fashion, colour, ornament,
> For him I imitate.
>   (3.4.389–93)

She does this so successfully that he can later simply step into the role and be what she imitates. Having internalized him (and, we assume, other friendly figures), Viola is secure in herself—unlike Orsino and Olivia. She can be an affectionate, responsive companion to others. She immediately strikes us as self-assured, especially in the context of the Duke's and Olivia's excesses and uncertainty. Viola is lively and vigorous, as her numerous ques-

tions and quick decisions indicate. She quickly strikes up a friendship with the Captain, and trusts him. Various figures are able to
help her—the Captain, her brother (as a memory and a model),
Orsino, and Olivia. Even more important, given the crucial need
to be able to be reparative, she can also help these figures.

As Cesario, Viola becomes an ideal companion for the Duke:
someone loyal, steady, and selfless who respects and understands
him in ways which are, apparently, new to him. He begins to grow
progressively less self-absorbed and a better companion. From his
first, restless speech we know that he longs for something or someone whose worth will satisfy and endure—will have meaning. We
discover from the opening lines of the first scene between him and
Cesario that he has evidently begun to find it:

> *Valentine.*   If the Duke continue these favours
>   towards you, Cesario, you are like to be
>   much advanced: he hath known you but
>   three days, and already you are no
>   stranger.
> *Viola.*   You either fear his humour, or my
>   negligence, that you call in question the
>   continuance of his love. Is he inconstant,
>   sir, in his favours?
> *Valentine.*   No, believe me.
>
>   (1.4.1–8)

Valentine sounds rather surprised at the Duke's quickly bestowed
favors. The issue of Orsino's constancy arises at once—as we
might expect, given the restlessness of his humor in the first scene.
He tends to fuse and to isolate, to idealize and to degrade. We
might expect this tendency to ruin his friendship. Several factors
allow for the new stability. For one thing, Cesario remains faithful
to the end, and shows no negligence; this quiets Orsino's fear of
inconstancy and loss. Another factor troubles critics more than
audiences: Orsino treats Cesario as a young man, and remains
oblivious to his true gender. Perhaps this is why Orsino never
feels tempted to fuse, or to isolate. Until the very end, he treats
Cesario as a reflection of himself—and what could be better? He
treats Cesario as a reflection of his own excellence.

This is literally Cesario's role when he takes Orsino's place in
wooing Olivia. As his surrogate, Cesario behaves assertively, even
boldly. He confirms—and obeys—the Duke's assertiveness: "Be

clamorous, and leap all civil bounds" (1.4.21). Cesario's vigor thus reaffirms Orsino's sense of his own strength. Because Viola loves Orsino, and is so sure of herself that she can endure the "barful strife" of wooing for him, she puts up with his obtuse, self-centered ways. She serves as a companion who makes him feel more secure in himself. Their relationship serves as a kind of adolescent friendship—a prelude to being ready, psychologically, to marry Viola.[12]

Viola behaves in the way a friend, or therapist, might in dealing with someone whose self-esteem is precarious because it fluctuates between the extremes of being too low or too grandiose. Her passivity allows a mild narcissistic elation to flourish in Orsino; and thus she bolsters his sense of worth by confirming his vigor, greatness, and perfection. She serves as a loving, selfless, respectful friend and servant. But also—in the most delicate of maneuvers—she tames his grandiose sense of himself and of his idealized object, Olivia. Cesario continually reminds him of the real nature of his situation: "Sure, my noble lord, / If she be so abandon'd to her sorrow / As it is spoke, she never will admit me" (1.4.18–20). Then Viola makes him take a close look at her by denying that Cesario's youth will draw Olivia's respect: "I think not so, my lord" (1.4.29). Now Orsino begins to notice that the person standing before him is not merely youthful, but has distinctly feminine traits: "Dian's lip," a maiden's voice, "and all is semblative a woman's part." Although right, he remains comically obtuse: what adolescent boy would relish hearing such a catalogue? Nevertheless, Orsino makes some tentative steps toward the reality which he hitherto scorns to acknowledge.

IV

Viola also helps to bring about changes in Olivia by her presence, by her personality. Here the effect is more comically dangerous. Olivia and Orsino ignore reality in its most basic aspect, the gender of the person they love, as if it were irrelevant to their longing for someone perfect. That they do so becomes compre-

12. Coppélia Kahn suggests that *Twelfth Night* deals with the "state of radical identity-confusion typical of adolescence, when the differences between the sexes are as fluid as their desires for each other"; in *Man's Estate: Masculine Identity in Shakespeare* (Berkeley: University of California Press, 1981), 208. There is certainly an adolescent quality to the relationship, but the play carefully understates sexuality. In terms of Grunberger's theory, the narcissistic and the instinctual are "unsynthesized" during most (or all) of the play (see n. 10 above).

hensible if we remember that this, in the end, is a longing for someone who will reflect their own perfection. This ultimate, narcissistic basis may explain their fondness. Orsino sees himself in "Cesario"; Olivia sees herself in the hidden Viola. This is only part of the truth, however, for Olivia and Orsino begin to establish contact with others, and move from the narcissistic realm into the realm of object relations. Olivia moves very quickly. She begins to evaluate herself more accurately, which is the crucial first step. At the outset of the play, we heard of Olivia's self-absorption in her role as mourner and cloistress. When Cesario appears at her gate and demands audience, Olivia forgets all this and comes alive. Like Orsino, she seems to have been waiting for someone like Cesario. He confirms her worth, yet draws her into a clear relation to reality—and right from the start:

> Most radiant, exquisite, and unmatchable beauty—I pray
> you tell me if this be the lady of the house, for I never
> saw her. . . . Good beauties, let me sustain no scorn; I am
> very comptible, even to the least sinister usage.
>
> (1.5.171–73, 176–77)

The costumes, and the characterization, of the two beauties preclude much confusion: Olivia is a languid lady in a veil, and Maria a spritely gentlewoman. Cesario's confusion is tongue-in-cheek, but serves to indicate that he really is also trying to look at Olivia—which is difficult, given the veil—rather than simply reciting a set speech. His curiosity is flattering, but witty and delicate; so is his defensiveness about being sensitive to the slightest incivility. Olivia soon answers the question about being the lady of the house: "If I do not usurp myself, I am" (1.5.187). Cesario has touched on just the right topic—on who and what Olivia is—and thus appears to understand her on the deepest level. He confirms her worth, the issue she plays with, and yet spots her defensiveness and isolation:

> Most certain, if you are she, you do usurp yourself: for
> what is yours to bestow is not yours to reserve. But this is
> from my commission.
>
> (1.5.188–90)

When Olivia and Cesario are left alone, Cesario asks to see her face. We suspect that Viola wants to see her competitor, but

coming from Cesario this request indicates that he speaks for
himself, and not by rote. She unveils, as if a work of art: "but we
will draw the curtain and show you the picture. Look you, sir,
such a one I was this present. Is't not well done?" (1.5.236–38).
She sounds grand, and yet tentative, needing a response. Someone
at last is there to mirror her beauty and worth, and she seems
pleased (as would any woman courted at a distance by Orsino).
Cesario sums up his sense of Olivia's looks and character: "I see
you what you are, you are too proud." He both confirms her pride
(she is beautiful), and tempers it (by finding it excessive because
unrelated to others—to Orsino, to having children). By the end of
this scene, Olivia begins to be what she admires in others (as we
know from her chiding Malvolio for "self-love"): she is "generous, guiltless, and of free disposition." Olivia falls in love with
Cesario, sends him a ring, and becomes vigorous—too much so,
given Cesario's true gender. Still, Olivia now is fully alive rather
than static and self-absorbed. She abandons her role as Diana
during her very first scene with Cesario, which indicates that her
sense of worth must not be so precarious as Orsino's. The process
is similar, however. Cesario mirrors and confirms her basic traits—
assertiveness, delicacy of sentiment, generosity—and also tempers the grandiosity implicit in Olivia's isolation. The process
here, as with Orsino, is roughly analogous to therapy, but without
the pain. And art is faster than life.

When Sebastian appears, Olivia is ready for marriage. We have
to assume that the twins are identical personalities: one male, the
other female. This is one arbitrary fact that Shakespeare relies
upon. However, Sebastian's character differs a bit from his sister's. He is masculine in his rough-and-ready battle with the knights;
but, unlike Cesario, self-effacing toward Olivia. Whereas Cesario
continually challenges her—tells her about her faults, refuses to
do her bidding, returns her gift—Sebastian is perfectly content to
marry this stranger, accept her gift, and do her bidding. Olivia
insists that he return with her: "Thou shalt not choose but go: /
Do not deny." He does so:

Sebastian.   What relish is in this? How runs the stream?
                Or I am mad, or else this is a dream:
                Let fancy still my sense in Lethe steep;
                If it be thus to dream, still let me sleep!

Olivia.	Nay, come, I prithee; would thou'dst be
	rul'd by me!
Sebastian.	Madam, I will.
Olivia.	O, say so, and so be.

(4.1.59–64)

When she provides a priest for a hasty wedding, he readily agrees. Viola has to be standoffish; but her twin proves very compliant. This reveals yet another aspect of Olivia's idealization of Cesario: she thought that she wanted a saucy lad, but what she needs—and gets—is a willing subject for her still rather imperious whims.

V

In the love scene (2.4) between Orsino and Viola we are prepared for the abrupt shift at the end of the play. The two scenes (1.1 and 2.4) are ripe for comparison: the first, a static musing of one man about love, surfeit, and abatement—using metaphors of appetite and the sea; the second, a man and the woman we guess he will marry in a lively dialogue about love, its changeability and constancy—using the same metaphors. In Viola's presence, Orsino begins to modify the view he developed in his very first speech:

> Give me some music. Now good morrow, friends.
> Now, good Cesario, but that piece of song,
> That old and antic song we heard last night;
> Methought it did relieve my passion much.

(2.4.1–4)

We can safely attribute to Viola's influence his new attitude to music. This central metaphor suggests both fusion, and a more harmonious relationship. Now music can comfort him. One reason is Viola's presence. Another is his awareness that music exists outside himself: he cannot have the song instantly, magically, as in the opening scene. Cesario is not to be the singer; a little frustration must be endured in waiting for Feste. "Music plays" behind their dialogue and presumably remains sweet since Orsino does not stop it. We find him beginning to experience someone as distinctly other than himself. A first hint is that he says "good morrow, friends" rather than simply ignore others as in his first scene. Cesario exists as a relatively autonomous person of whom he asks a series of questions, and listens to the answers; and with whom he begins to transcend his rapt concentration of interest upon himself. Orsino takes a more serious interest in others, although he is still the center of attention:

> Come hither, boy. If ever thou shalt love,
> In the sweet pangs of it remember me:
> For such as I am, all true lovers are,
> Unstaid and skittish in all motions else,
> Save in the constant image of the creature
> That is belov'd. How dost thou like this tune?
>
> (2.4.15–20)

An ordinary question, but new to him, and one to which Cesario gives an extraordinary reply: "It gives a very echo to the seat / Where love is thron'd." For Viola, music gives an echo to an inner feeling: she finds a reciprocal relation, rather than, as Orsino did, loss of sweetness. He thought of filling up Olivia's "sovereign thrones" with "one self king" (1.1.38–39), but Viola conceives of "the seat / Where love is thron'd" as an internal object, an inner certainty which returns the value outward rather than spoil it because it can never be adequate. Her more complex and active response differs from his attempted merger with music; it prepares us for a new sense of satisfaction in both music and love.

In one of Orsino's rare compliments—itself a sign of new generosity—he says "Thou dost speak masterly." He thinks of Cesario as a reflection of himself, yet also separate: "young though thou art, thine eye / Hath stay'd upon some favour that it loves." Viola begins a series of hints to which he proves comically obtuse—"A little, by your favour"—but which also make him actually look at Cesario as someone other than himself: "What kind of woman is't?" "What years, i'faith?" He even, vaguely, puts himself into a woman's situation:

> Let still the woman take
> An elder than herself; so wears she to him,
> So sways she level in her husband's heart:
> For boy, however we do praise ourselves,
> Our fancies are more giddy and unfirm,
> More longing, wavering, sooner lost and worn
> Than women's are.
>
> (2.4.29–35)

He still idealizes women; we know that Olivia has forgotten her

brother and giddily begun wooing Cesario. Orsino now says that
women love in a better way than men do. He sees some chance
for stability, for women can provide constant and devoted love.
Since he speaks to a woman without knowing it, we spot the irony.
Steadfast Viola says, perhaps eagerly, "I think it well, my lord."
She must hope for one, and only one, shift in his fidelity. The
ironic exchanges and Viola's poignant good humor make his deprivation begin to seem ludicrous. The song mocks his excesses; in
"Come away, come away death" no one is even to know the
whereabouts of the bones of the lover "slain by a fair cruel maid."
The humor introduces a sense of reality to Orsino's misgivings
and qualifications.

In a typically grand manner, he directs Cesario—rather than
himself—to be assertive: "Get thee to yond same sovereign cruelty." Cesario again interjects a realistic note: "But if she cannot
love you, sir?" In his self-absorption, Orsino declares: "I cannot
be so answer'd." With wonderful tact, Cesario confirms Orsino's
self-esteem, but in doing so forces him to realize that others also
exist:

> Sooth, but you must.
> Say that some lady, as perhaps there is,
> Hath for your love as great a pang of heart
> As you have for Olivia: you cannot love her:
> You tell her so. Must she not then be answer'd?
> (2.4.89–93)

The example is set up so that Orsino finds that his wishes must
of course be obeyed. At the same time, the example forces him
to entertain the idea that someone other than himself, "some
lady," has a will of her own (and thus the volition to yield to his
wishes). At this point, when Orsino has to consider that some
woman may actually love him—rather than, like Olivia, be the
inert material of his imaginings—he seems to change. On one
level, he remains obtuse and self-centered: no woman can match
his constancy. However, Viola-Cesario has just confronted him
with the possibility that some lady really may have "as great a
pang of heart / As you have for Olivia"; this seems to make him
alter his view of himself and of an idealized object. He asserts that
no woman's heart is:

> So big, to hold so much: they lack retention.

Alas, their love may be call'd appetite,
No motion of the liver, but the palate,
That suffers surfeit, cloyment, and revolt;
But mine is all as hungry as the sea,
And can digest as much.

(2.4.97–102)

Again, he debases women—"they lack retention"—and seems as restless and longing as at the start of the play; but his hunger seems sharper, more focused on a love object. Orsino sees himself in relation to women, rather than to music, or to some bodiless "spirit of love." Now, it seems, he can truly feel love. Indeed, no woman's heart is "so big, to hold so much." This differs from his wish to surfeit, which he now identifies with the palate—and tries to distance from himself as a feminine trait.

At this point he no longer thinks of himself as having a distempered appetite. He can avoid the surfeit and abatement which formerly bothered him. The reason, we can easily assume, is that Viola stands before him. Now he sees himself as having a liver whose needs must be met, whereas formerly he used the term only to refer to Olivia's "liver, brain, and heart" (1.1.37). The liver, the traditional metaphor for the seat of sexual passion, is also used here as an organ of digestion. True love, he says, leads to "retention," not to a cloyed palate or to loss. At the very moment when he explicitly joins love with sexuality, he combines the two key metaphors of his first speech in the play, and comes up with a potential resolution. It allows for constancy, for incorporation rather than loss by surfeit or abatement: his love is "all as hungry as the sea, / And can digest as much." The metaphor is curious. It allows for a nice distinction between palate and liver—between a fickle hunger and one which leads him to hold and digest. The sexual implication makes sense, particularly if we conceive of his narcissism, his self-love, as now invested in the love of another.[13]

An unfortunate implication creeps in. We might easily accept the notion that desire still cries, "Give me some food"; but the idea that the beloved might be digested is unsettling—especially when it comes from a character who previously thought of killing

13. It augments his instinctual drives rather than remain unadapted and anachronistic (as Grunberger puts it, n. 10 above). Hearty psychoanalytic critics may want to pursue Grunberger's idea that "capture, digestion, and absorption"—are a mode which characterizes anality: the crucial first stage in developing a sense of reality, and in mastering it (*Narcissism*, 143–64).

off all her other affections and of filling up all her thrones. Perhaps
this is why Cesario immediately presents Orsino with an instance
of "what love women to men may owe." This clarifies the difference
between subject and object, and avoids the implication of fusion
in Orsino's speech:

> My father had a daughter lov'd a man,
> As it might be perhaps, were I a woman,
> I should your lordship.
>
> (2.4.108–10)

This makes Orsino ask her history—makes him consider her as
separate from himself, and women as separate from men. Cesario
enigmatically presents the sister as someone with a will of her
own, even if she never told her love:

> But let concealment like a worm i' th' bud
> Feed on her damask cheek: she pin'd in thought,
> And with a green and yellow melancholy
> She sat like Patience on a monument,
> Smiling at grief.
>
> (2.4.112–16)

Cesario offers a glimpse of how calmly the sister (Viola) can endure frustration—unlike Orsino—and of how much women need
to be loved, rather than serve as the material for fantasies of the
sort in which Orsino still indulges. Cesario concludes that "we
men . . . prove / Much in our vows, but little in our love." Once
again, this deflates Orsino's omnipotence—men are not perfect—
but in a way which affirms the camaraderie between Orsino and
Cesario, and among all men. Cesario takes the Duke seriously, but
relates him and his failings to those of most men, of ordinary men.
When Orsino asks: "But died thy sister of her love, my boy?"
Viola-Cesario forces him to think, and frustrates him for a necessary moment: "I am all the daughters of my father's house, / And
all the brothers too: and yet I know not." An actor playing Orsino
could take careful, puzzled note, and make us feel that he gets
some part of her meaning before insisting that *his* love "can give
no place, bide no denay."

Shakespeare puts Orsino in the extraordinary position of someone who never has to face the difference between his idealization
of a perfect beloved, and the ideal woman he marries. Viola
actually measures up to his unrealistic demands by being thor-

oughly constant, selfless, and generous. A plucky Rosalind would
never do for Orsino, nor would a demanding equal such as Beatrice, or a formidable Portia—or even Olivia, given her bold,
changeable, imperious character.
Perhaps the greatest puzzle is Viola herself. She gets Orsino,
and seems genuinely fond of him. Since she is so secure in herself
and in a benign inner world, we assume that she must know what
she wants. Olivia makes us think that the Duke has many virtues
(1.5.262–66). Still, he disconcerts us at the end of the play. He
turns on Cesario, calls him a dissembling cub. With comic stub-
bornness, Orsino persists in idealizing Olivia; when at long last
she enters, he exclaims: "now heaven walks on earth." But when
he finds that she has wed Cesario he degrades her to a "marble-
breasted tyrant." We may simply regard this as the death throes
of his former ways. Still, his wish for revenge on Cesario has
narcissistic overtones:

> But this your minion, whom I know you love,
> And whom, by heaven, I swear I tender dearly,
> Him will I tear out of that cruel eye
> Where he sits crowned in his master's spite.
>   (5.1.123–26)

He will "sacrifice the lamb that I do love, / To spite a raven's heart
within a dove." The situation—and rhymes—insure that we do
not take this as much more than comic excess. And Viola's willingness to die is another—now preposterous—indication of her
constancy. Still, we hardly need to have these traits emphasized
once again. If we are at all attuned to Orsino's narcissistic mode,
this outburst suggests that he has not entirely changed.[14] We are

14. Kernberg in *Borderline Conditions and Pathological Narcissism* continually
addresses this issue. Kohut does so in "Thoughts on Narcissism and Narcissistic
Rage" (1972), reprinted in *The Search for the Self: Selected Writings of Heinz
Kohut: 1950–1978*, vol. 2, ed. Paul H. Ornstein (New York: International Universities Press, 1978). Kohut says that "such bedevilment indicates that the aggression was mobilized in the service of an archaic grandiose self and that it is
deployed within the framework of an archaic perception of reality" (p. 643).
Malvolio's threat of revenge also has such overtones.
    Shylock can also be viewed from such a perspective; his irrational fury stems
from narcissistic wounds which many viewers find painful to contemplate. I do
not overtly discuss this aspect of his character in my chapter on *The Merchant*
because it would distort the play. However, when I refer to Shylock's and Antonio's fluctuation between omnipotence and impotence during the trial, I have a
narcissistic imbalance in mind.

left with the possibility that Viola idealizes Orsino, thinks him better than he is—and right up to the end.[15]

VI

The subplots divert our attention from what worries us about the lovers: perhaps fantasy is merely fantasy, and invention an imposition upon reality which leads to trouble. In the case of the household characters other than Malvolio—Feste, Toby, Andrew, and Maria—their prosaic, commonsensical approach makes the lovers' fantasies seem enriching (as I suggest in the next section). Malvolio, however, outdoes the lovers in being "high-fantastical," yet meets defeat. As G. K. Hunter says: "The happiness of the lovers would seem to have been bought at a price which excludes Malvolio, and we may feel that this circumscribes and diminishes the final effect of their happiness" (p. 48). There is another possibility. Excluding Malvolio stabilizes our sense of the lovers' happiness by confirming the essential difference between him and them: they idealize from a basic sense of trust in others which allows them to appreciate whoever stands before them (whatever the gender). Malvolio's appetite is far more distempered. He wants to possess Olivia solely for the purpose of carrying out his grandiose, exhibitionistic fantasy of ruling the household. That she may love him is based on the fact, Malvolio says, that "she uses me with a more exalted respect than any one else that follows her" (2.5.26–28). This is not simply delusion but a perverse kind of reality testing; he subjects bits of the outer world to scrutiny—like Olivia's handwriting—rather than simply make a leap of faith as Orsino, Olivia, Viola, and Sebastian do. Malvolio offers an example for his presumption: "The Lady of the Strachy married the yeoman of the wardrobe." Suddenly, and with no indication of any affection, he leaps past the marriage and past the wedding night to "having been three months married to her, sitting in my state" and "calling my officers about me, in my branched velvet gown, having come from a day-bed, where I have left Olivia sleeping." So much for the bride. He concentrates upon himself, the detail of *his* costume, and upon the omnipotent con-

15. For this reason, I am not so certain of the final result as Coppélia Kahn: "*Twelfth Night* traces the evolution of sexuality as related to identity, from the playful and unconscious toyings of youthful courtship, through a period of sexual confusion, to a final thriving in which swaggering is left behind and men and women truly know themselves through choosing and loving the right mate" (*Man's Estate*, 210–11).

trol which he would exercise over the disrespectful members of the household: "telling them I know my place, as I would they should do theirs." He will chastize Toby, "quenching my familiar smile with an austere regard of control." Maria's plot works so brilliantly because she plays on his desire to be the absolute center of attention. She creates a role for him, right down to explicit details of dress and behavior.

It is difficult not to feel sympathy for such a character. He gets left out in the cold after a brief and self-destructive fling at trying to confirm his sense of worth. He wants unlimited praise, and unlimited control of the household. During their midnight cater-wauling, for instance, Sir Toby attacks Malvolio's attempt to keep order:

> Out o' time sir? ye lie! Art any more than a steward? Dost thou think because thou art virtuous, there shall be no more cakes and ale?
>
> (2.3.113–15)

Maria, and many a critic, assumes that Malvolio is "the best persuaded of himself, so crammed (as he thinks) with excellencies, that it is his grounds of faith that all that look on him love him" (2.3.149–52). However, as Melvin Seiden puts it, Malvolio's actions are "the very opposite of what they pretend to be: not the firm conviction of integrity but a self-destructive sense of inferiority."[16] I think that our confusion about this distinction causes much of the trouble we have with Malvolio at the end. If he is merely conceited, then the trick might be good for him, take him down a bit—or at least be deserved ridicule. Yet if he lacks self-esteem, then he is pitiful and sad, and the characters and the play treat him cruelly. Critics opt for one or the other of these responses, yet neither seems fully satisfactory. The reason Malvolio annoys us is that he cannot take in anything good or, therefore, *allow* it to be good. Olivia appreciates him, deplores the trick, and wants to see justice done:

> Prithee, be content;
> This practice hath most shrewdly pass'd upon thee.
> But when we know the grounds and authors of it,

16. Melvin Seiden, "Malvolio Reconsidered," *University of Kansas City Review* 28 (1961): 111.

Thou shalt be both the plaintiff and the judge
Of thine own cause.

(5.1.350–54)

Fabian immediately confesses his guilt so that "no quarrel, nor no
brawl to come, / Taint the condition of this present hour" (5.1.355–
56). Olivia compassionately says, "Alas, poor fool, how they have
baffled thee!" But Feste teases Malvolio and taunts him for his
nasty remark at the start: " 'Madam, why laugh you at such a
barren rascal, and you smile not, he's gaged'? And thus the whirli-
gig of time brings in his revenges" (5.1.373–76). This rebuke provokes Malvolio's unsettling exit line: "I'll be reveng'd on the
whole pack of you!" Olivia tries to be sympathetic still, as does
the Duke, yet they—and the audience—are momentarily overwhelmed by all this fuss, and by its inappropriateness. Unlike
Fabian, Malvolio is so self-involved that he apparently neither
notices the newly paired-off couples, nor the twin Cesarios—or,
if he notices, he cares not a hoot. Olivia has confirmed the validity
of his grievance, and given him a kindly hearing; still, he remains
furious, having spoiled the good gestures and been stung by Feste.
Malvolio has not only lost the chance for unlimited praise and
control as Count, but become the butt of those whom he wanted
to impress and manipulate. All this is very true to character, to
the "distempered appetite" which Malvolio conveys in all its sad
unpleasantness. He dwells only on himself since he feels so wounded
and exposed. He spoils everything which he tastes—even good
things, such as his mistress's compassion and protection. He failed
to get what he grandiosely demanded—an idealized role for himself—and thus scorns the considerable crumbs which reality offers.
Feste's taunts provoke his rage; they are particularly galling because they allude to his having made a fool of himself by his
ridiculous smiling during the letter scene. All this overwhelms
him: his self-esteem is so precarious that even Olivia's kindness
cannot confirm his identity. What he lacks is the balanced view
which Olivia demonstrates when she says, as he leaves, "He hath
been most notoriously abus'd" (5.1.378). She echoes his own complaint, yet means well. Even when we are consciously aware of
why he behaves as he does—and Olivia appears to be—it is difficult
not to feel annoyed and punitive. He tries to pull us into his
delusion by spoiling everything good, such as the happy reunion
and wondrously effected marriages. He vents his infantile rage
upon characters with whom, to various degrees, we identify. The

disproportionate time which they—and critics—devote to Malvolio during the last scene indicates that we are confronting a narcissist. He demands attention far out of proportion to what he ought to get because none of it really *means* anything to him. The great positive effect of his usurpation here—and of his narrow and unrealizable invention as Count Malvolio—is to make us feel that Orsino and Olivia have grown beyond such tedious and disturbing self-involvement, and are ready to appreciate the twins who fulfill more realizable inventions.

<h2 style="text-align:center">VII</h2>

The other subplots in *Twelfth Night,* wonderfully comic in dialogue and situation, seem static in characterization. This partly stems from the almost complete absence of idealization or ideal formation. Feste has none. Orsino's fellow suitors for Olivia, Malvolio and Sir Andrew, act solely from self-interest and a shaky sense of worth. Sir Toby wants only a good time; his rapid satiety, like that of other characters, with food, drink, music, and jests— and their consequent abatement in value—spurs him to none of Orsino's melancholy, romantic attempts. Toby does marry Maria, but in recompense for her trick on Malvolio—about as unromantic an incentive as possible.

Antonio, however, seems more like the lovers in his penchant for idealization, and in the fact that at the end he more firmly bases it on reality.[17] His friendship for Sebastian is a model of selfless love, in direct contrast to Sir Toby's exploitation of Sir Andrew. Antonio seems almost too selfless, and finally ends up being arrested for aiding Cesario (whom he thinks Sebastian). We have no reason to believe Sebastian a "false idol," but Antonio's choice of "idol" is precise in its connotations. No one is perfect, but Sebastian's friendship seems close to being so. At the end of the play, the marriage of Sebastian to Olivia allows for transition to a clearer relation between the men—one confirmed by Sebastian's extravagant but now more plausible greeting of his friend (5.1.216–18). One result of their near-perfect friendship is to make Sebastian appear worthy of Olivia in that he, like his sister, is so good.

Unlike Antonio and the four lovers, Feste holds no ideals at all. Like most of the members of the subplot, he helps to throw the inventiveness of others into relief. Stage fools, of course, rarely

17. L. G. Salingar feels the pain here and speaks of Sebastian as actually being a "false idol" in "The Design of *Twelfth Night*," *SQ* 9 (1958): 131.

hold ideals, the Fool in *Lear* being an exception. Salingar finds
Feste "a moralist with a strong bent toward skepticism"; "what
he sees at the bottom of the well is 'nothing' " (p. 136). Feste
devotes himself to assessing what lies before him; unlike Antonio
and the lovers, who test reality only briefly and in limited ways,
he finds nothing. Although Feste gets caught up in the foolish
excesses of the household when they trick Malvolio, he generally
stays neutral and detached. His only "inventions" (other than
playing Sir Topas) are his unusually fanciful authorities and allu-
sions—to old hermits of Prague, Quinapalus, Pigrogromitus,
Vapians—which draw attention to themselves as pure nonsense;
they testify to his basic distrust of fanciful creations. Feste sees no
disparity between ideal and actual because he sees *only* the actual.
He regards Olivia's mourning as simply an aberration, not a sign
of constancy. The truth lies somewhere between what Feste and
Orsino perceive—as it also does, say, in the implicit mockery of
Feste's song "O mistress mine" when seen in the light of the play
(2.3.40–53). Perhaps the sentiments expressed in the song are not
Feste's (he simply sings the song). Still, here and in "Come away,
come away death" (in the next scene), he voices a consistent
attitude. All three vigorously mock inventions and opt for common sense. The "mistress mine" could be taken as a reference to
Olivia who should "stay and hear, your true love's coming, / That
can sing both high and low" (a reference to Cesario). The song
advises the lady to "trip no further": "In delay there lies no plenty,
/ Then come kiss me, sweet and twenty: / Youth's a stuff will not
endure." By implication, Olivia ought to take what lies before her,
rather than concentrate (like Orsino and Viola) on such questions
as "What is love? 'Tis not hereafter." So downright a response on
the part of the mistress of the household might appear eminently
practical, but since Olivia has already pinned her hopes on Cesario, we know that she had better delay. Similarly, "Come away,
come away death" mocks Orsino's extreme constancy to "a fair
cruel maid," and makes him seem extravagant and perverse; we
are particularly sensitive to this because Viola stands patiently
before him. Yet here, too, lies the point: the song makes fun of
extreme constancy at a time when we also sense its value if it can
be shifted from Olivia to Viola.

   In the final song Feste (or the narrator) finds that as one grows
up, foolish things are no longer accepted as trifles; knaves, thieves,
swaggerers, and drunkards get into trouble. The song's haunting
quality, especially in the refrain about the wind and the rain,

derives from its insistence upon putting human activity—from a child's play to a man's love—in context. Adverse elements such as wind and rain remind us what life is like, as they do in the Fool's use of the same refrain when he sings for Lear on the heath. Strangely, the Fool's song in the midst of tragedy consoles, whereas Feste's at the end of comedy discomforts. Lear has just expressed concern for the Fool, who reassures him that "He that has and a little tiny wit . . . Must make content with his fortunes fit"—must adjust to the vicissitudes of life—"Though the rain it raineth every day." Even though the rain strikes, we can rise above adversity, as do so many characters in *Lear*; ideals persist through the thick of the storm. In contrast, Feste sobers us with his insistence upon a commonsensical acceptance of life: he subjects all invention to a realist's view—"a foolish thing was but a toy." The final song emphasizes the return to such a world after a prolonged experience of inventions apparently divorced from reality. Viola contributes to this new spirit by insisting that Sebastian give superfluous details of his background before she concludes the obvious: he is indeed her lost brother. Similarly, Orsino persists in referring to Viola as Cesario until she can return, after the play's time span, dressed as a woman; then, but not now, she will be "Orsino's mistress, and his fancy's queen."

Roy Schafer says of literature that "we deal also with the reader's wish to find that such grandeur exists, existed, or can be conceived of . . . with his wish to discover ideal objects in the outer world, even if only imagined ones. These give form, stability, and use to his own inventions."[18] The existence of such perfection would reaffirm our own. *Twelfth Night* confirms our wish to idealize, "to discover ideal objects in the outer world, even if only imagined ones." The play makes the wish plausible—despite its apparent madness and folly—because the lovers who idealize others actually find them. *All's Well* and *Measure for Measure* present a far more skeptical view of this all-too-human wish. From now on, reparation is not so easily effected: autonomy yields to self-absorption; trust becomes distorted by confusion about whether good objects and ideals actually exist or are defensively imagined. All difficulties are no longer easy, as these comedies draw closer to the frustrations of real life.

18. Roy Schafer, "Ideals, the Ego Ideal, and the Ideal Self," in *Motives and Thought*, Psychological Issues 18/19, ed. Robert R. Holt (New York: International Universities Press, 1967), 170.

~6~
All's Well that Ends Well
Longing, Idealization, and Sadness

All's Well that Ends Well fully reveals the danger of inventing what one wants, of idealizing others beyond what seems a reasonable extension of actual traits. Unlike *Twelfth Night,* this comedy confronts us with characters whom it would seem difficult to imagine perfect. Orsino may not seem quite worthy of Viola, but Olivia pronounces him "virtuous . . . noble, / Of great estate, of fresh and stainless youth; / In voices well divulg'd, free, learn'd, and valiant, / And in dimension, and the shape of nature, / A gracious person" (1.5.262–66). Thus it is easy for Viola, and us, to see him as ideal. Bertram never receives even modest praise without its being severely qualified; nevertheless, Helena imagines him an ideal husband. She herself is commended by everyone but Bertram for her goodness and virtue; but since she imposes herself upon him—twice—it is difficult to think her as admirable as other characters do. They idealize Helena.

Critics follow the characters in their impulse to distort reality in quest of something or someone perfect. Some critics, like Helena, deny Bertram's bad points—deception, cowardice, cold-heartedness—in favor of his good one: honor through battle; they transform his tepid repentance into a sign of his being a better man. Other critics follow the lead of the King, Countess, Lafew and most of Helena's world by denying her bad points—being obtuse, manipulative, willful—in favor of her heroic persistence and willingness to give all for love. Such idealization is precarious and puts off other critics; they degrade either Helena and her

121

society, or Bertram, in an opposite but directly consequent response to idealization—and equally a distortion of reality. Many
pronounce the play radically flawed, a failure. No matter what
their view of *All's Well,* most critics search for something extremely good—and either distort the work to find it or, failing to
find what they want, degrade it. Their approaches are especially
informative and worth looking at in detail.

First it is necessary to admit that *All's Well* is an odd play, and
to accept this rather than to deny aspects which we do not like or
think inappropriate to Shakespeare's comedies. G. K. Hunter
sums up a widely held view: "The play has undoubtedly a strongly
individual quality, but it is difficult to start from this, since it is
mainly a quality of *strain,* of striving through intractable material
for effects which hardly justify the struggle, a quality of harsh
discord which seeks resolution, but achieves less than is sought."[1]
We ought to start from this observation and adjust our focus
accordingly: to "achieve less than is sought" precisely defines the
play's poignant effect and its "success." One reason why we look
for success in Shakespeare's works can help us to understand
something about ourselves and about the characters in *All's Well.*
We, like them, seek to preserve our sense of goodness: we want
Shakespeare and his works to be consistently excellent—by which
we apparently mean that in comedy the characters should achieve
what they want, and plots should result in concord. All should end
well. Yet in doing so, we distort in our quest for something extremely good, just as Helena and most of her world do. Because
of this impulse critics either find some aspect of the play ideal,
where it really is not, or declare the work a failure because, for
instance, Helena idealizes Bertram—or the King idealizes her—
and this makes critics wary. Let us look at the process in some
detail.

G. Wilson Knight praises Helena as "almost beyond the human,"
underestimates her sexual interest in Bertram, and denies her
intrusiveness (she "will only have Bertram on terms just to him").[2]
Knight grudgingly admits that "it is hard to see Bertram as an apt
partner, but this is an old story, and we feel the same about other
of Shakespeare's young heroes" (p. 160). He refuses to admit that

1. G.K. Hunter, "Introduction," in *All's Well that Ends Well,* Arden ed.
(London: Methuen, 1959) xxix. Throughout this chapter all references to G. K.
Hunter are to his introduction and editorial comments.
2. G. Wilson Knight, *The Sovereign Flower* (London: Methuen, 1958), 131.

Bertram is unsuitable for Helena: Bertram is "no coward, far from it" (p. 112), but he can "be blamed for positively disliking" her; still, there is "a possible undercurrent of satire against such conventional and arbitrary marriages" (p. 116). Knight never thinks of the satire as working against Helena, although she forces herself upon an unwilling man. Knight very much wants to make Bertram worthy, and thus says that when he hears news of Helena's death "it affects him deeply. . . . True, he speaks lightly of her death soon after . . . but we later find him admitting his faults, and claiming now to love her. It is here he mentions Lafew's daughter" (p. 129). This is wishful thinking; Knight's excellent reading of Helena shows how beautifully, and dangerously, in tune he is with her penchant for idealization.

Philip Edwards also finds Helena supremely good: an "angellike wife to safeguard him [Bertram] from the consequence of his actions"; but "the imbued irresponsibility, selfishness and shallowness of a Bertram remain intact" despite her and providence and family.[3] Edwards sees the flaw not in her, or even in Bertram: "he is unredeemable: Shakespeare could not save him" because Shakespeare's "conscience [would not allow him] to alter a character whose alteration would be, simply, incredible"; it would be to change "the soul of the play" (p. 114). Edwards rightly observes that "the obstinancy [of a Bertram] is in humanity as Shakespeare saw it before it is in his dramatic fiction" (p. 114). The great question is why Edwards, like so many, finds "the failure of *All's Well* . . . in [its] insistence on a happy ending in spite of the evidence" (p. 110). The evidence, "the soul of the play," is the play itself; *we* insist upon a "happy ending" whereas the play provides something else.

Critics fault the play—or Helena, or Bertram, or their society. M. C. Bradbrook sees through Bertram, but then her vision clouds. She lists what is wrong with him:

> his petulance, his weakness, his cub-like sulkiness, his crude and youthful pride of rank. His charm has to be accepted because Hellen loves him, but there is little other evidence for it. Hellen's love . . . is a devotion so absolute that all thought of self is obliterated; yet her action cannot but make her appear, however much more modestly to an

3. Philip Edwards, *Shakespeare and the Confines of Art* (London: Methuen, 1968), 114–15.

Elizabethan than to us, a claimant, and a stickler for her bond.[4]

Where is his charm? Or Helena's absolute selflessness? Bradbrook honestly admits the flaws, but then denies the implications. She rightly terms Helena "a voice of despair breaking into the play; at other times a pliant lay-figure on which the characters drape their admiration" (pp. 169–70). Critics also drape their admiration, and most probably because they find it painful to admit the despair; Bradbrook avoids it by saying the play is flawed: it began as a moral play on honor but is bisected by the human problem of unrequited love (p. 162).

Harold S. Wilson (like others) admits Helena's defects implicitly by claiming that Shakespeare degraded Bertram to help develop "the virtue and appeal of the heroine."[5] How does it improve the virtue and appeal of a heroine by having her pursue a degraded man? A. P. Rossiter sees Bertram, even at the end, as "a weak, cowardly, mean-spirited, false, and ill-natured human being,"[6] and relegates discussion of Helena's character to a note appended to his lecture, having said:

> I take [Helena] for granted, which is the right way with her. Analysis only results in confusion; for if you analyze her, you find that her only *noble* qualities are courage and the Stoical reserve.... The rest ... a possessive passion for her man; an unconquerable determination ... an accomplished opportunism.... The sum total of all this as "virtue" is not ethically satisfying.
>
> (pp. 99–100)

Rather than deal with this problem, Rossiter explains it away by saying Helena is a "traditional" storybook female (p. 100). He

4. M. C. Bradbrook, *Shakespeare and Elizabethan Poetry,* 169. E. M. W. Tillyard nicely conveys this ambivalent feeling, but does not see it as a problem: at the end "Helena has got her man; and he needs her moral support with such pathetic obviousness that she never need fear his escape"; in *Shakespeare's Problem Plays* (Toronto: University of Toronto Press, 1949), 122.

5. Harold S. Wilson, "Dramatic Emphasis in *All's Well that Ends Well,*" *Huntington Library Quarterly* 13 (1950): 222–40; reprinted in *Discussions of Shakespeare's Problem Comedies,* ed. Robert Ornstein (Boston: D. C. Heath, 1961), 47, n. 3.

6. Rossiter, *Angel with Horns,* 91.

excuses Helena on the same grounds which Knight uses for excusing Bertram. Rossiter concludes that the play "came from an unresolved creative mind, in which sentimentality tried to balance scepticism" (p. 105). Critics toss problems raised by the characters and the play back into Shakespeare's lap. Jonas A. Barish admires the play's special poignance and austere beauty, yet finds a "defect of artistic management, a relatively imperfect fusion of elements with which Shakespeare worked throughout his career."[7] Barish excuses Bertram as being at the center of an insufficiently worked out morality plot, and finds him not "disagreeable," but "insufficiently interesting, too defective in nerve-tissue, too blunt in sensibility and wooden in his reactions, to command the attention that the plot would seem to be claiming for him" (p. 366).

II

The uneasiness, strain, and sadness which many seek to explain away, are central to the experience of the play and to its psychological value. In life we, like Helena and her society, cannot make all end well, although we want to. *All's Well* makes us experience the longing and sadness which causes us to idealize—and which often result from our attempt to do so. Unless we admit the essential sadness of the human condition, we remain out of touch with reality and unable to feel the concern for others which stimulates reparation.[8] It is the viewer who can attain such a state through *All's Well*; what Helena and others feel toward the end

7. Jonas A. Barish, "Introduction," to *All's Well that Ends Well* in *William Shakespeare: The Complete Works,* ed. Alfred Harbage (Baltimore: Penguin Books, 1969), 365.

8. Heinz Kohut discusses this process in terms of a "transformation" of narcissism: a genuine detachment from the self "can only be achieved slowly by an intact, well-functioning ego; and it is accompanied by sadness as the cathexis [investment] is transferred from the cherished self to the supraindividual ideals and to the world with which one identifies. The profoundest forms of humor and cosmic narcissism [i.e., 'supraindividual and timeless existence'] therefore do not present a picture of grandiosity and elation but that of a quiet inner triumph with an admixture of undenied melancholy"; in *The Search for the Self,* 1:458. However, I think that the narcissistic component remains, as is evident in the "quiet inner triumph." On this, see Béla Grunberger, *Narcissism.*

There is clearly a narcissistic grandiosity in Helena's heroic pursuit, especially since her aim is not so selfless as she says. However, we lose sight of this self-absorption because her society (unlike, say, Orsino's) completely agrees with her view.

we do not know. Her persistence and manipulation indicate that she does not feel the sort of sadness caused by being fully in touch with reality. In addition, she lacks a sense of humor which might make us feel that she can observe herself with accuracy. We know that she is not disinterested when she makes bawdy jokes with Parolles; her playfulness, unlike his, seems suspect. Helena's minimal sense of humor helps to account for the play's unpopularity: we are more wary of her than of Viola, or even Vincentio, for she seems to have no humorous detachment from herself—or sad awareness of reality.

Poignant moments in the festive comedies heighten the positive overall tone; in the problem comedies, the sadness becomes pervasive and exists simultaneously with a relatively happy conclusion. In *Troilus and Cressida* this realistic mixture never comes into being, for the play deals entirely with extreme idealizations— or degradations—of love, war, and the heroic past. The play seems a glimpse of chaotic unreality. The romances, in Shakespeare's next phase, are reparative in a different way because they employ magic and encourage omnipotent thinking: someone good—Prospero or Paulina, for instance—is effective and in charge. The romances often show characters working through their failings, as Leontes and Prospero do, but this does not necessarily make these plays more true to life. Few people ever work through deep-seated failings. One of the attractions of the problem comedies is that by their inconclusive nature and strained tone they imitate life as we know it. The longing for goodness remains, along with the *awareness* that we long, and that we can be only partly satisfied. To admit the sadness, and that the wish for goodness is just that, a wish, can make us realize that there are no perfect solutions in which all's well. This admission helps us to realize that no omnipotent benign creatures exist: no Helena who can earn a man's love; no one who can make Bertram grow worthy of her or of his station. *All's Well that Ends Well* pulls us up short, and in this lies its reparative effect if we are willing and able to accept it.

Most critics exactly catch the tone of strain and negation; they begin, and sometimes end, by treating a series of negatives: problems, flaws, and failures. The negation, however, is an integral, coherent attitude or even structural device: we find it in the language, character, and plot. For a moment, let us look at the language. Helena tells the Widow:

> If you misdoubt me that I am not she,
> I know not how I shall assure you further
> But I shall lose the grounds I work upon.

(3.7.1–3)

Characters often speak so oddly that critics assume the text must be corrupt. These lines are involuted yet comprehensible, unlike the numerous inscrutable ones which plague editors into offering alternative meanings followed by question marks. The characters, like many an interpreter, define by plunging into a thicket of negations, just as Helena does here. Hunter finds that there is often an appearance "of neat rhetorical balance within couplets of simple construction; but the intellectual complexity of the antitheses is such that the neatness of structure is felt as cramping and frustrating" (p. lviii). In a footnote he alerts us to what I find most striking about the language: "the extent to which definition . . . is achieved by a negative process of exclusion. We learn most often and with greatest vividness what people cannot, will not, or do not wish to do." For example, when Helena tries to persuade the King to attempt another cure, which he is loathe to do, she says:

> It is not so with Him that all things knows
> As 'tis with us that square our guess by shows;
> But most it is presumption in us when
> The help of heaven we count the act of men.

(2.1.148–51)

Hunter remarks that, among other problems, "the relation between human ignorance and human presumption is too complex to be expressed satisfactorily by the trite *But most* in l. 150." I would also stress that Helena proceeds in a manner peculiar to this play: she defines what we are by stating what we are not, and what she can do by what she cannot do. Her method continues in this speech; she says try—"not me"—but heaven; "I am not an imposter"; "my art is not past power, nor you past cure" (2.1.152–56). Hunter observes that in Shakespeare's romances an "extremely loose parenthetical syntax . . . allows an expression of complex relationships and contradictory levels of experience without tying them to set forms [couplets]; thus the relationships are suggested and implied, not pursued through labyrinthine detail. In the more relaxed style the positive evocation of value in images of sensuous warmth and the communication of emotional drive behind the words becomes a possibility" (pp. lviii–lix). He thinks that "there is a general failure in *All's Well* to establish a medium in verse which will convey effectively the whole tone of the play" (p. lix). Logically, of course, the verse and prose must effectively convey the play's tone: they create it. As Hunter points out, the tone is bare and dissonant, nervous, brittle, and above all one of longing and pursuit.

III

The play most often defines character and action, like the language out of which they are created, by "striving through intractable material for effects which hardly justify the struggle." Let us begin with Helena, the most fully developed character. In the first scene she responds to Lafew's kindly farewell remark, "you must hold the credit of your father," by launching into a soliloquy beginning: "O, were that all!" To underscore this negation of what we expect she says "I think not on my father. . . . What was he like? / I have forgot him; my imagination / Carries no favour in't but Bertram's" (1.1.77–81). Why must she deny the memory of her father to concentrate on Bertram? This is quite unlike Rosalind's roughly similar remark to Celia when reporting that she spoke to her own father without his knowing who she was: "But what talk we of fathers, when there is such a man as Orlando?" (3.4.34–35). Part of the brittleness of Helena's remark may result from her father being dead, or from her attempt to replace him with Bertram, as her riddling earlier comment indicates: "I do affect a sorrow indeed, but I have it too" (1.1.50). It is also characteristic that she feels strain where we would never expect it. She denies her father, sets forth her new love for Bertram, and then immediately despairs of gaining him: " 'twere all one / That I should love a bright particular star / And think to wed it" (1.1.83–85). No one can marry "a bright particular star"; her paradoxes persist into the action itself and haunt us to the very end. So far, all we have seen of Bertram is his vague attention to the elders' talking about loss and death. Helena, as so often during the play, "follows Bertram on stage to interpret his conduct through her love"; perhaps his "conduct is to be reconsidered in the light of her love" (as Price concludes).[9] But this would be *yielding* to her idealization; instead, we should attend to her activity, not simply to his conduct. Helena severely restricts the terms by which she evaluates Bertram, and talks only about his noble birth and his good looks. On these points she cannot be controverted. She attempts no assessment whatsoever of his honor (apart from birth), his virtue, or his goodness—or any of those qualities so crucial in the discussion which precedes her soliloquy and which concern characters throughout the play. She describes him as ideal without ever employing the terms which she and other characters find so essential. This clearly indicates that she creates him mostly out of her wish. Since she quietly ignores the standards of her world, she more easily deceives herself—and the viewer. She continually evaluates every character except Bertram in terms of honesty, virtue, and goodness. She also condemns herself for her failings in such matters, but only rarely—and late—does she hold Bertram to these standards. Because she idealizes him, viewers are encouraged to do so, and thus to seek what the play will not render up: a clear sense of Bertram being worthy.

Critics attempt to find Bertram honorable, or at least not objectionable. We expect that Helena, someone presented as good and wise, must have found a worthy beloved, especially since she remains painfully loyal to him. From the start she persists in seeing Bertram as "so above me. / In his bright radiance and collateral light / Must I be comforted, not in his sphere" (1.1.85–87). Since we hardly know anything about him when she tells us of her love, we can easily be fooled. The play delays letting us know what Bertram is like so that we can appreciate her invention of someone eminently good. And yet we know how dangerously idealized her view is by her treatment of Parolles, Bertram's supposed friend. He enters, ironically, as a "relic": Helena finishes her soliloquy by saying that Bertram has gone "and my idolatrous

9. Joseph G. Price, *The Unfortunate Comedy: A Study of "All's Well that Ends Well" and Its Critics* (Toronto: University of Toronto Press, 1968), 140. Like Price and many others, I see Helena as the central character. Richard P. Wheeler continues another tradition by emphasizing Bertram: "the forced marriage to Helena deflects [Bertram] from his quest for a masculine identity and toward a sexuality he fears" (*Shakespeare's Development,* 40). Wheeler argues that Shakespeare's treatment of Bertram expresses the hostile component of a deep ambivalence that in the sonnets has been suppressed or turned back against the poet's self (p. 73).

fancy / Must sanctify his relics. Who comes here?" Helena knows
the contradictory nature of her fancy: it is both idolatrous and yet
sanctifies. I see no reason to assume that she "despises herself for
it" (Arden edition). She seems simply to appreciate the paradox,
as she does when she says "I love him [Parolles] for his [Ber-
tram's] sake," although she knows Parolles to be a liar, a fool, and
a coward. She labors to transform this wretched stuff into someone whom she can like, which results in her turgid comment:

> Yet these fix'd evils sit so fit in him
> That they take place when virtue's steely bones
> Looks bleak i'th' cold wind; withal, full oft we see
> Cold wisdom waiting on superfluous folly.
>   (1.1.100–3)

Perhaps the text is corrupt, but such involuted passages usually
occur at moments when a character tries to make someone better
than he is.

Helena manages to like Parolles, despite his faults—just as she
manages to love Bertram, although in his case she rarely notes
how far he is from ideal. Such adaptability is heroic, and crucial
to the preservation of a sense of goodness; yet it becomes dangerous, for she deceives herself. Her deception seems almost conscious. She knowingly suppresses her distaste for Parolles; we
cannot be sure she does not do the same with Bertram later on.
Somehow, it would be easier to tolerate her blinkered response to
Bertram if we felt that she unconsciously denied his faults, rather
than consciously suppressed them in an effort to find someone
extremely good. That she may know his failings makes her seem
not only sadly self-deceived, but willfully wrong headed. The play
never clarifies this, and indeed makes us believe that her whole
society shares her propensity for delusion. The elders—the King,
Countess, and Lafew—see Bertram's faults, but never try to dissuade Helena. They fail to point out that he is not so desirable or
suitable; nor do they suggest that her pursuit may be quixotic, or
unseemly. No other Shakespearean comedy has so many parental
figures who actively support a love match—and no other match
is so inappropriate. Helena and her society are at one in their
willful idealizing.

When Parolles and Helena talk they bandy sexual jokes in a way
which led the scene to be excised for a long time as too ribald for

an audience, and too improper for Helena. Because she discusses
something real, sexual attraction, without trying to deny or idealize it, the language suddenly becomes comprehensible (if we can
keep up with the bawdy puns), and utterly dissimilar to the gno-
mic quality of most of the dialogue. Sex is real to her and to
Bertram, their only shared interest. Helena talks about sex and
marriage without relating them to the moral worth of the husband. She deludes herself by testing only one aspect of reality, and
is "realistic" at the expense of losing her bearings. In this Helena
and Bertram share an ominous trait, for he later resorts to similarly narrow reality testing when he beds, as he thinks, Diana.

In talking to Parolles, Helena suddenly decides that her situation only appears hopeless. With that practicality which makes
her at once admirable and, because of the circumstances, willful,
she realizes that she can use her virginity to gain Bertram. When
Parolles asks "Will you anything with it?" (1.1.159), she creates
an extraordinarily expansive account of what she will become:

> Not of my virginity yet:
> There shall your master have a thousand loves,
> A mother, and a mistress, and a friend.
> (1.1.161–63)

(I see no need to emend the Folio punctuation as the Arden editor
does: "Not my virginity; yet . . .") She will not give up her virginity yet: "there," in her virginity, "shall your master have a thou-
sand loves." Rather than present a catalogue of the varieties of
love available to Bertram at court (as Hunter and many others
suggest), Helena creates "a definition of perfect love, which labours
for its object's good" (Knight, p. 140). She defines her role, not his.
Knight thinks that "Helena's love sees Bertram as he potentially
is," but she dwells only on the actual, sexual attraction. She speaks
about moral and social attributes only in relation to herself, to
what she might be: "A mother, and a mistress, and a friend." She
will be "his humble ambition, proud humility." We learn nothing
at all about what she thinks of his character, or his potential for
growth at court. She concentrates upon herself and what she might
become, which is why she begins with "a mother," the only
unfamiliar term in the courtly titles and phrases which follow
(phoenix, goddess, traitress). The word "mother" strikes interpreters as out of place (Arden edition), but not if we realize she

talks about herself, not court ladies. When Bertram takes her virginity he shall find her a mother: this is the whole point of the task which he later sets her. Again, this mismatched couple have one thing in common, sex, but she thinks of it positively as the means to becoming an ideal wife—and he as the means to negate her longing.

At the end of this wonderfully inclusive catalogue of paradoxical roles, Helena turns to Bertram's role:

> Now shall he—
> I know not what he shall. God send him well!
> The court's a learning-place, and he is one—
>   (1.1.171–73)

Her abrupt, mysterious shifts may reflect reticence before Parolles, yet she could easily fool him—or resort to soliloquy—if she wanted to articulate her feelings. She clearly does not want to assess what Bertram is, or might become. This seems to be sensible, for no one can guess what a young lover may turn out to be; it is wise not to pride oneself on the excellent effect one might have. Still, Helena refuses to evaluate him as a person of certain achievements and propensities. Parolles tries to pursue her remark that Bertram "is one" by asking: "What one, i' faith?" She dodges: "That I wish well. 'Tis pity" (1.1.173–75). Parolles persists: "What's pity?" and she turns from Bertram himself to her wish:

> That wishing well had not a body in't
> Which might be felt, that we, the poorer born,
> Whose baser stars do shut us up in wishes,
> Might with effects of them follow our friends,
> And show what we alone must think, which never
> Returns us thanks.
>   (1.1.177–82)

Again, the contortions in the verse suggest the strain of her thinking. She apparently indicates a desire to "show the effects of [her] wishing in terms of physical action" (Arden edition); she persists in dwelling on her wish, not on who he is or what he might be.

Helena's feelings progress during this key scene. First she thinks it impossible to gain Bertram, then the bawdy talk about her virginity being used leads Helena to list active roles which she could play as his wife. In her second soliloquy her longing grows less passive, the physical aspect of love more real, and finally she becomes active and hopeful: "Our remedies oft in ourselves do lie" (1.1.212–25). She abandons her crucial awareness of the difference between longing for something good, and finding it. We all need to believe that "the fated sky / Gives us free scope," yet this can be a dangerous wish: it ignores real-life limitations and verges on omnipotent thinking. No one can be certain, although Helena says she is, that "only doth backward pull / Our slow designs when we ourselves are dull." She attempts to deny the play's insistent awareness of the inevitable tension between hope and loss (one established again and again during the first sixty lines of the play):

> Who ever strove
> To show her merit that did miss her love?
> The king's disease—my project may deceive me,
> But my intents are fix'd, and will not leave me.
> (1.1.222–25)

Her project will deceive her in a way which she never anticipates: she will gain merit without gaining Bertram's love. From this point onward Helena's comic mode, with its emphasis on remedial action and taking chances, begins to diverge from the ironic mode of *All's Well* and its implacable insistence upon the difference between conception and realization.[10]

The play, however, never allows us to forget this gap. In the following scene Bertram decides to win merit in a war which has its own vagaries and produces its own deceptive gain; of this more later. The third scene completes our sense of the distinguishing traits of Helena's love. The bawdy talk about marriage and cuckoldry by the Countess and her Clown makes an earthy and deceptively realistic background for Helena's idealization. Her taut and complex discussion with the Countess, like the Countess's exchange with Lafew earlier, creates a sense of community in their mutual acceptance of the difficulties of those in love.

Here, long before she learns how sorely Bertram will wound her, we find Helena's last full assessment of her love. She still

10. Roy Schafer correlates Northrop Frye's four literary modes to psychoanalytic views of life in *A New Language for Psychoanalysis*, chap. 3, (New Haven: Yale University Press, 1976).

dwells not on how it might be returned, but on what she feels. "I love your son," she confesses to the Countess, and at once dwells upon the negative: "Be not offended, for it hurts not him / That he is lov'd of me" (1.3.189,191–92). Although we and the Countess know Helena plans to go to Paris and cure the King, Helena says: "Nor would I have him till I do deserve him; / Yet never know how that desert should be" (1.3.194–95). "My project may deceive me," she has said, "but my intents are fix'd, and will not leave me." Her speech about her endless ability to pour out love is at once heroically selfless and, in the light of future events, painful:

> I know I love in vain, strive against hope;
> Yet in this captious and inteemable sieve
> I still pour in the waters of my love
> And lack not to lose still.
>
> (1.3.196–99)

She explicitly refers to her hope, and imagines Bertram as "the sun that looks upon his worshipper / But knows of him no more." She obsessively sees herself as a worshipper, knows nothing particular about her idol, and vaguely feels some error: "Indian-like, / Religious in mine error, I adore / The sun." Her metaphor, "inteemable sieve," is startlingly appropriate: she claims to "strive against hope," yet only by her image do we guess why; she never voices doubt. Helena thinks of herself as giving all in the most quixotic of gestures, pouring the waters of her love into a sieve which can neither contain nor return that which she pours into it. Rarely does a lover see her beloved as a sieve so early in the game—and without, apparently, giving much attention to the utter irrationality of her hopes about him. For Helena the problem lies simply in Bertram being of higher rank, but for us there are weightier problems: so far he has given no indication of being interested; soon he shows that he does not love her—or respect the King—and has no intention of keeping his word to either of them.

IV

Helena's invention of an ideal beloved remains constant throughout the play, with minor alterations; now she turns to action. At once, and as always in this play, negation persistently intrudes.

For example, the King resists another attempt to cure him. And when Helena succeeds, it is not easy to see her cure as "miraculous" (as Bradbrook does, p. 168). Parolles interrupts and makes fun when Lafew tries to describe the cure for us. Bertram says not a word about the wonder of it all. Also, Helena heals the King not out of affection and altruism but, as she makes clear, to gain Bertram. These details significantly diminish our joy at what ought to be an awesome moment, and in so doing nicely prepare us for the consequences which lie in store for the King, for Bertram, and for Helena. When Helena exercises her right to choose, she first denies all the courtiers who would accept her. Lafew, in keeping with the play's mood, assumes that they deny *her*. When Bertram refuses Helena he disobeys the King's command; when he capitulates and marries her, he runs away.

At this point the dismaying series of negations extends into almost every nook and cranny. When Helena finally summons up the courage to ask for a kiss before Bertram leaves her, she says:

> I am not worthy of the wealth I owe,
> Nor dare I say 'tis mine—and yet it is;
> But, like a timorous thief, most fain would steal
> What law does vouch mine own.
>
> (2.5.79–82)

Bertram asks what she wants, and Helena replies:

> Something, and scarce so much; nothing indeed.
> I would not tell you what I would, my lord.
> Faith, yes:
> Strangers and foes do sunder and not kiss.
>
> (2.5.83–86)

Like so many of her attempts, this is brave, sad, and unsuccessful. Even here she resorts to a negative illustration about "strangers and foes" in hope that this will somehow make Bertram kind. When she fails, she says, "I shall not break your bidding, good my lord," which in its attitude seems close to her earlier remark: "Sir, I can nothing say / But that I am your most obedient servant" (2.5.70–71). She continually describes her desires and her simplest responses in terms of what she is not, or will not do.

Bertram's two letters push her further into this position. He writes the Countess to complain of being "undone": I have wedded her, not bedded her, and sworn to make the 'not' eternal." His mother catches the "not": "This is not well" (3.2.26). In his letter to Helena, he deliberately denies hope even as he raises it: "When thou canst get the ring upon my finger, which never shall come off, and show me a child begotten of thy body that I am father to, then call me husband; but in such a 'then' I write a 'never.' " He concludes: "Till I have no wife I have nothing in France"; to which his mother says, again in the fashion which predominates: "Nothing in France until he have no wife! / There's nothing here that is too good for him / But only she." Even her support gets stated in terms of what is not the case.

The tasks which Bertram sets are in themselves negatively intended, tasks designed with the express purpose of being unfulfillable. Helena readjusts her sense of what she must do to maintain her ideal; she can act positively only by renouncing her role: since he will have no wife in France, she will leave France. Rather than blame him, she blames herself for driving him to the wars (although we know that he was chafing to leave before she chose him). She reveals her love in an astonishing passage about a bullet's flight:

> O you leaden messengers,
> That ride upon the violent speed of fire,
> Fly with false aim; move the still-piecing air
> That sings with piercing; do not touch my lord.
> (3.2.108–11)

She cannot know what the end result will be although the stunningly simple "do not touch my lord" shows the intensity of her wish. She can only hope that all will turn out well.

The heroine in Boccaccio actively and forthrightly seeks her husband, but Helena simply leaves. She happens to find herself in Florence. The play would not have us dwell on such coincidence, as indicated by her roundabout route to St. Jaques (of Compostella?) by way of Florence; Shakespeare needs her in Florence, but avoids suggesting that she pursues Bertram. That Bertram and Helena both leave France prefigures the series of "removes" by which the King manages to get back to Paris. Helena sought the King in Paris to get Bertram; once rebuffed, she (and the King) tend to *leave* one place rather than to seek another. So pervasive is this pattern of denial that when we first meet the Widow and Diana in Florence, they surmise from a tucket that they have failed to be in the right place to see the returning soldiers: "We have lost our labour; they are gone a contrary way" (3.5.7–8). Then, seventy lines later, the troops do come their way. We glimpse in this minor detail a pattern which informs the whole work: the ladies get what they seek—such as it is—by enduring the apparent negation of their hopes. At this point in the play Helena recedes into the background; we learn little more of her feelings, and see little of her as the bed trick gets under way. She cannot appear to be so much in control as she actually is.

<h2 style="text-align:center">V</h2>

When we shift our attention to Bertram and the events in Florence we discern a similar pattern: definition in terms of negation, and yet—this seems crucial—with none of Helena's creativity and resilience in the face of adversity. Bertram seeks an ideal, honor through fighting in Florence. Let us examine the nature of the war. We find France neither officially at war with Siena, nor on the side of Florence. The King states that, for some reason we never learn, "our cousin Austria . . . Prejudicates the business, and would seem / To have us make denial" (1.2.5–9). Austria has "arm'd our answer, / And Florence is denied before he comes." This mysterious business ends in an ambiguous compromise: "Yet, for our gentlemen that mean to see / The Tuscan service, freely have they leave / To stand on either part." Shakespeare elaborates the source to intensify the prevailing mood of his play. In Painter's translation of Boccaccio's story, Beltramo leaves his wife and goes to Tuscany "where understanding that the Florentines and Senois were at warres, he determined to take the Florentines parte" (Arden edition, p. 148). Beltramo simply makes a choice. Bertram, on the other hand, fights in a war defined by an ambiguously negative attitude: the King will not openly take sides; his men opt for the very one which Austria wanted the King not to take. Joseph Price, among others, thinks the vagaries involved in the merits of the opposing forces do not suggest a cynical attitude toward the war, but I cannot see it as "merely setting for the involvements of Bertram and the exposure of Parolles" (p. 146). A mere setting need not be so elaborately contrived; we certainly do not need to hear about these mysterious political maneuverings for reasons of plot or characterization. All this cannot help but taint the positive value of Bertram's fighting.[11]

The King sends the men off, but denies Bertram permission to join them; Bertram refuses to abide by the King's decision and steals away—after the marriage he did not want, and will not consummate. Immediately after Bertram leaves for war (2.5), the play again undercuts the value of the battle. In response to an account of the dispute given by the Duke of Florence (an account which we do not hear), a Lord comments "Holy seems the quarrel / Upon your Grace's part" (3.1.4–5). Why the haunting "seems"? Another Lord then conveys a sense of France's own ambiguous position: "The reasons of our state I cannot yield," although he can guess; but as an outsider he "dare not / Say what I think of it, since I have found / Myself in my incertain grounds to fail / As often as I guess'd." Such statements disconcert us. We certainly do not need to hear of the Lord's reasons, or the Duke's puzzlement, or the King's understanding with Austria, just so that Bertram can have an offstage war in which to fight. The play undermines the ideal of simple martial honor even before Bertram gains it. Martial honor is still valid, but the circumstances make us wary.

No sooner does Bertram gain honor in the field than he begins to sully it. The seduction of Diana has much of the negative coloration so prevalent in *All's Well*. His siege leads to an assignation which, so far as he knows, will be characterized by its negative nature: he deflowers a virgin, neither sees her nor speaks to her in bed, and has no intention to wed her. The trick itself depends upon denial: it assumes that the lovers' bodies exist separately from their personality. An audience may be troubled by such implications. And rightly so; even Helena, its hopeful perpetrator, expresses dismay that lust plays "with what it loathes [taking it] for that which is away" (4.4.25). *Her* perversity—or so we are free to assume—is pursuing such a man.[12]

Just after Bertram has been deceived in a trick which might well trouble us for his sake, and for Helena's, the play forces us to face yet another instance of his unvarying bad character. Before leav-

11. For different reasons, Howard C. Cole also finds this ironic; he sees the play's irony as "faithful to its story's questioning of reasons and rationalizations [in leaving] no character untouched" in *The "All's Well" Story from Boccaccio to Shakespeare* (Urbana: University of Illinois Press, 1981), 134.

12. The bed trick bothers many critics. Jonas A. Barish rightly notes that "events are moving darkly": "a Bertram who really could not tell Helena from

ing to bed Diana he received a letter from his mother which the second Lord says "stings his nature, for on the reading it he chang'd almost into another man" (4.3.3–4). Critics make much of this in an attempt to show a change for the better in Bertram. However, when the same Lord hears that Helena has died, news brought in the letter itself, he remarks: "I am heartily sorry that he'll be glad of this" (4.3.61). Bertram has not changed "into another man." He immediately enters, breezily listing various "businesses" which he has performed that night: taken leave of the Duke, "done my adieu with his nearest, buried a wife, mourn'd for her, writ to my lady mother I am returning, entertain'd my convoy, and between these main parcels of dispatch effected many nicer needs" (that is, bedded Diana). Within the space of ninety lines we are told that he has changed, but not with regard to Helena; and then we see him behaving with his usual callousness, eagerly making preparations to return to France now she is dead. We, like the Lords, may *want* to believe that Bertram can grow into a new man, but the play defeats us at every turn. Long before he appears in court and thoroughly disgraces himself, we are alerted to expect little that is admirable except martial honor— and no propensity to change for the better. Tillyard thinks "the stage was adequately set for (what would be much nearer Boccaccio) an effective return of the repentant prodigal to the forgiveness which Helena can secure for him" (Arden edition, p. liv); but the alleged "hammer-blows that Bertram sustains" in 4.3 glance off him with no effect.

VI

The unmasking of Parolles—like the exposure of Bertram in the fifth act—results in an apparently irreparable loss of honor. This loss, however, leads to the creation of some sort of value: in the case of Parolles, through his own attitude and effort; in the case of Bertram, through Helena's effort. *All's Well* continually reveals some positive potential, especially if we shift our attention away from Bertram and onto the more creative character whom he

Diana in bed would not belong in a play by Shakespeare at all, nor would a Helena who thought such a deception possible" ("Introduction," 367). And yet Bertram cannot tell the women apart, which seems quite in character for him; and Helena knows it possible. We need to adjust our sense of the characters accordingly, for the obtuse and problematic qualities of the trick alter our sense of Bertram and Helena.

serves as a foil. Although the lords design the drum incident
largely for Bertram's benefit, his response proves ludicrously inadequate. Instead of feeling ashamed of himself for being misled
by Parolles, Bertram merely calls him a cat—three times. Barish
observes that "such an inadequate response to an event of such
magnitude robs the episode of much of its proper and legitimate
weight" (p. 366). However, the response shows just how shallow
Bertram is, and how unredeemable. The episode brilliantly conveys his inadequacy, if only we will accept the play's view (and
not hope that Bertram must be, or must have been intended to
be, better than he is). Parolles, not Bertram, benefits here—just as,
in the love plot, the value comes not from Bertram's responses but
from Helena's. The play frustrates us as a means of making us
more aware of the human condition, and of our wish that it were
better.

In a very nice tactic, eminently suited to the play's tone, Shakespeare makes the hoax depend upon the soldiers negating language itself. Dogberry and Verges simply misuse words in *Much
Ado;* the soldiers speak a nonlanguage, one which no more exists
than does Parolles's honor. The Lords, also defamed by Parolles,
can nevertheless admire his complete denial of all soldierly values: "He hath outvillain'd villainy so far that the rarity redeems
him" (4.3.264–65). The Lord perceives something positive even
in Parolles's cowardly lies; Bertram, typically, fails to see this and
tiresomely remarks: "A pox on him! He's a cat still" (for his fourth
use of the maligned animal). Most important of all, Parolles creates a new, somewhat more positive role for himself. He rises
from the ashes of all that he pretended to be, and evolves into
another creature based on the extremely limited potential remaining to him. Having been proven foolish, he decides to live by
exhibiting his folly. His self-awareness and vitality make Bertram's dull-witted and lifeless responses here—and during his
own unmasking in the last act—all the more patent. Parolles,
unlike Bertram, even speaks a soliloquy (4.3.319–29). As we should
by now expect, he first points out what he is not: "Yet am I
thankful. If my heart were great / 'Twould burst at this." He can
no longer be a captain, yet "simply the thing I am / Shall make
me live." Parolles always knew that he was not what he pretended
to be, unlike his master, and perhaps this allows him to be so
adaptable. When one "ideal" is destroyed for Parolles, that of
being a valiant captain, he invents another and more realistic one:

"being fool'd, by fool'ry thrive. / There's place and means for every man alive." Instead of falling apart as we expect, he adjusts himself to new circumstances and adapts to a new standard of excellence and perfection. "I'll after them," he says, which is more positive and courageous under the circumstances than any of his valiant gestures as a braggart soldier. In his adaptability he resembles, in his own limited and comic way, Helena herself.

VII

When attention shifts back to Helena at the end of the fourth act, she sounds plangent variants on the play's title. She reassures the Widow and Diana that "All's well that ends well; still the fine's the crown. / Whate'er the course, the end is the renown" (4.4.35–36). When she learns that the King has removed from Marseilles, she comforts the dismayed Widow by saying—less assertively— "All's well that ends well yet, / Though time seem so adverse and means unfit" (5.1.25–26). At the end of the play, the King rings changes on this phrase which add a more tentative quality than that implicit in Helena's use of "though" in her second version: "All yet seems well, and if it end so meet, / The bitter past, more welcome is the sweet" (5.3.327–28). In the epilogue he maintains his sense of the conditional: "All is well ended if this suit be won, / That you express content." Between Helena's initially bold assertion of the proverbial idea, and the King's conditional affirmation of it, comes the puzzling conclusion.

Dr. Johnson, disturbed by the ending, brings up an aspect which deserves further attention. When Bertram returns from Florence, he should not so readily be forgiven of the "double crime of cruelty and disobedience, joined likewise with some hypocrisy." Johnson sees how the Countess might forgive her son, but asserts that the King "should more pertinaciously vindicate his own authority and Helen's merit."[13] Johnson has good reason to be puzzled here. It has nothing to do with Shakespeare "hastening to the end of the play" (a favorite Johnsonian explanation), or already having enough to deal with in the remainder of the scene. Shakespeare invents most of this material; he vastly complicates the conclusion suggested by his source. There the wronged Giletta presented herself, along with two sons and the ring, and asked the Count to "observe the conditions" which he had set. He

13. Johnson, *Works of Samuel Johnson*, 7:400.

asks for an explanation; she tells him how things came to pass, and—in contrast to Shakespeare's baroque invention—"in order." Then the Count readily receives her as his wife. Clearly neither Shakespeare's haste nor impatience to end leads him to create the strange denouement. He contrives it just as he does the rest of the play: negation yields to some approximation of a positive result. The King refuses to make Bertram account for his behavior:

> Let him not ask our pardon;
> The nature of his great offence is dead,
> And deeper than oblivion we do bury
> Th' incensing relics of it. Let him approach
> A stranger, no offender.
>
> (5.3.22–26)

The King attempts to deny the offense, rather than confront it—or Bertram. That the King tries to "bury" what he terms a "great offence" hardly sets an audience at ease. Bertram says: "My high-repented blames / Dear sovereign, pardon to me." The King frustrates this attempt, however, by interrupting: "All is whole. / Not one word more of the consumed time." Bertram's brief remark at the end of the play—"Both, both. O pardon!"—makes us wonder why he should be discouraged here; we have no reason to believe that his offenses really are "high-repented" before this point (see his totally inadequate mourning of Helena at 4.3.82–89). That we never see him take full responsibility for his action makes us uncomfortable. Nor—what is equally disturbing—have we ever found anyone in the play *expect* him to be responsible. By way of contrast, the Duke in *Measure for Measure* forces Angelo, Claudio, Juliet, and Lucio to repent—and makes Isabella and Mariana ask mercy for someone who wronged them. Members of an audience with a well-developed conscience might well worry, as Johnson does, about things being swept under the rug.

This uneasiness increases when Bertram refuses to accept his guilt: he protests that his evil deeds were the unfortunate result of his long-standing love for Maudlin (news to us, and to the characters). We can barely understand what Bertram tries to say (Arden edition, p. lvii). Bertram never before or after attempts such complex metaphorical language. He consistently speaks more simply than any major character; even Parolles puns with Helena and tries to imitate Lafew's courtly language in describing the wonder of the King's cure. The King finds it "well excus'd. / That didst love her [Helena? Maudlin?], strikes some scores away / From the great compt." An excuse, nevertheless, differs from repentance, as the King indicates in his grand generalization about guilt, loss, and remorse: "remorseful pardon slowly carried ... turns a sour offence." In sum, the King refuses to demand repentance; but Bertram asks pardon, and then excuses his conduct; the King says the excuse is good, but denies its adequacy. That Shakespeare devotes seventy lines of the final scene to such strange stuff is difficult to justify unless he seeks to prepare us for the hauntingly inadequate affirmations at the end.

From this point on Bertram lies so brazenly that he loses all honor. First he gives a troth-ring for Maudlin to Lafew, who claims that the ring was Helena's. Bertram denies this: "Hers it was not." The ring, Shakespeare's addition to the source, provokes an unwitting lie, yet inexorably begins the process of definition by negation rather than by the straightforward assertions which Shakespeare found in the source. The mood extends to the smallest details. For no clear reason, Lafew feels uncertain that he should be present (twice: 4.5.85–86 and 5.3.12). Even the Gentleman who merely brings in Diana's letter uneasily begins: "Whether I have been to blame or no, I know not" (5.3.129). In lines like these, and throughout the play, "know" and "no," "not" and "knot," sound the same and contribute to the strained tone as they awkwardly jingle with one another.

When the Widow and Diana enter, the King asks Bertram: "do you know these women?" To which he evasively replies: "My lord, I neither can nor will deny / But that I know them" (5.3.165–66). He denies Diana is his wife; Lafew denies Maudlin will be his wife. Diana baroquely tells the King to ask Bertram "if he does think / He had not my virginity." That she confronts Bertram (rather than Helena, as in the source) allows this series of nullifications: she neither slept with Bertram, nor thinks she has; Bertram never suspects that he did not sleep with Diana. Beyond the situation itself, almost all details incessantly lead to negation. Diana does not want to call Parolles as her witness, for she is loath "to produce / So bad an instrument"; Bertram tries to undermine Parolles's testimony as coming from a proved liar. When this discredited witness appears, he equivocates; then, after telling the truth, he says, "I will not speak what I know."

The King's interrogation produces denial upon denial. To the question of how Diana got the ring, she says: "It was not given me, nor I did not buy it"; "It was not lent me neither"; "I found it not." Exasperated, the King asks: "If it were yours by none of all these ways / How could you give it him?" Diana caps this dizzying series: "I never gave it him." She persists in refusing, then produces a flourish of negatives which create a larger paradox (5.3.283–87) and lead to the statement which introduces Helena: "So there's my riddle: one that's dead is quick, / And now behold the meaning." We expect Helena's appearance to clear the air, but instead of resolving the tension she manages to prolong it. The King wonders if she is real; she replies: "No, my good lord; / 'Tis but the shadow of a wife you see; / The name and not the thing" (5.3.300–302). Whatever strength Bertram's affirmation and request for pardon have must derive from our relief at its being simple, straightforward, and positive: "Both, both. O pardon!" Yet we have good reason, by his previous lies, not to believe him.

A minor detail of great significance helps to sustain the uncertainty at the end: Helena alters the terms which Bertram set in his letter. When she appears she reads the crucial parts: "When from my finger you can get this ring / And is by me with child, &c" (5.3.306–7). The startling shift in grammar, knowledge of the old tale, or a good memory would remind us that Bertram actually wrote: "and show me a child begotten of thy body that I am father to" (3.2.57–58). Perhaps this alteration is a slip, or change of mind, on Shakespeare's part; yet it alters the mood exactly the way all his other changes do. In the source Giletta produces two sons rather than the one son demanded of her; they are not mere babes, but "carefully . . . noursed and brought up" to be "faire young boyes" (Arden edition, pp. 151–52). In contrast to Giletta's characteristic overachievement of the tasks set her, Helena is simply pregnant: she cannot as yet show the requisite child to Bertram.

In a scene so much more elaborate than in the story, this alteration shows the coherence of Shakespeare's design. The denouement involves a highly punctilious working out of questions about identifiable rings replete with histories and symbolic meanings (especially the ring Shakespeare adds). At the same time, he alters the actual, realized child of Bertram's instructions (and the source) into a potential child, one not yet born let alone "carefully noursed and brought up." Critics ignore this detail—perhaps because of their search for an unambiguously happy, or unhappy, ending.

Until recently it was not possible to assume that being pregnant almost means having a child in one's arms. Giletta's two sons add joy because they better ensure succession than one easily lost son. That Helena is simply pregnant suits the insistently tentative quality of the play. She stands as a perfect symbol of potential, one which contributes to the play's haunting sense of longing for something good which may, or may not, be realized.[14]

The obliquely positive, conditional tone extends throughout the conclusion. Helena asks Bertram: "Will you be mine now you are doubly won?" Her tone seems poignant, "doubly won"; or, this phrase may convey her intolerable persistence, especially to Bertram who again (as when she chose to wed him) turns to the King, not her: "If she, my liege, can make me know this clearly / I'll love her dearly, ever, ever dearly." Helena herself counters with a conditional statement rather than an affirmation: "If it appear not plain and prove untrue / Deadly divorce step between me and you!" She then asks: "O my dear mother, do I see you living?" Helena and Bertram seem determined to be uncertain about everything, no matter how obvious it may be. In this they are wise, given what they have experienced.

This might have been a conclusion in which Bertram fully admitted guilt for his scorn of Helena and "requited" it—as Benedick does in *Much Ado*. But Helena herself has been so manipulative that she—like Beatrice—should meet him halfway; in doing so, she would have to free him, for we have no sign that Bertram loves her. Straightforward reparation vanishes in the problem comedies, and may be the reason why they rarely get a positive reception. As I suggested at the start, *All's Well* can restore us in a deeper, more basic, sense by clarifying the relationship between ideals which sustain (such as many of those in *Twelfth Night*) and idealizations which prove limiting and dangerous (such as most of those in *All's Well*). *Twelfth Night* blurs this crucial distinction. *All's Well* clarifies it by mirroring and confirming our need to find something extremely good, and then frustrating it so that we recognize the wish is a wish—a longing. The play tempers the sort of near-grandiose elation which such plays as *Twelfth Night* can create. Now the sadness implicit, say, in Viola's quest is openly revealed (too openly, many feel). We can see *All's Well* as precipi-

14. John Arthos sees this "unknown birth" as "an uncertain image of all the confusions and hopes that have reigned before"; in *The Art of Shakespeare* (London: Bowes and Bowes, 1964), 104.

tating *Measure for Measure* and its more radical questioning of ideals. What makes these two comedies so problematic is not their arbitrary plots or unattractive characters, but their focus on what is problematic in life itself: not the grandeur of tragedy or the elation of the earlier and final comedies, but the mixed sadness and pleasure of our condition.

~7~
Measure for Measure
Adapting to an Unidealized World

Surely the greatest irony of this ironic play is that it provokes in
its audience the very responses denied to members of its own
world: an urge to embrace idealizations and to mete out punishment to those who fail to live up to them. For instance, is the
Duke an ideal ruler, or a self-centered manipulator? Are we to
admire Isabella when she is furiously chaste, or when she puts
herself at the Duke's disposal in deceiving Angelo—or not at all?
To many viewers, the characters are woefully unable to practice
what they preach. Rosalind Miles thoroughly demonstrates that
"extreme and opposed views mark out [the play's] critical history,
from the earliest recorded comment down to the present."[1] She
rightly says that "all the characters have ultimately to learn to live
in the world of compromise," but her heart is not in it: "Shakespeare's compassion springs directly from his ironic detachment
. . . he has created a set of generally unlovable people, and he
directs us throughout not to make judgements on them" (pp.
283–84). To find the characters "generally unlovable" is to make
a judgment, to be unwilling to abide a world of compromise.

Much of the time, we follow the lead of the characters in idealizing. The Duke, Isabella, Angelo, and others (such as Claudio) are
vulnerable to stringent judgment by one another, and by us. In
All's Well the penchant for idealizing is more hidden than in
Measure for Measure; now the play openly explores the isolation
of ideals from the context of human fallibility. The Duke is, on

1. Rosalind Miles, *The Problem of "Measure for Measure,"* 1.

147

the one hand, a good ruler, despite some shady dealings; but he is not perfect, as his quixotic, vacillating nature indicates. If we look back at instances of idealization in *All's Well* and *Twelfth Night,* we see how much more conscious *Measure for Measure* makes us of the thin line between viable ideal and dangerous idealization. Orsino's view of love—and of Olivia and Viola—is self-centered and vulnerable, yet he finds someone who perfectly fits his grandiose conception of what a beloved should be. In *All's Well,* Helena finds no perfect mate; we presume that she knows it, but she never acknowledges how far he falls short of being what she wishes; nor does she try to integrate this knowledge into her own love for him. *Measure for Measure* brings the conflict between idealized and actual into the open. We find conflict of an intensity never found in the other comedies, and rarely surpassed in other of Shakespeare's dramas.

The characters in *Measure for Measure* adapt, insofar as they can. The audience can also adapt to these uncomfortable compromises—but only if it resists the pressure toward idealization. The play and our own natures subject us to a great deal of pressure; this may be one reason why Dr. Johnson feels that "the grave scenes . . . have more labour than elegance."[2] The play provokes us to seek perfection in human behavior. The title alerts us to a Christian context: "measure for measure" is a phrase from the Sermon on the Mount which the Duke later uses when sentencing Angelo. Christ alludes to the old law in teaching the new: "Judge not, that ye be not judged. For with what judgment ye judge, ye shall be judged, and with what measure ye mete, it shall be measured to you again" (Matt. 7:1–2). Christ warns against censure of others; yet in doing so he invokes talionic law: you will be judged exactly as you judge. He replaces one absolute with another. This is very important: he wants us not to exact an eye for an eye; but if we do we will be punished in talionic fashion, measure for measure. In addition, he directs us to be nonjudgmental—but invariably so. And we are to eschew revenge—completely; indeed, "love your enemies . . . do good to them that hate you." This may be a better code, but it is certainly not a more flexible one. Flexibility is the last thing he has in mind, for he admonishes his followers to outdo even the scribes and pharisees in strict observance of the laws. Christ is often represented as someone who lifts the burden of the old law, but he does nothing so simple.

2. Johnson, *Works of Samuel Johnson,* 7:216.

He increases the burden of conscience by defining sin not only as deeds and acts, but as thoughts and intentions—as in lusting after a neighbor's wife.

The phrase "measure for measure" refers us to the Sermon, and heightens our sense of the play's ethical problems: especially the fierce equation between thought and deed. The characters are continually ensnared in similar paradoxes, and either acquiesce (as the Duke tries to in avoiding judgment), or catch the letter but not the spirit (as Angelo does in rendering talionic judgment), or reject Christian teaching out-of-hand (as the bawdy characters do with regard to sexual behavior)—or, and this is the common reaction, shift back and forth between embracing grandly conceived ideals, and spurning them. The play demands a detached alertness to standards of behavior; and yet it assumes the validity of some which are basic to Christianity. Religious and social problems, each involving strict standards, conflict with one another, as in the case of justice versus mercy. In other instances, high standards subvert one another: Isabella cannot behave in a manner both charitable and chaste. The play not only pits Christian virtues against each other, it brings them into conflict with social and legal demands, as in the incredibly knotty relationship between church and state views of legal marriage.

We strongly desire certainties and clearly ideal, or nonideal, figures; *Measure for Measure* deeply frustrates us. Here, I think, is a clue to its reparative effect: we can vicariously experience characters who seek what we seek, and then find our frustrations in theirs. Although the longing for one is great, no ideal figure exists in *Measure for Measure*; nor does the play offer an ideal solution to any of the problems raised by the interaction between sexuality and aggression. Neither the marriages nor the legal decisions smack of perfection. To hope for perfect solutions is dangerous. Rather than find ideals largely attained, as we do in most of these plays, we find odd compromises. For instance, the Duke turns out to be far better at his task than he thought, but still not a model for rulers. When he uses the phrase "measure for measure" during the trial he plays with the concept—partly uses it, partly reveals its drawbacks; he intrudes a grim, yet humorous sense of reality which precludes taking the dictum at face value. In similar fashion, the play can assist us to bring idealized figures and wishes back to earth, to the actual mess and confusion which so vividly define Vienna right up to the end.

II

Critics of very different persuasions idealize the Duke, and in doing so reveal a common desire that he be better, rather than be what he is. J. W. Lever surveys many versions of "the disguised ruler" from early sixteenth-century legends to James I (and James's use of the role, and discussion of it in *Basilicon Doron*); Lever concludes that Vincentio exemplifies "what most of Shakespeare's contemporaries would regard as the model ruler of a Christian polity."[3] Richard P. Wheeler, approaching the Duke from an entirely different angle, says that "In order to present Vincentio as the ideal ruler in Vienna, Shakespeare displaces the conflict away from the central figure and into the world around him" (that is, other major characters).[4] Wheeler suggests that "*Measure for Measure* is divided within *itself* by Shakespeare's attempt to protect and identify with an ideal of paternal authority while responding also to the flesh and spirit of a very worldly Vienna" (p. 143). Other critics find the Duke far from ideal, and rightly so, yet they degrade him.[5] It seems clear that they also expect too much from him. Critics generally impose their expectations on the Duke, and then either rejoice to find them confirmed, or deplore the fact that they are not.

Vincentio invites us to see him as ideal, but at the same time betrays his own inability to believe it. This makes him a strange character for the center of one of Shakespeare's comedies, but a welcome relief after Orsino's and Helena's self-deception. Vincentio is not in love, but we can all too readily see conflicted

3. J.W. Lever, ed., *Measure for Measure,* Arden ed. (London: Methuen, 1965), li; further references to Lever are to his introduction and editorial comments.

4. Wheeler, *Shakespeare's Development,* 133. The following critics also idealize Vincentio: Josephine Waters Bennett, "*Measure for Measure" as Royal Entertainment* (New York: Columbia University Press, 1966); M. C. Bradbrook, "Authority, Truth, and Justice in *Measure for Measure,*" *Review of English Studies* 17 (1941), reprinted in *Discussions of Shakespeare's Problem Comedies,* ed. Ornstein, finds the Duke "is at least the representative of Heavenly Justice" and "represents unerring Justice ... and Humility" (pp. 78–79); G. Wilson Knight, "*Measure for Measure* and the Gospels," in *The Wheel of Fire,* rev. ed. (New York: Meridian Books, 1957), says that the Duke "is lit at moments with divine suggestion comparable with his almost divine power of fore-knowledge, and control, and wisdom" (p. 74). Also see Roy W. Battenhouse, "*Measure for Measure* and the Christian Doctrine of Atonement," *PMLA* 61 (1946): 1029–59. For further discussion see the Arden edition, lvii–lviii.

5. The following critics highly suspect the Duke's goodness. Philip Edwards ("Healing Power of Deceit," 118), focuses upon the implications of deceit: Vincentio's deceptions bring "quite extraordinary emotional distress" to Claudio, Juliet,

feelings of aggression in him, and perhaps of sexuality as well. The Duke has an inner life richer than has been assumed, one all too lifelike in its longing and self-contradiction.

At the start of the play he sets forth a concept of government so grandly conceived that it startles us if we come to the play directly from the sources. At the outset of the tale in the *Hecatommithi* the Emperor Maximian, an exemplary ruler, instructs Iuriste: "I can forgive you all other failings, due either to ignorance or negligence . . . but any deed which is contrary to justice shall receive no pardon from me." At the start of *Promos and Cassandra,* the deputy of another perfect king announces that he has been sent to rule "That styll we may to *Iustice* have an eye. . . . No wylfull wrong, sharpe punishment shall mysse, / The simple thrall, shalbe iudgde with mercie, / Each shall be doombde, euen as his merite is." Shakespeare's ruler raises the level of expectation from merely being "just" to a larger process:

> Of government the properties to unfold
> Would seem in me t'affect speech and discourse.
>   (1.1.3–4)

Vincentio apparently is more diffident. He does not indulge in the simple pronouncements which governors parade forth in the sources; but he creates an almost impossibly high standard by making an issue of the ruler governing through being virtuous:

---

and Isabella—and he merely "defuses the crisis which he himself has caused," but makes "no progress at all in his initial objective" of cleaning up Vienna.

Herbert Weil, Jr. in "Form and Contexts in *Measure for Measure,*" *Critical Quarterly* 12 (1970): 55–72: "Shakespeare parodies the melodramatic structure he took over from his sources. He reveals a hero pompous and apparently successful, yet failing to recognize his own weaknesses" (p. 70)—and the comic inadequacy of his solutions.

William Empson in *The Structure of Complex Words* (London, 1951), 270–84, reprinted in *Discussions of Shakespeare's Problem Comedies,* ed. Ornstein, remarks on the Duke's "pomposity . . . touchiness, the confidence in error, the self-indulgence of his incessant lying . . . [which must] always have been absurd" (p. 108); "the higher you pitch the ethics of the Duke, the more surprising you must find his behaviour" (p. 109).

A. P. Rossiter (*Angel with Horns,* 168) thinks, as do others, that it is impossible to find a consistent characterization of the Duke: there is "the ideal shadow of the end (flawed . . . by lack of magnanimity) and the realist of a pessimistically-contemplated world-order" in the "Be absolute for death" speech.

> Heaven doth with us as we with torches do,
> Not light them for themselves; for if our virtues
> Did not go forth of us, 'twere all alike
> As if we had them not.
>
> (1.1.32–35)

Being just, the ideal held out to the deputies in the sources, seems easy by comparison. Vincentio never even mentions the rudimentary concept of "justice" during the opening scene. He remarks that Escalus knows "the nature of our people, / Our city's institutions, and the terms / For common justice" (1.1.9–11), but the word here means "conditions for administering, or technical terms of, the common law" (Arden edition).

When the Duke directs Angelo to let "mortality and mercy in Vienna / Live in thy tongue, and heart" he again inflates the ideal while seeming to bring it down to earth. By pairing "mortality" with mercy, rather than "justice," he defines justice in terms of pronouncing a death sentence, and suggests that the judge's sense of his own mortality should qualify the need for justice. Editors gloss these lines as "I delegate to thy tongue the power of pronouncing sentence of death, and to thy heart the privilege of exercising mercy" (Arden editor, following Douce). This creates precisely the separation which the Duke's phrasing avoids. He makes the process of governing an integral part of the ruler's life, avoids naming "justice" or separating it from mercy, and refuses to localize these powers in opposed parts within the judge. By averting the usual dichotomies and compartmentalized responses, Vincentio emphasizes that "mortality *and* mercy," "tongue *and* heart," must work together. This uneasy coexistence may lead the editors to offer their gloss—and may account for why the Duke tries to abandon his task.

He already appears uneasy about living up to the ideal which he has created. He regards the ruler's "soul," not the law itself, as the ultimate standard: "Your scope [Angelo] is as mine own, / So to enforce or qualify the laws / As to your soul seems good" (1.1.64–66). He explicitly gives Angelo the option of qualifying the laws, something to which Angelo pays no attention until he lusts for Isabel and his soul is no longer able to guide him.

Having given directions in the first scene, the Duke mysteriously takes his leave. In the second scene, Lucio suggests that the Duke must be off on a political mission. During this scene we discover from the highly aggressive and sexual world of low-life Vienna that Angelo has been left with an intractable people. We also find that he has begun to enforce the law with unheard-of vigor, and that Claudio has been arrested. Finally, in the third scene the Duke disposes of another possibility: "the dribbling dart of love," he curiously volunteers, is not the cause of his leaving Vienna. The Duke's statement that he had to leave because things were too out-of-hand after his years of being lenient is not convincing, as the Friar immediately, pointedly, says: "It rested in your Grace / To unloose this tied-up justice." "I do fear [it would seem] too dreadful" is the Duke's, again not very convincing, reply. Since turning his power over to a deputy hardly makes things less tyrannous, we are at a loss to know what motivates the Duke—especially since he then announces that, despite his having claimed to love "the life remov'd," he will at once return to Vienna in disguise "to behold [Angelo's] sway." The Duke suspects Angelo is too "precise": "Hence shall we see / If power change purpose, what our seemers be" (1.3.53–54).

All the historical precedent in the legend and history of the disguised ruler seems unable to explain why Shakespeare should make Vincentio appear so culpable (even Friar Thomas alerts us to this). I think that we are to be *disabused* of the notion of an ideal ruler even before we discover the utter tyranny of Angelo. And also, we are to see Vincentio as a complex, self-contradictory character of the sort which we expect at the center of one of Shakespeare's plays—especially one with such brilliantly characterized figures as Angelo and Isabella. The Duke first presents governance as a going forth of the ruler's virtue, then he abandons his state. Apparently he has no reason, but then we find he has a chilling one: he wants to see what his suspect deputy will do. Beneath this lies an apparent connection: Vincentio stresses the ruler's virtue, leaves the state because he feels inadequate, and then tests someone who seems too virtuous. His self-esteem is fragile—like Angelo's and Isabel's and Claudio's. Like them he distrusts himself, especially his aggressiveness; his taking over would be "too dreadful." Unlike the three major characters, however, we get no clear sense of how his sexuality is implicated in his fear of being assertive. We know that he resists the dribbling dart of love too confidently, grows fond of Isabella, and proposes to her; still, this turns out to be very schematic and unrealized. On the other hand, *Measure for Measure* is not a romantic comedy,

but one in which aggression and sexuality are so problematic as
to preclude love. It may be that Vincentio identifies with Angelo's
sadistic aggression, and even exorcises it through identification
with him. The Duke may identify with Claudio's sexual loathing,
and exorcise it—or, more likely, dodge the whole issue. We
simply do not see enough of this side of the Duke to be certain;
however, we see enough to be sure that he is no mere figurehead,
and no ideal ruler—but, given everything, a good one.

One character with whom the Duke seems to identify is a surprise: Lucio. They cling to one another like burrs throughout the
play—to our amusement, usually, but never to the Duke's. Lucio
insists upon those aspects of the Duke which the Duke himself
finds intolerable: potential sexual activity; lenience; and a predi-
lection for mystery, dissembling, and being at the center of attention. What allows the Duke to function so well once he puts on
a disguise is that as a Friar he cannot readily be aggressive. Also,
by watching Angelo be too precise (a tendency he shares) he can
be assured that his own rule could not help but be an improvement—and that he was right, is right, to qualify the laws as to his
soul seems good. By voluntarily giving up his power, the Duke
finds himself in a situation where he must be assertive: he has no
choice. What I suggest helps us to guess his motivation and to
understand the odd actions he takes: his irascibility; his passive
tolerance; his apparent degradation of all values in the speech "Be
absolute for death"; his questions about what the Duke is really
like (3.2); and his whole elaborate plan to save the day by, and this
is not incidental, placing himself at the center of all plots and in
view of the populace whose aves he claims to dislike.

If we look at Vincentio from this perspective we can begin to
see aspects of him which critics pass over, such as his sense of
humor. If the Duke is an ideal ruler, this would be unseemly; if
he is reprehensible, it would be either irrelevant or a sign of
frivolity. When Vincentio tells the Friar his reasons for his departure from Vienna, he describes what is wrong with the state:

> We have strict statutes and most biting laws,
> The needful bits and curbs to headstrong jades,
> Which for this fourteen years we have let slip;
> Even like an o'er-grown lion in a cave
> That goes not out to prey.
>   (1.3.19–23)

That the citizens in Vienna can be seen as "headstrong jades" shows a better sense of proportion than we expect from a ruler who fears to be too dreadful, too tyrannous. He sees his people as spoilt horses, and the laws as "bits and curbs" by which to restrain them; this is all very down-to-earth for a ruler who brilliantly and too scrupulously eschews "justice" in favor of "mortality" in relation to mercy. Vincentio makes the situation appear less awesome than we expect by defining these "strict statutes and most biting laws" with a series of incongruous similes. He compares himself to "an o'er-grown lion in a cave / That goes not out to prey." The point is now easily misunderstood; he refers not to his impotence, but to his craftiness.[6] The ancient story comes from a highly favored schoolbook of the times: "an old lion, pretending to be sick, invited the other animals to visit him in his cave, thus saving himself the trouble of going out to catch his prey." There is self-deprecation, and a sense of humor too, for he sees himself not as dreadful, or culpable, but as a storybook-animal hero. Vincentio continues:

> Now, as fond fathers,
> Having bound up the threatening twigs of birch,
> Only to stick it in their children's sight
> For terror, not to use, in time the rod
> Becomes more mock'd than fear'd.
> (1.3.23–27)

Since "fond" means "affectionate," as well as "foolish," it is hard to restrict his meaning to a sense of being impotent; he also acutely perceives his ridiculous position—ridiculous, not desperate, and thus more easily remedied. To follow his metaphor, if used the rod can soon inspire considerable fear. For a line and a half he grows abstract and avoids similes; this restores our sense of his serious point: "so our decrees, / Dead to infliciton, to themselves are dead" (1.3.27–28). This is the only line which is so doggedly earnest as critics see most of the speech. He at once reverts to homey similes:

> And Liberty plucks Justice by the nose,
> The baby beats the nurse, and quite athwart

6. Wheeler (*Shakespeare's Development*, 109), for example, reads this speech earnestly. I use the Arden footnotes extensively here.

Goes all decorum.
                                        (1.3.29–31)

A wonderful sense of the ludicrous plays over his view of the
supposedly dire—and certainly bad—results of his reign. That
Justice should have a nose, and that it should be plucked by
Liberty, hardly befits so august an abstraction as Justice; nor does
Liberty (recently equated with lechery by Claudio and Lucio)
seem particularly dreadful. That the baby beats the nurse is indec-
orous, yet comically absurd. The Duke suggests here—and in the
whole speech—that things are not really so bad as he likes to
think. Or, perhaps, he hopes that they are not so bad as they seem
to be. At the end of the play, once he knows exactly how vicious
his subjects can be, his tone grows more somber:

> My business in this state
> Made me a looker-on here in Vienna,
> Where I have seen corruption boil and bubble
> Till it o'errun the stew.
>   (5.1.314–17)

Since he speaks in disguise, however, this evaluation has ironic
overtones: he blames himself, the absent Duke, for all this. In
addition, he still has an antic, if not humorous, tone. In *Macbeth*
we find the simile "Like a hell-broth boil and bubble"; however,
the pun on "stew" as "brothel" and a "preparation of meat with
vegetables" has a bizarre effect. Perhaps he intends no pun, but
the next sentence has a similar effect. There are, he complains,

> Laws for all faults,
> But faults so countenanc'd that the strong statutes
> Stand like the forfeits in a barber's shop,
> As much in mock as mark.
>   (5.1.317–20)

He refers to a barber-surgeons' "jocular lists of graded penalties
. . . for bad manners on their customers' part." This is antic humor,
but here as in what Vincentio tells Friar Thomas, he sounds
surprisingly down-to-earth, and reluctantly tolerant of human failings.

Vincentio's general assessments of mankind fall short of complete condemnation, even though he has ample opportunity for it. Much of the time he resorts to irony's comforting distance, but he also involves himself intimately with the lives of his subjects: he both defends himself *and* risks ridicule for the sake of others. What he most worries about is whether he can be a good ruler. When he comments on what the ideal ruler should be (at the start of the play, and again at the end of act 3), he sounds rather stiff and fastidious, but when he tries to see his principles in perspective he grows wry and humorous. His tone takes on the sort of shifting coloration which indicates an attempt to keep in touch with everyday life: by the engagement of humor, as well as by the detachment of irony.

III

Measure for Measure reveals virtually every ideal as fragile and unrealistic. The Duke articulates his standard of good governance while he abdicates because he cannot fulfill it. Angelo cannot even live up to his own narrow ideal, and quickly becomes monstrously unjust. Isabella not only fails to attain the stricter confinement which she seeks, but after Lucio's visit she becomes mired in a situation where she cannot help but prove deficient. High standards meet immediate frustration. As Gervinus long ago stated, the play "calls us universally from all extremes, even from that of the good, because in every extreme there lies an overstraining, which avenges itself with the contrary reaction."[7]

We know from the start that Angelo and Isabella cling to a grandiose self and to grandiose standards. Like the Duke, they try to live up to ideals too extreme, too straitly conceived and out-of-touch with human reality. The chimera of perfection can also lead audiences astray by making them condemn the characters. In one of the earliest critical comments, however, Charles Gildon points out that the play carries "an excellent Moral, and a just Satire" against those who would "bring us to a Perfection Mankind never knew since the World was half peopled."[8] Critics still open themselves to just satire, for they lament the imperfection of one or another of the characters—or all of them. They expect that some character ought to be faultless, but the play scrupulously avoids

7. Arden edition, lix, gives Gervinus's view from his *Shakespeare Commentaries,* trans. F. E. Bunnett (1875), 504.

8. Charles Gildon, *Remarks on the Plays of Shakespear* (London, 1710); printed as vol. 7 of Rowe's edition (1709), 342.

providing one.

When Angelo bends the law to serve his own sexualized aggression he defeats our expectation that he might succeed at being austerely just; the play encourages condemnation until the very last moment. He orders the execution of Claudio, ravishes the virgin whom he assumes to be Isabella, and tries to lie his way out at the end. (That some critics see Angelo as just seems incredible, a sure sign of how much we want to idealize.)[9] Angelo perverts justice because he refuses to admit that human beings are involved in the process of judging and governing. Thus he cannot admit extenuating circumstances; nor can he admit the judge to be a person until he himself has been overwhelmed by lust. Even then he resists the humility which this knowledge should bring.

The Duke's own idealized standard of a good ruler apparently drove him to abandon the task, and to take it up only in disguise. Still, he knows from the start that justice and ruling must intimately involve the person of the governor. Unlike Angelo, he continually employs physical, human terms when he talks of the governor's role, as in his metaphor of "tongue, and heart" and his speaking of having "drest [Angelo] with our love, / And given his deputation all the organs / Of our own power" (1.1.19–21). Angelo sees himself, in metaphor, as metal:

> Let there be some more test made of my metal,
> Before so noble and so great a figure
> Be stamp'd upon it.
>
> (1.1.48–50)

When the Duke replies he reveals the difference between their concepts:

> No more evasion.
> We have with a leaven'd and prepared choice
> Proceeded to you.
>
> (1.1.51–53)

9. W. M. T. Dodds in "The Character of Angelo in *Measure for Measure*," *Modern Language Review* 41 (1946):88, reprinted in *Discussions of Shakespeare's Problem Comedies,* ed. Ornstein, writes that Angelo "typifies strict justice. The contention between Angelo and Isabella is, as well as the personal issue, the greater issue of Justice and Mercy. . . . [Angelo] is a man whose ideals of abstract Justice are clear, and to be revered, whatever his own practice as a 'justicer' may be." Abstract concepts, however, are the great danger in the world of this play.

The modifier "leaven'd" suggests a lively and homey activity, yeast causing bread to rise—a complete contrast to Angelo's conceit about stamping out coins. In a similar tone, Angelo later says:

> We must not make a scarecrow of the law,
> Setting it up to fear the birds of prey,
> And let it keep one shape till custom make it
> Their perch, and not their terror.
>
> (2.1.1–4)

He thinks in terms of what we must not make the law—we must not turn an abstract concept into a scarecrow—rather than think, as the Duke does, about what we ought to make it. The change which Angelo contemplates certainly cannot be in the direction of something more humane. He sees the citizens as birds of prey (in itself hyperbolic: what they "prey" upon is only crops). The Duke, on the other hand, sees the citizens as headstrong jades, children, nose-tweaking libertines, and nurse-beating babies. Escalus recalls the Duke's tone when he answers Angelo: "Ay, but yet / Let us be keen, and rather cut a little, / Than fall, and bruise to death."

Like Angelo, many critics seem to think that justice can be treated in the play as an abstraction with an unvarying meaning. However, in *Measure for Measure* the meaning changes with the user and with the situation. Angelo's sense of justice is relentlessly mechanical: "What knows the laws / That thieves do pass on thieves?" (2.1.22–23); and "It is the law, not I, condemn your brother" (2.2.80). However, Pompey's trial, which takes up most of 2.1, impresses upon us the difficulty of knowing what is just; Angelo, maddened or bored by the wonderfully absurd complexity of the hearing, leaves it to Escalus (which repeats the original pattern of the Duke leaving Vienna to his deputy). That the trial is so humorous and inconclusive puts other trials in the play in perspective: "truth," like "justice," will not yield itself up to those who are impatient or ill-humored. Angelo so isolates himself from the humanity of the judge and the plaintiff that his sense of justice remains a grandiose standard unrelated to reality. As soon as he discovers himself to be all too human, he finds that his ideal cannot possibly be of use to him.

When Isabella first speaks to Angelo, she, too, divorces her ideal of mercy from actual circumstances:

I have a brother is condemn'd to die;
I do beseech you, let it be his fault,
And not my brother.

(2.2.34–36)

Angelo questions her logic: "Condemn the fault, and not the actor
of it?" Yet he is from the start in tune with her. Both cannot relate
the person to what he does; nor can they understand what makes
a situation unique. That Claudio is a particular person in a particular situation plays virtually no role in her speeches. She pleads
for humanity in general. Shakespeare keeps her ignorant of the
strongest extenuating circumstance, her brother's quasi-legal marriage to Juliet, for if she had this fact at her disposal she might be
pushed beyond comfortable abstractions about justice and mercy.
Nor does Angelo see Claudio as an individual, until, significantly,
the possibility of the brother taking revenge occurs to him.

IV

Sexuality and personal relationships are so problematic that love
is not possible in *Measure for Measure*. Even Claudio and Juliet,
instead of adding a romantic interest, contribute to the prevalent-
ly brittle tone. They are caught between chastity (in the sense of
sexual abstinence) and marriage—valid each in its own way but
locked into conflict. Shakespeare complicates this sitution in a
way which ties it to basic social and religious problems of his
time. Ernest Schanzer points out that "two opposed and irrecon-
cilable objectives on the part of the Church" led to the vulnerability of the young couple. The Church wanted to make "legal marriage
as easy as possible in order to encourage people to live in a state
of matrimony rather than 'in sin,' " and hence "decreed that any
de praesenti contract . . . constituted a legal marriage."[10] Claudio
has a point when he claims to be wed by "a true contract . . . save
that we do the denunciation lack / Of outward order" (1.2.134–
38). However, as Schanzer notes, "to counteract the obvious evils
to which such laws were bound to give rise, the Church also

10. Ernest Schanzer, "The Marriage-Contracts in *Measure for Measure*," *Shake-speare Survey* 13 (1960): 82–83. Recently, Karl P. Wentersdorf in "The Marriage Contracts in *Measure for Measure*: A Reconsideration," *Shakespeare Survey* 32 (1979):143–4, says: "In this play, more strikingly than in any other, the dramatist comes to grips with the ambiguities and imperfections of the legal system and with the ramifications of its impact on the lives of the people."

insisted that, though valid and binding, such secret marriages were sinful and forbidden, and that, if they took place, the offenders were to be punished and forced to solemnize their marriage *in facie ecclesiae"* (p. 83). He cites Harrington's *Commendacions of matrymony* (1528) wherein "matrymony clandestinat ... is forboden by the lawe ... not withstondying that matrymony is valeable and holdeth afore God in to so much that and the one of the same forsake the other and take other they lyue in a dampnable aduoutry." Harrington also finds consummation of such "lawfully made" matrimony a deadly sin if not "approued and solempnysed by oure mother holy chyrche" (Schanzer, p. 83). Shakespeare uses the Church's contradictory ideals to place Claudio and Juliet in their peculiar dilemma. The sources do not touch upon this religious and legal conflict; it replaces forcible seduction of a virgin in *Hecatommithi,* and mutual consent based on expectation of marriage in *Promos and Cassandra.* The play treats a situation where *both* religious ideals are good in themselves, yet so out-of-touch with reality as to fall into opposition even with one another (much to the confusion of people who try to live by such precepts). If *de praesenti* marriage binds so fast that breaking it becomes adultery, why are such marriages forbidden (as well as encouraged)? Or their consummation a deadly sin? Evidently questions not to be asked.

Of all the characters in the play, only Claudio and Juliet want to marry for love, and seem able to adjust their wishes to the demands of reality (the need for a dowry, the hope that her "friends" will drop their opposition, and the quasi-legal status of their secret marriage). This compromise early in the play fails partly because of external pressure: the rigor of Angelo's concept of the law, and the ascetic and churchly disapproval of the Friar-Duke. When sent off to jail Claudio still seems realistic: he thinks the sentence is rigid and capricious, justice arbitrary, the deputy new and perhaps desirous of making a name for himself.

However, Claudio and, to a lesser degree, Juliet, reveal such conflicted views of love, sex, and guilt that they, too, seem vulnerable because of their propensity to idealize—and then, consequently, to degrade. Claudio denigrates sexuality in a way more horrifying than Angelo and Isabella do, for he refers to sexual relations with the woman he loves, and to whom he is married; he explains the cause of his being jailed as having been too "liberal" with Juliet:

Our natures do pursue,
Like rats that ravin down their proper bane,
A thirsty evil; and when we drink, we die.
(1.2.120–22)

Lucio, rightly baffled by this, asks if Claudio's offense is murder.
When Claudio says "no," he asks, if it is "lechery" then. Rather
than at once deny this, Claudio replies "Call it so," and begins to
talk about his "true contract" with Juliet. This is unsettling, and
has led some critics to deny what Claudio says so as to make him
sound—as we expect—a proponent of normal human sexuality.[11]
   Claudio, the play's one true lover, degrades sex as an expression
of love. The play resigns the only positive expression of sexual
love to Lucio, a rake who at the end regards marrying his whore,
the mother of his child, as worse than death. Lucio speaks these
moving words in, of all places, a convent and to a novice:

Your brother and his lover have embrac'd,
As those that feed grow full, as blossoming time
That from the seedness the bare fallow brings
To teeming foison, even so her plenteous womb
Expresseth his full tilth and husbandry.
(1.4.40–44)

Shakespeare might easily have had Claudio say something like
this, but instead has him compare sexual relations with his wife
to eating rat's poison. This strange reversal startlingly reveals the
two poles between which characters veer. The rake Lucio idealizes
sex and love, and also virginity: to him Isabel is "a thing enskied
and sainted / By your renouncement" (1.4.33–34). Claudio and
his wife degrade sexual relationships and embrace ascetic notions
which might give pause to a hell-fire preacher. This strange activity on the part of the lovers indicates that they, like the precise
Angelo and the chaste Isabella, feel extreme ambivalence. Neither
the idealization nor the degradation can fully account for "reality," for a commonsensical approach to sexuality; these distorting
responses suggest that terrible anger lies smoldering just beneath
the surface.

   11. For example, Derek Traversi, *An Approach to Shakespeare* (1957; London:
Hollis and Carter, 1969), 65–83. I discuss his view in chap. 7, sec. VII.

Of Juliet's views we know less, but in her confession of guilt to
the Friar-Duke she capitulates to the extremist view: "I do repent
me as it is an evil, / And take the shame with joy" (2.3.35–36).
She asserts her autonomy by accepting the guilt and shame, but
why say "with joy"? She briefly considers Claudio's execution:

> Must die to-morrow! O injurious love,
> That respites me a life, whose very comfort
> Is still a dying horror!
>   (2.3.40–42)

However, the "love" she refers to is not love for Claudio, or even
love in the abstract, but its physical effects: her unborn child,
whom the Friar just referred to as "the sin you carry." The lovers
begin by seeming properly rebellious toward their rigid, cruel society, but soon suffer from scruples with the rest of the major
characters.

Claudio's request that Lucio ask Isabel to help him, sensible as
it is, also reveals his inability to perceive reality in all its complexity, including the needs of others. She is a novice in a convent,
intent upon taking further vows, yet her brother sends Lucio, a
rake and a pimp, to ask her to plead with Angelo for him. Claudio
does so with a full sense of her sexuality and of its usefulness:

> For in her youth
> There is a prone and speechless dialect
> Such as move men; beside, she hath prosperous art
> When she will play with reason and discourse,
> And well she can persuade.
>   (1.2.172–76)

"Prone," "move," and "play" are, as the Arden editor notes, all
capable of suggesting sexual provocation. That Claudio should
put her in such a position, and with his eyes open to its potential
outcome, helps to explain the depth of her outrage when Angelo
propositions her—and when Claudio insinuates that it may not
be so wicked since fornication is the least of the seven sins.

V

Before Claudio and Isabella meet in prison and flare into incan-
descent rage, the Duke begins to intervene with a baffling speech.

When the Duke advocates that Claudio "Be absolute for death: either death or life / Shall thereby be the sweeter" (3.1.5–6), he seems not only ineffectual, for Claudio asks Isabella to help him right after the speech, but cruel. Why should Vincentio deny all that is good in life, and yet avoid the consolation of religion which such a speech from a Friar ought to confirm? Just before the speech, Vincentio asks if Claudio has any "hope of pardon from Lord Angelo," to which he replies:

> The miserable have no other medicine
> But only hope;
> I have hope to live, and am prepar'd to die.
> (3.1.2–4)

This sounds sensible, and makes the Duke's long speech on death all the more mystifying. I think that the Duke spots in Claudio a tendency common to characters in this play. Claudio idealizes figures by making them omnipotent, and seeks to gain strength by merging with them. When this fails, as it must, he degrades them. He hopes that his sister can save him; when she refuses, he roundly denounces her. (The interaction between Angelo and Isabella is roughly similar; critics make excellent sense of the conflict.)[12]

In his speech on death, the Duke confronts Claudio's attempt to deny reality—which, especially here, means to deny ambivalence and guilt. Claudio's contempt for his relationship with Juliet shows how unable he is to accept the blame for what happened. What got them into trouble is not sex, nor even Angelo's new enforcement of the law: it is he and Juliet. She accepts this psychological and religious truth (to the point where her zeal makes us suspect that she cannot be quite so guilty as she thinks). Claudio does not. He tries to get a pardon, which is sensible, natural, and yet an attempt to avoid guilt. This reveals itself in his ambivalence toward sex and toward his sister—and in his anger in this scene. The Duke tries to kill Claudio's false hope, and with it his denial of responsibility. This seems cruel, but as a result Claudio grows calmer. His fantasies draw into a closer relation with external reality; his ambivalence and anger recede, and with them his need to idealize Isabella—or Angelo—as a savior.

The Duke's speech is only the first step in this process, but a

12. See, for example, Harriet Hawkins, "'The Devil's Party,'" 105–13; and Wheeler, *Shakespeare's Development*, 106–20.

crucial one: not only for Claudio, but for the Duke himself—and for the drastic shift in the play's movement from tragic confrontation to comic reparation. Claudio needs to abandon hope since it depends on Isabella, and (as we know, but he does not as yet) this would mean the sacrifice of her identity. It would also mean that Claudio would have to tolerate not only his guilt for getting Juliet in trouble, but also for making Isabella commit a sin. The Duke's speech helps to make Claudio realize that no one can or should solve everything for him: that he must stop idealizing them (in hopeful expectation) or degrading them (in hurt and disgust). He must accept his own responsibility—accept, in a word, the real world. The Duke denies the value of everything in life: man is but a "breath" (not a "soul") and "servile to all the skyey influences"; not noble; "by no means valiant"; has no friend; his children, far from loving him, are eager for his death; and riches, youth, age, even the passing moment are of no value. Unlike Jaques in his caricature of the seven ages of man, the Duke hits home. As Wheeler says, there is little here "that could conceivably sweeten the experience of living" (p. 117). And yet, in a paradoxical way, there is: the denial of everything good and potentially ideal, leaves an even stronger need for *something*. This would make sense in Christian terms if the Duke held out the prospect of salvation; but he does not.[13] I think that he deliberately fails to do so. The Duke seems determined not to allow Claudio to revert to idealization. If God were invoked, then the proclivity for idealizing could not be fully confronted. This reason, and not the author's or the Duke's agnosticism, is relevant here; later, once Claudio has admitted his guilt and stopped exaggerating the ability of others to save him, the Provost refers convincingly to immortality and heaven (4.2.63,68).

In psychoanalytic terms, being able to confront death and the negation of everything helps to diminish the obsession with finding perfection. As Kohut remarks, the full attainment of wisdom "includes the emotional acceptance of the transience of individual existence, [but] we must admit that it can probably be reached by only a few and that its stable integration may well be beyond

13. For the un-Christian nature of the speech see the Arden edition, lxxxvii. Also see F. R. Leavis, "The Greatness of *Measure for Measure,*" *Scrutiny* 10 (1942): 238; and Wheeler, *Shakespeare's Development,* 116–20. For a religious interpretation, see Arthur C. Kirsch, "The Integrity of *Measure for Measure,*" *Shakespeare Survey* 28 (1975):97–98.

the compass of man's psychological capacity."[14] Here, then, is one reason why critics and viewers—and Claudio—find it so difficult to admit the full force of this speech. Nevertheless, its point seems clear. Until we can accept that we will never get all that we want (say, from a self-object), we feel deprived; we experience severe ambivalence and resort to imagining that different aspects of life are all good or all bad. When the Duke insists that *nothing* is good or valuable, he produces an inevitable response: something must be worthwhile, simply because it *is*. In the face of utter negation, a person (unless quite mad) has no choice but to face the world as it actually is: not perfect—or, the exact opposite, not irredeemably horrendous. Rossiter points out that "there is no redemption, no hint of immortality in the whole" speech. Without meaning to do so, he precisely indicates its value: "The only certitudes are existence, uncertainty, disappointment, frustration, old age and death."[15] These irreducible certainties are—to be grim but accurate—a crucial part of reality. Claudio and virtually all the major characters find it difficult to endure this perception; instead they deny it by making grand idealizations, or by making grand degradations. In the shuffle, reality gets lost. Since the characters have a propensity for creating extremely high standards of perfection, the Duke's speech mentions values only as delusions; this is because Claudio, Isabella, Angelo (and the Duke himself), use "values" to shore up, desperately, their delusional sense of self and of life.

Claudio responds to the speech by claiming: "To sue to live, I find I seek to die, / And seeking death, find life" (3.1.42–43). But he no sooner says this than, in the next line, Isabella calls from within. The Duke replies: "Dear sir, ere long I'll visit you again"; when we look back on it, the Duke may suspect that his speech has not yet brought Claudio around. He is right; as soon as Vincentio pretends to leave, Claudio asks: "Now, sister, what's the comfort?" This question, and the heated scene between brother and sister, indicate that he is not ready to die, nor yet willing to accept his guilt; instead he sees Isabella as his salvation. When she too tells him he must resolve to die, he sexualizes death: "If I must die, / I will encounter darkness as a bride / And hug it in mine arms" (3.1.82–84). His metaphor is too appropriate; it can refer

14. Heinz Kohut, *The Analysis of the Self* (New York: International Universities Press, 1971) 327.

15. Rossiter, *Angel with Horns*, 166.

to his own bride—the "cause" of his death sentence, the woman whose sexuality he equated with rat's bane.[16] Claudio continually tries to see death in exaggerated terms rather than accept it as our common end. At this point he is almost ready to assume his guilt so long diverted by false hopes. However, he still tries to make others save him, and his manipulation drives Isabel into sadistic rage:

> Take my defiance,
> Die, perish! Might but my bending down
> Reprieve thee from thy fate, it should proceed.
> I'll pray a thousand prayers for thy death;
> No word to save thee.
>
> (3.1.142–46)

Now the Friar has two guilt-ridden, guilt-projecting figures to deal with. As I suggested in my introduction, his strategy is to reduce the level of guilt to what each can tolerate. He tells Claudio that Angelo was only testing Isabella, and since she "made him that gracious denial which he is most glad to receive," Claudio, by implication, can rise to the occasion: "therefore prepare yourself to death. Do not satisfy your resolution with hopes that are fallible; tomorrow you must die; go to your knees, and make ready" (3.1.164–69). Claudio now accepts some guilt: "Let me ask my sister pardon; I am so out of love with life that I will sue to be rid of it." Next the Duke praises Isabella's goodness (given what she has just said, a half-truth), and he suggests a way in which she can protect her honor and do good for Mariana and her brother. Rather surprisingly, she immediately acquiesces to the idea of leading Angelo on, and having Mariana substitute for her in bed; this is all the more noteworthy since Isabella just accused Claudio of being so loose and despicable. The shift is to reparative action on her part; both characters are now able to feel some of their guilt and become responsible for themselves and for others.

VI

An intriguing issue remains: how did Vincentio himself reach this

16. Isabel herself sexualizes the situation. Janet Adelman explores Isabel's potential sexual fantasies in "Mortality and Mercy in *Measure for Measure*," in *The Shakespeare Plays: A Study Guide* (Delmar, Calif.: University Extension, University of California, San Diego, and Coast Community College District, 1978), 111–12.

positive state? Until now he has merely visited Juliet and con-
fessed her; he has been as passive as he was during his reign. "Be
absolute for death" is his first major speech as Friar (and so far
the Duke's longest one). The perspective on life which he takes is
just as important as his advice or its effect. "Be absolute," he says,
be "positive," "free from all doubt" about death. The topic suits
him, for he conceives of justice as "mortality," and has a generally
negative view of life and of himself. Still, it is curious to find
Vincentio so certain of anything, given his vague reasons for
abandoning and then returning to his state. Like so many other
characters, the Duke tends to idealize, or to degrade; here he
reaches the point of utter negation. Wheeler is right about Vincentio seeming "bereft of life," but not for the whole play. Vincentio
discovers the instability of Claudio, witnesses the scene between
brother and sister, and hears what Angelo is up to. He then comes
to life. He begins to take action, to assert himself. Now he need
not simply "rule," an activity which he disliked. Nor need he
conceive of his dealings with people simply in terms of "justice,"
an abstraction which makes him uneasy. Instead, he can act in the
manner which he held up to Angelo as ideal: use his virtue, "So
to enforce or qualify the laws / As to . . . [his] soul seems good."

Vincentio's ideal seemed unrealizable to himself and perhaps
to us; he could not get in touch with it, could not use it: he felt
unworthy. Now he begins to integrate his ideal into his character
and abilities, and for several reasons. One is the emphasis on
doing good, rather than—as at the outset—dealing with wrongdo-
ers. Another is that his reflection on death and the worthlessness
of life has an effect on him similar to what it has on Claudio: it
forces him to tame his idealization, his search for perfection. The
denial of all values and meaning results in a confrontation of the
process of idealization/degradation: between these two poles lies
what is actually there, ambivalently felt reality. Vincentio wants
Claudio to realize that no one will take care of everything—a
realization which the Duke himself has been forced to make because of Angelo's perfidy.

We cannot see Vincentio as an ideal ruler, but we can begin to
appreciate him. He begins to accept imperfect reality, starting
with the most basic kind: his own nature and deeds. Like Claudio
and Isabella he seems to accept his guilt for actual or imagined
destructiveness. In the Duke's case we can only assume that this
happens, but with a degree of certainty; there is no better way to

account for his becoming assertive and responsible, and at this very moment of the play. (Unless, as some argue, the plot is faulty, or the Duke has no feelings, or he stands for the divine intervening in human life; all are possible, yet seem unable to account for what I see as an intensely human response to the result of his deeds.) Now it can no longer escape Vincentio that his vacillation and abdication have led to a potentially disastrous situation: not only is Angelo, as he feared, too precise, but worse; and the relatively innocent Claudio and Isabella are wrought up to an extreme pitch, as well as in physical danger. The Duke begins to repair the damage, and seems almost uncanny in his ability to manage Claudio and Isabella. They have begun to act out their rage and destructiveness; so, in an excellent therapeutic move, he offers them "plans" to contain and redirect these otherwise self-fragmenting activities: to Claudio, a fabrication about Angelo's test of Isabella and advice to prepare for death; to her, a plan to help her brother, Mariana, and—not incidentally—herself. Indeed, the Duke offers himself a plan to divert his own acting out (or, Shakespeare does): his withdrawal because of ambivalence about asserting himself can now be curbed and channeled into constructive deeds.

VII

Like the major figures, the characters in the subplot are vivid and full of life: not with the intensity of Angelo, Claudio, and Isabella, but with all the ease of the utterly amoral. Dr. Johnson, stern and apparently relentless moralist though he seems to be, remarks that "the light or comick part is very natural and pleasing," unlike the "grave scenes" which were written with "more labour than elegance" (p. 216). He faults the major characters on moral grounds, yet lets the disreputable ones off scot-free. I think that many people share his emotional relief. The bawdy characters do not implicate us in their situations; instead they neutralize our tendency to idealize or debase.

That we strain after idealization can be seen in some critics' view of sexuality in the play. Derek Traversi finds "a balance between two aspects of human passion: the natural and proper instinct upon which it rests and the dissolution and disease to which its unchecked indulgence leads" (p. 80). David L. Stevenson says that Lucio's "sturdy amoral view of human passion as the sheer act of sex . . . rudely mitigates the serious element in Angelo's perfidy by reminding us of the neutral, mechanical, com-

mon denominator to all lovemaking."[17] However, we never see
"the natural and proper instinct" from the lovers' perspective,
and only they could convince us; to Claudio sex is poison swal-
lowed, and to Juliet shame taken "with joy." Only Lucio sees the
natural and proper aspect of their lovemaking, but since he is a
loveless rake we suspect that he idealizes it.[18] The citizens accept
sex as "natural," but give no sense of it being other than degrading
and disease inducing. Lucio may see fornication as "neutral, mechanical," but that hardly makes Angelo seem less perfidious,
especially since his thoughts and deeds are so tinged with sadism.

The play relentlessly deprives sexuality of positive connotations, and instead figures spiritual or physical diseases in it. This
leads to problems in the main plot where characters idealize or
degrade. In the subplot, however, the amoral tone of the characters helps set such mental processes to rest. The sleazy characters
expect so little of each other that we can more easily resist being
involved in their view. Instead, we seem ready to regard it as
"realistic." The various bawds, whores, and customers find disease everywhere, and probably are right to do so, just as they are
right to see few compunctions in themselves. Pompey ignores
Escalus's warning, and goes off to jail, oblivious of guilt. Lucio
refuses to bail him and makes fun of his plight. Abhorson finds
Pompey "a discredit to [our] mystery"—as he is, comically. Lucio
has no qualms about abandoning Kate and his own "teeming
foison." Only Mistress Overdone has a heart of gold, and keeps
the child. We are usually aware of a cool, cheerful irresponsibility
among the low characters.

The Duke's tone in dealing with the citizens is often so stern
and fastidious that they engage our sympathy despite everything.
When he first encounters them as Friar, he exclaims: "O heavens,
what stuff is here!" (3.2.5). He makes ironic little jokes:

Elbow.   Bless you, good father friar.

17. David L. Stevenson, *The Achievement of Shakespeare's "Measure for Measure"* (Ithaca, N.Y.: Cornell University Press, 1966), 59.
18. Traversi (*An Approach to Shakespeare,* 66), sees only the positive side of the
speech, and finds it an instance of "strong and simple emotion." In the 1979
Riverside Studios production (Hammersmith) directed by Peter Gill, Hugh Thomas
made the speech utterly ironic and hypocritical. This interpretation worked brilliantly and added consistency to Lucio's characterization, but at the expense of
obscuring the play's own larger irony in giving such convincing sentiments to a
rake.

Duke.   And you, good brother father.

                                              (3.2.11–12)

But Vincentio often grows so irrate and ponderous that Pompey,
for instance, can hold his own:

Duke.   Fie, sirrah, a bawd, a wicked bawd;
                   The evil that thou causest to be done,
                   That is thy means to live.
                   . . . .
                   Canst thou believe thy living is a life,
                   So stinkingly depending? Go mend, go
                   mend.
Pompey.   Indeed it does stink in some sort, sir. But
                   yet, sir, I would prove–

                                           (3.2.18–20,25–27)

Pompey turns the moral outrage expressed in "So stinkingly depending" into a bland acceptance of actuality: "Indeed it does
stink in some sort, sir." The Duke appears too fastidious in the
world of smell and of moral niceties. The subplot characters accept sexual misdeeds as banal facts of life, rather than invest them
with moral energy. They do not sentimentalize or debase themselves in relation to any grandiose conception. They serve as a
relief. Our impulse is so strong, however, that critics sometimes
idealize amoral sexuality itself. One even tries to sentimentalize
Barnardine, the only unambiguously criminal character. About
him Rossiter concludes that in the play's "world of tottering values and disordered will, Barnardine stands out as admirable. His
will is single: mere will-to-live; and in him the will to be oneself,
and to manage others in action by force of mind, reaches a limit"
(p. 166). Still, Barnardine is admirable only in the sense of being
utterly realistic: he has the Duke over a barrel by refusing to
repent, or to die unrepentant; he knows that the Duke has compunctions, and uses them.

     The idealization in which the central characters indulge at least
indicates their potential for finding some realizable standards for
themselves. Lucio considerably tames Vincentio's grandiosity,
and helps us to see him for what he is. In Lucio's first encounter
with the Friar-Duke, he blandly remarks that "it was a mad,
fantastical trick of him [the Duke] to steal from the state" (3.2.89–
90). Indeed it was. Lucio also rightly says that "a little more lenity

to lechery would do no harm in him [Angelo]." The Duke knows this, but replies that lechery "is too general a vice, and severity must cure it." Since as Friar he has just dreamed up the bed trick (hardly the model of severity toward Angelo's vice), we cannot see him as entirely in possession of his wits or his honesty. The Friar-Duke seems under some constraint, one which Lucio intensifies by saying that the absent Duke would never have condemned Claudio because "he had some feeling of the sport; he knew the service; and that instructed him to mercy." Worse yields to worst: Lucio accuses the Duke of being "a very superficial, ignorant, unweighing fellow" (3.2.136). Instead of brushing this aside—or revealing who he is—the Duke tries to argue with Lucio, fails, and begins to sound truculent. Finally, he soliloquizes:

> No might nor greatness in mortality
> Can censure 'scape. Back-wounding calumny
> The whitest virtue strikes. What king so strong
> Can tie the gall up in the slanderous tongue?
> (3.2.179–82)

Royalty is notoriously prickly, but Vincentio actually takes Lucio's slander to heart, and soon asks Escalus, as if to reassure himself: "I pray you, sir, of what disposition was the Duke?" "What pleasure was he given to?" (3.2.224–27). The audience need not hear the answers, unless we have been disconcerted by the Duke's ludicrous position. But if so, it would be better to have Escalus offer some positive remark, rather than be prompted by Vincentio. He needs reassurance, and for good reason: Angelo proved worse than he suspected; lechery cannot readily be cured by "severity" since Angelo is in the process of propositioning Isabella. Vincentio has also just watched Pompey and Mistress Overdone go off to prison, and heard of their repeated wrongdoing over the years. In charging the Duke with lechery, Lucio hits wide of the mark. In charging him with being an "unweighing fellow"—"injudicious"—he gets too close to home. The Duke is angry with Lucio, and, it is easy to assume, with himself. Lucio's slander gives voice to Vincentio's own unstated guilt and his strongly implicit lack of self-esteem. The Duke does not have "the whitest virtue," but he strives to live up to such an idealization—as we see in the soliloquy with which he ends the scene:

He who the sword of heaven will bear
Should be as holy as severe:
Pattern in himself to know
Grace to stand, and virtue, go:
More nor less to others paying
Than by self-offences weighing.
(3.2.254–59)

He is now more explicit than at the start of the play when he told Angelo to use his virtue. Now he sees the *need* to bear the sword of heaven, to use the sword of justice deputed to him by God. And he more explicitly realizes the need to base his actions on what he knows about himself: the "pattern in himself," the precedent for his judgments in his own conduct; and the need to weigh "self-offences." He also blames Angelo: "To weed my vice, and let his grow!" (3.2.263). It must be Vincentio's own vice he refers to: what has happened to the state because of his lenience, and by leaving Angelo in charge. (The Arden editor follows Jenkins in thinking that the Duke speaks as "everyman" and about the vice of "other persons in contrast to Angelo's own.") Angelo's inhumanity—which the Duke suspected because he himself is too much a perfectionist—makes him now ready to assert himself, although still in disguise and thus at Lucio's mercy. Lucio's continual insistence upon the Duke's failings, and at the end upon the "Friar's" failings, forces Vincentio to tame his penchant for self-inflation. The Duke is by no means so bad as Lucio says, but on the other hand he is not (as many critics argue) "as holy as severe." The gibes make Vincentio testy and tetchy. The audience, now about to watch him manipulate all the characters over a long period of time, can see him, in some ways, as ludicrous. Lucio can wound the Duke because he still regards himself as having "the whitest virtue," despite his unidealized nature—a nature which also makes him, although he seems unaware of it, human and likeable.[19]

VIII

Audiences are easily won over by the rapid succession of surprising events during the long final scene; but critics worry it, feel that

19. Miles notes that being disguised as a friar in plays of the period inspired mirth, not religious awe as is now assumed (*The Problem of "Measure for Measure,"* 173).

it does not fully resolve the issues or release the tensions which the play has created. Janet Adelman suggests, on the other hand, that "in our disappointment at [Angelo's] reprieve, we are brought face to face with that part of our own natures that needs to be tempered by mercy" (pp. 109–10). I think that this process occurs over and over during the last scene: disappointment confronts us with the need to temper idealizations—for example, about "justice." Isabella strikes some as too merciful. The Duke strikes others as too harsh when sentencing Lucio, too lenient when judging Barnardine, and too cruel in deceiving everyone about Claudio being dead. Critics find Vincentio's behavior during the trial too self-centered for an ideal ruler—or too omnipotent. Finally, some think the ending itself imperfect, a comic ending artificially tacked onto an essentially tragic action.

If we step back for a moment, we can perceive the culmination of a psychological process which the whole play encourages: the frustration of grandiose ideals causes anger which, when confronted, leads to guilt; guilt, once admitted, forces adaptation to an unidealized world, the much-maligned reality in which we find ourselves. If we can tolerate our often intensely ambivalent responses to the final scene, we can—as some of the characters do—find ourselves in touch with life again and capable of reparation.

First, let us look at two critics, Johnson and Coleridge, who rightly express dismay over the problematic nature of the trial. Since they lived during an age closer to Shakespeare's and far more Christian than ours, their indignation must make us wary of any religious allegorization which resolves too many problems. To Johnson, "Angelo's crimes were such, as must sufficiently justify punishment, whether its end be to secure the innocent from wrong, or to deter guilt by example; and I believe every reader feels some indignation when he finds him spared" (p. 213). Johnson cannot understand how Isabel could find extenuating circumstances for Angelo's crimes; since she thinks that he has executed Claudio, "the only 'intent' which 'his act did not overtake,' was the defilement of Isabel." Of her argument that he was good " 'till he looked on me," Johnson indulges in a joke: "I am afraid our varlet poet intended to inculcate, that women think ill of nothing that raises the credit of their beauty, and are ready, however virtuous, to pardon any act which they think incited by their own charms." Why does Johnson find it impossible to accept her forgiveness, or acquiesce in the Duke's pardon? Coleridge also balked: "The pardon and marriage of Angelo not merely baffles the strong indignant claim of justice (for cruelty, with lust and damnable baseness, cannot be forgiven, because we cannot conceive them as being *morally* repented of) but it is likewise degrading to the character of woman."[20] Coleridge must suspect the *sincerity* of the repentance; if we cannot conceive of such crimes as being morally repented, then what does repentance mean?

These critics respond as many of us do: they judge, condemn, and wax indignant. The play tantalizes us with absolutes—justice, mercy, chastity, virtuous government—and then pulls us up short: Angelo should be punished, but is forgiven; Isabella wants to be a nun, but the Duke proposes marriage; he gave up ruling Vienna because he was too lenient, but now—although he could be strict without seeming tyrannous—he dispenses a more quixotic and lenient sort of justice than ever before. The play encourages us to hope for a clear resolution, yet disappoints us every step of the way.

Let us look at the events of the final scene in schematic outline. The Duke appears in his role as ruler; then Isabella accuses Angelo, Lucio accuses the absent Friar, Mariana accuses Angelo. The Duke leaves at line 258 and returns as the Friar; then Lucio accuses him, he accuses the absent Duke, and Escalus charges him (the Friar) with slander for doing so. The scene creates a crisis analogous to that reached during the first half of the play. Then the scene, like the second half of the play, turns from multiple accusations to reparative measures once the Duke appears as himself: Angelo confesses and is married to Mariana; she pleads for his life, as does Isabella. Finally, the Duke unknots all the problems. Strangely, though, he begins by accusing the most innocent character, the Provost; he frees the guiltiest character, Barnardine; and concludes by punishing the least guilty one, Lucio. In outline the action seems musical in its sense of form: a recapitulation of the destructive intents and accusations of the first half of the play, followed by the quirky reparative efforts of the second half.

The last act seems designed to expose idealizations and to con-

---

20. *Coleridge's Shakespearean Criticism,* ed. T. M. Raysor, Everyman ed. (London: Dent, 1960), 1:102.

front the characters—and us—with our disappointment that nothing can be perfect, or even get very close to being so. The ending further reveals the law's arbitrariness. This is not, for instance, the case in *The Merchant*; there we are led to believe that the wisdom of the law itself protects citizens, not just that Portia does. *Measure for Measure* makes us suspicious in several ways. Immediately before the final scene, Isabella chafes at speaking "indirectly": "I would say the truth, but to accuse him [Angelo] so / That is your part [Mariana]; yet I am advis'd to do it . . . to veil full purpose" (4.6.1–4). This is not the sort of remark to make us rest easy. From the start, the scene exposes justice to the glare of irony. The Duke commends the deputies on the "goodness of your justice." Isabella pleads for "Justice, O royal Duke," yet her repeated calls for justice remind us that she cannot really be seeking it: her accusation is false; Angelo has not defiled her. Nor, as we and the Duke know, has Claudio been executed.

In an especially tricky maneuver, the Duke affronts our sense of justice when he tells Angelo to be "judge / Of your own cause" (5.1.168–69) and repeats the noxious idea (5.1.255–56). Many critics seem deceived by this, yet Vincentio never allows Angelo to judge. The Duke remains firmly in charge until he leaves at line 258; Angelo simply asks Mariana some questions and describes why he left her. When Vincentio leaves, Escalus—not Angelo—takes over. Angelo never even speaks until the Duke returns in disguise, and then discusses only the Friar, not Isabella and Mariana. Nevertheless, the Duke as Friar insists upon the inequity:

> The Duke's unjust
> Thus to retort your manifest appeal,
> And put your trial in the villain's mouth
> Which here you are come to accuse.
>   (5.1.298–301)

Vincentio teases us into thinking his actions are manifestly unjust. Shakespeare also makes Escalus suddenly appear despotic, rather than his reasonable self. When the Friar objects to the Duke letting Angelo judge his own case, a perfectly valid point, Escalus wildly accuses him of suborning the women and slandering the Duke:

> To th' rack with him!—We'll touse you
> Joint by joint, but we will know his purpose.
> What! Unjust!
>
> (5.1.309–11)

And again, when the Friar remarks that Vienna bubbles over with corruption, the Duke's and everyone's view, Escalus bursts out:

> Slander to th' state!
> Away with him to prison!
> (5.1.320–21)

At this point in the play we can hardly be meant to see much depth of characterization in Escalus, only the bizarre injustice of his actions. He placidly accepts Lucio's accusation, and denounces the Friar for his incontrovertible observations. Again, in a wish to idealize aspects of the play, some critics ignore that Escalus is hardly a representative of equity after his outburst.[21] The Duke, Angelo, and Escalus behave so high-handedly that we not only sense the arbitrariness of judges, but grow ambivalent about the value of justice. As Johnson and Coleridge indicate, we grow indignant—and, as Adelman suggests when thinking of Angelo, our indignation verges on being vindictive.

We tend to be disappointed and frustrated not only with justice, but with most of the characters. There is a great deal of ambivalence toward virtually everyone in the main plot, and not just the Duke and Isabella. The bed trick implicates Mariana in the sort of deception which makes us suspicious. Even when she tries to show the need to tolerate Angelo's wickedness we can be frustrated by her:

> They say best men are moulded out of faults,
> And, for the most, become much more the better
> For being a little bad.
>
> (5.1.437–39)

---

21. John W. Dickinson in "Renaissance Equity and *Measure for Measure,*" *SQ* 13 (1962):297, finds Escalus rational and equitable as distinct from being merciful, the Duke's approach; Dickinson sets up a triad of approaches: justice (Angelo's attempt), equity, and mercy.

Angelo was more than "a little bad," he was monstrous. None of
the characters is capable of sounding both good *and* realistic.
Isabella demonstrates that no one here is allowed to have or to be
an ideal. Instead, characters remain significantly out-of-touch with
life. Isabella asks for mercy for Angelo, a great improvement over
her attitude toward Claudio; still, we are not permitted to regard
even her mercy as entirely valid. She seems too merciful, too
willfully inflexible in this, as in her previous virtues:

> Look, if it please you, on this man condemn'd
> As if my brother liv'd. I partly think
> A due sincerity govern'd his deeds
> Till he did look on me.
>
> (5.1.442–45)

She strains to be fair, and her virtue is now an active force; but
she tries to argue her case, and it is a weak one. She raises more
problems than she can handle. Rather than simply say that the
quality of mercy is not strained, and leave it at that, she uncon-
vincingly argues that:

> My brother had but justice,
> In that he did the thing for which he died:
> For Angelo,
> His act did not o'ertake his bad intent,
> And must be buried but as an intent
> That perish'd by the way.
>
> (5.1.446–51)

As far as she knows, Angelo did execute Claudio; this would not
have been just, given the circumstances, nor can we feel very easy
about his own sister assuming that it would be. Also, Angelo's act
actually did "o'ertake his bad intent": he intended to ravish Isabella;
that Mariana was in her place does not undo the evil intention or
act—only (perhaps) the result. Isabella, like her fateful opposite
Angelo, remains too remote from commonsensical reality.

Angelo rigidly insists on being punished for his evil, and tempts
us to long for a good beheading. It is very difficult to feel ambivalent about him, but we are forced to see the vindictiveness of our
wish that he get what he deserves. He can conceive of no other
possibility: "let my trial be mine own confession. / Immediate
sentence, then, and sequent death / Is all the grace I beg" (5.1.370–

72). He repeats this when married: "I crave death more willingly than mercy" (5.1.474). As we have seen, some critics get caught up in Angelo's own rigid code of an eye for an eye, but he himself shows how grandiose and inhuman the ideal of talionic revenge is. The play alludes in its title to the Sermon on the Mount. This directs us to no easy answers—say about mercy—but to a sermon every bit as problematic as the play. Many of the issues are the same: intent in relation to deed, especially with regard to sexuality; the paradox of needing to judge on earth, but not being good enough to do so. But most of all, I think, the Sermon reveals Christ's attempt to transform rigid codifications of ideals into more flexible ones better in tune with the human condition. For instance, Christ internalizes, quite literally, the old ideal of an eye for an eye: "If *thy* right eye cause thee to offend, pluck it out, and cast it from thee: for better it is for thee, that one of thy members perish, than that thy whole body should be cast into hell" (Matt. 5:29). He also reinterprets guilt to include inner intent and self-recrimination, as well as external deed and punishment. But this higher ideal quickly loses touch with life and becomes a pernicious idealization. Everyone has so many evil thoughts that feeling guilty for each of them can bring on the charge—as it often does in confessionals—of searching for scruples, of excessive self-importance, of pride. At several points Christ seems to acknowledge the tendency of ideals to rigidify into extremes out-of-touch with actual circumstances. For example, he expands the command "thou shalt not kill": "whosoever is angry with his brother unadvisedly shall be culpable of judgment" (v. 22). The qualification is crucial: "unadvisedly," or (in the King James Version) "without a cause." Similarly, his idea that women be protected from arbitrary divorce contains an exception as a bow to necessity: "whosoever shall put away his wife (except it be for fornication) causeth her to commit adultery" (v. 32). What Shakespeare's play has most in common with the Sermon is that both acknowledge the tension between viable ideals and rigid idealizations.

Although the Duke seems for a long time to conceive of Angelo's guilt just as severely as Angelo does, when he judges him he uses the phrase "measure for measure" to indicate that he is *not* about to follow talionic law:

> The very mercy of the law cries out
> Most audible, even from his proper tongue:
> 'An Angelo for Claudio; death for death.
> Haste still pays haste, and leisure answers leisure;
> Like doth quit like, and Measure still for Measure.'
>
> (5.1.405–9)

He characteristically conceives of justice in human, physical terms rather than abstractions, and adds a whimsical touch: the audible cry from the tongue of "mercy" really comes from the tongue of "justice." Also, haste and leisure are strange amplifications of the concept of measure for measure, death for death. (The Arden note cites, for instance: "Blood cries for bloode, and murder murder craves"; Marston's *Antonio's Revenge*.) That "haste still pays haste, and leisure answers leisure" is so temperate an analogy that it tames the grand biblical invocation of "Measure still for Measure." The Duke condemns Angelo to die on the place where we know no one died: "the very block / Where Claudio stoop'd to death, and with like haste."

In a remarkably moving scene Mariana, and then Isabella, plead for Angelo's life. The Duke prolongs the suspense, brings on the Provost with Barnardine, Claudio (muffled), and Juliet; Claudio is revealed to be alive, and at this moment of revelation—which ought to clear up everything, preferably with a brief hint at explanation—the Duke turns to Isabella:

> If he be like your brother, for his sake
> Is he pardon'd; and for your lovely sake
> Give me your hand and say you will be mine.
> He is my brother too: but fitter time for that.
>
> (5.1.488–91)

The shift here is difficult for an actor to make: the Duke's brilliant *coup de théâtre* justifies his high-handed manner during the last part of the play, but he continues to astonish us, and this seems perverse given the situation. He could simply pair off the couples and offer to withdraw to his palace where, offstage, he could make all clear. Instead he proposes to a novice, one bent, so far as we know, on becoming a nun—and only recently extricated from attempted rape by the Duke's own deputy.

The strange proposal heightens the play's insistence that no one *be* ideal, or *have* a realistically grounded ideal. There is a strong sense of the grandiose, exhibitionistic self in the Duke's maneuver and in his goal, just as there is in Isabella's spendid plea for mercy by denying Angelo's wicked intent. Vincentio—like her, like Angelo, and like Claudio in the great prison scene—loses touch with reality. He has accomplished much that is good, and demonstrated his new-found ability to rule. He has tamed his idealization of the good ruler, and can now endure seeming tyrannous (perhaps too readily), yet still lenient (again, perhaps too much so). We know that the citizens remain beyond his efforts, but with the courtiers he does quite well. Nevertheless, he is unable to rest content with this success.

Instead, we see the remains of his persistent need to call attention to himself and to attempt goals which seem quixotically unrealistic. Isabella can hardly refuse the Duke, but we have no idea that she would welcome a proposal, and no reason to think that the Duke has been leading up to this all along. Vincentio seems to want to bolster his self-esteem, yet again. The self-aggrandizement is rather comic: he announces his proposal at the very moment when two oddly matched and thoroughly shaken-up couples stand before him. Isabella never replies, but certainly ought to look a bit dazed. (She should not look furious, as actresses sometimes play it; the latter interpretation, harkening back to Angelo's proposition and Claudio's seconding of it, makes *her* seem too self-aggrandizing as virginity besieged.)[22]

Vincentio has just demonstrated how much control he has as a ruler; now he undermines all this by revealing that he lacks control, and in a variety of ways. Just before his proposal to Isabella, he dismisses Barnardine since he can do nothing with him; nor—we are quite sure—can the Friar to whom he entrusts him. Like the intransigent citizens of Vienna, Barnardine cannot be controlled for his own good; that the Duke resigns him to someone else suggests, uncomfortably, his turning over the state to Angelo at the start of the play. Then comes the unanswered proposal: "but fitter time for that." When the Duke tells Angelo to love Mariana, "her worth, worth yours," we suspect irony: Angelo's worth has been rather tarnished, and Mariana's deception does not exactly make her a paragon of worthiness. If we take

22. Isabel's fury in the 1979 Riverside production, demonstrated by her gestures and by upstaging the Duke, diluted his exhibitionism with confusing effect; viewers have more than enough to deal with at this point.

the remark as straightforward, the Duke seems distracted. He turns, finally, to Lucio, to one of the most uncontrollable subjects in his dukedom. As I suggested, Lucio's bite is sharp because he reminds the Duke of traits which he would like to forget: his own repressed sexuality, his excessive lenience, and his apparent foolishness; the Duke sums up these charges:

> You, sirrah, that knew me for a fool, a coward,
> One all of luxury, an ass, a madman:
> Wherein have I so deserv'd of you
> That you extol me thus?
>
> (5.1.498–501)

We find an interchange between the Duke and Lucio, rather than between the Duke and any one of a number of more suitable figures (or none at all). As always, he comes off the worse for dealing with Lucio. The Duke not only judges him too severely, but behaves so manipulatively that we are reminded of his previous, more justifiable, maneuvers. He sentences Lucio to be married to his rejected whore and then hanged; next he forgives him and at the same time coerces him into submission. This uncomfortably recalls the Duke's manipulation of Angelo's marriage and reprieve, and his tight control of Claudio and Juliet. The result is largely comic, but with connotations which sully the Duke's recent display of skill at managing his wayward subjects.

This odd coda to the Duke's disposition of the major characters tempts us once again to judge someone harshly for failing to be as perfect as he would like to think himself. Critics and audiences often yield to the temptation. They conclude that the Duke once again demonstrates that he is not so ideal as he, or they, supposed. They further conclude that the comic ending is awkward, problematic, and contrived. In many ways they are right. Like the major characters, they embrace or even introduce idealizations: Vincentio should be as he wishes, an exemplary ruler; his resolution of the conflict (or Shakespeare's) should be thorough, unproblematic, and convincing. This should be the sort of comedy which Shakespeare earlier wrote—an *As You Like It* or a *Twelfth Night*—or was later to write: a *Winter's Tale* or *Tempest*. People who find such deficiencies seem more puzzled than one might expect, for in finding them they validate the larger process of *Measure for Measure:* their response is the very human one of wishing that things were better, the brittle hope for something perfect. *Measure for Measure* should mirror and confirm their longing for an ideal; yet it does not, and instead leaves us, as Adelman puts it, creatures of the middle state.

Conclusion

The assumption that something exists which is extremely good characterizes all of Shakespeare's comedies. Even in *Measure for Measure* an ideal such as the good ruler remains valid if thoroughly tempered by an awareness that he will be more like Vincentio than a divinity. *Measure for Measure* gains strength by more comprehensively imitating life than *All's Well*: several characters confront the danger of idealization; the robust, amoral citizens treat ideals as irrelevant notions. Another source of strength in *Measure for Measure* is that so many of its characters participate in reparative action. Here and in the comedies as a whole such action provides us with a model. Because the play deepens our sense of fierce conflict *and* of the possibility to surmount it, the impulse for restitution seems all the greater. From here it is only a short step to the late comedies, but several years intervene during which Shakespeare produced his great tragedies. The problem plays may have precipitated them, for they bring to a head Shakespeare's reliance upon idealization—in the comedies, sonnets, and the *Henriad*—and reveal just how dangerous it can be.

Recently, critics have begun to feel that Shakespeare understates the role of sex in the comedies: say, in the emphasis on the artifice of courtship, or on the frequent use of women disguised as boys. In *All's Well* and *Measure for Measure,* he shows sexuality to be more disruptive than critics previously have allowed. For instance, some think that Helena's sexual interest in Bertram blinds her to his real worth; others argue that Bertram fears the possibility of an incestuous relationship. In *Measure for Measure* it is sexuality which forces many characters to idealize or to degrade: not just Angelo, but also Isabella, Juliet, and Claudio; the Duke seems to repress it. For some reason, sex is not very convincingly integrated into the reparative effect of these comedies. Perhaps Shakespeare's own bias accounts for this. Or perhaps we are wrong to look so diligently for a strong sexual component; we may be too Viennese. Or, it may be that the reparative effect of these comedies over the years and for so many different people, may owe its resilience to the fact that they understate sexuality; when they do not, in the problem comedies, the plays falter and audiences stay away. The festive comedies allow greater leeway: relationships can seem as sexual as we like. This is an option which Restoration comedy, for example, does not allow.

Whatever the reason, when sexuality enters this series of comedies as frankly as it does in *Troilus and Cressida,* the reparation abruptly ends. Probably this play is not a comedy at all, but a satirical history or a tragedy—despite its comic parts. Certainly *Troilus and Cressida* cannot restore our sense of ourselves or of life as benign. It explores the pernicious results of idealization so trenchantly that it serves as a preamble to the tragedies. Ideals in love, war, and about the heroic past—ones which prove viable to some degree in previous comedies, tragedies, and histories—turn out to be completely degraded. Helen might launch a ship or two, but not for grand or savory reasons. The acerbic brilliance and accuracy of observation of this play speak to our inner world in its most chaotic and destructive state.

The tragedies also do so, but at the same time they convey ideals and the possibility of great goodness. At times this value is located in the past, as at the end of *Hamlet*; at others, it exists in the play's framework: the Venetian civilization to which Iago will be returned provides a standard against which to measure his and Othello's barbaric deeds. As I noted in my introduction, *King Lear* confirms a restorative impulse by the deeds of idealized children which nearly succeed, and by the value which survives, if only as a possibility, to the exhausted survivors at the end.

Perhaps it is a reflection of our contemporary interest in psychology, but sexuality appears strongly implicit in the failed idealization and tragic degradation of Lear and his daughters; of Hamlet and Coriolanus and their mothers; and of Macbeth and Othello and their wives. The sexual implications add a depth of feeling to the tragedies which never presents itself in the comedies. This is curious. We find a firm sense of sexuality in the tragedies which (except for *Othello*), have as their main interest other matters such as gaining or keeping political power, but not in the comedies which have as their main interest love and marriage. Shakespeare portrays the tragic potential of sexuality more convincingly than the positive one. This is true also of the romances, but in them the sexual dimension enriches the reparative effect. Except for *The Tempest*, ferocious emotions, often sexual, are given full expression so that we find a full cycle: ambivalent love overwhelmed by hate and destruction, and rescued through guilt and reparation. The late comedies confirm that Shakespeare's works consistently address our reparative impulses. They introduce destruction and loss so as to contain and repair them: not just for the characters, but for us. Even Shakespeare's tragedies often do so: at times by formal gestures such as the return to a normal, civilized state of things (as in *Othello* and *Lear*—and, with some qualifications, in *Coriolanus* and *Hamlet*); and at other times by presenting a transcendent experience (as in *Antony and Cleopatra*). *Macbeth* is unusual in giving the full turn of the wheel: it plunges us into the depths of wickedness, and surfaces at the end in the utter clarity and goodness of Malcolm (and Macduff, Siward, Ross—plus Fleance and Donalbain). What makes *The Winter's Tale* so different is that one character, Leontes, grows from being like Macbeth to being like Malcolm—but as a sexual being, not a virginal knight.

Shakespeare's persistent concern for reparation must be the cause of his persistent resort to idealization. Even in the romances, for all their profounder acceptance of sexuality and of the inherent sadness and imperfection of mankind, Shakespeare resorts to idealized figures: completely trustworthy female characters of intelligence, virtue, and strength; and in the last of all his plays, a magician. Prospero is what Vincentio aspired to be: a grandiose, exhibitionistic ideal of a ruler, slightly tempered by realistic attitudes and an awareness of human imperfection. When Prospero says "And what strength I have's mine own, / Which is most faint," he does so after the action of the play, and after he himself has determined to renounce his omnipotence.

In *The Tempest* Shakespeare writes the quintessence of a reparative comedy. He creates his own plot for the first time since *Love's Labour's Lost* and *A Midsummer Night's Dream* (both dependent upon idealization qualified by a more realistic attitude). Shakespeare subordinates humor, romantic love, sexuality, and even festive elements to the grand theme of reparation. Prospero says that he seeks to regain his dukedom, but as soon as he gets his enemies in his power he has in effect done so. His real aim is to bring the wayward to feel guilt and become the better for it. Shakespeare thus reduces the love plot to two elements: Miranda and Ferdinand are made to feel, if not the burden of guilt, the potential for wrongdoing; and by marrying them off Shakespeare symbolizes the reparation of the two fathers' wrongs and wrongdoing. The brilliance of the verse adds richness to this courtship, but it is severely subordinated to the restoration plot. Once again, we find a minimal sense of sexuality except as a destructive force (potentially so for Miranda and Ferdinand, actually so for Caliban). In contrast, we find a maximal sense of ideal goodness in an omniscient, omnipotent controlling character who creates a better world—but not, we know, a perfect world.

One reason why this play is so moving in the context of Shakespeare's career is that an enduring bias remains: he idealizes in order to preserve the possibility for something extremely good. Perhaps this leads him to write plays and sonnets which distort human sexuality by idealizing or degrading it. There are numerous exceptions, of course, but even in *Antony and Cleopatra* we can spot this distortion in the extreme ambivalence of the lovers. Shakespeare's weakness may be the source of his creativity and strength. It helps him to create tragic heroes who convey with terrible accuracy the destructiveness inherent in idealizing and degrading: the eternal struggle between fusion on the one hand, and isolation on the other. And it allows him to create comic heroines (and occasional heroes) who convey with wonderful effect the possibility that someone ideal exists who can create or preside over a benign and trustworthy world. Such idealization is dangerous. One pays for it, as Shakespeare's characters demonstrate in a multitude of ways. And yet his own propensity gives his reparative strategies a conviction which a more tempered view could never give. Shakespeare feels the need for an ideal so intensely that it suffuses almost all his work—sonnets, histories, tragedies, and especially the comedies—and speaks to our deepest longing.

Index

190   Index